DAVID WHITWELL

AMERICAN MUSIC EDUCATION: THE ENIGMA AND THE SOLUTION

WHITWELL BOOKS

American Music Education: The Enigma and the Solution
Dr. David Whitwell

Copyright © 2016 David Whitwell
All rights reserved.
Published in the United States of America.

Cover image:

ISBN-13 978-1-936512-89-8

Whitwell Publishing
Austin, TX 78701
WWW.WHITWELLPUBLISHING.COM

I want to express my appreciation for my colleague, Craig Dabelstein of Brisbane, Australia, for his contribution to this volume. It is quite impossible for me to describe for the reader the contribution of Craig Dabelstein in bringing my books back into permanent digital status and publication. He has devoted himself without a fee to the production of nearly one book per month for five and a half years. Moreover his own background in editing, design, art work and his own professional activity as a performer and conductor of the highest standards helped immensely in creating a more valuable final product. Without his selfless dedication innumerable books and early editions of original band scores would have been lost to the world.

Contents

I The Enigma of American Music Education — 9

Introduction — 10

1 What is Music? — 19
- Ancient Descriptions of Music — 20
  - On the Myths and Muses — 20
  - On Ancient Gods of Music — 23
  - On Natural Science and the Listener — 27
  - Is Music a Branch of Mathematics? — 34
- On the Physiology of Music — 41
  - On Early Music Therapy — 43
  - Is Music Genetic? — 51
  - On Movement and Music — 60
  - The Location of Music (and us) in our Bicameral Brain — 69
- The Debates on Reason versus Emotion — 72
  - Is Man Ruled by Reason or Emotion? — 72
  - Early Intuitions on the Bicameral Mind — 84
  - On the Importance of the Experiential — 93
  - The Baroque: Emotion takes Precedence over Rules — 101
- Music as a Language — 114
  - Music is the Language of our Emotions — 117
  - Music as the Language of Truth — 125

2 In the Beginning — 137
- What was the Earliest Music Like? — 137
- What was Early Music Education Like? — 142
  - Plato on Music Education — 146

    Aristotle on Music Education 154
    Music Education in Ancient Rome 168
    Quintilian on Music Education 171

3 The Arrival of Notation 173
    A Brief History of Western Notation 176

4 The Great Divide 183
    Musica speculativa vs Musica practica 183

II The Reformation of American Music Education 201

Professional Prerequisites for the Reformation of American Music Education 205
    The Musical Excellence of the Teacher 205
    Music Learning must be through Performance 211
    Concepts cannot describe Music 212
    The Grammar of Music is not Music 219
    Music Repertoire must be of High Aesthetic Level 223
    Catharsis—The Educational Purpose of Music 229
    Catharsis is the End Goal for Public School Music Education 240
    Ethics 101: A Concert is not a "show" 244
    Contesting Bands: The Great Pretense 252

Unique Benefits of Performance based Music Education, not possible under the Conceptual Music Education Doctrine 267
    Students receive the only Direct Right Hemisphere Education in the School 268
    Students receive the only Present Tense Education in the School 269
    Students experience a Direct Association with Great Minds 271
    Students Discover and Develop their Unique Emotional Template . . . 275
    Students experience Beauty as a form of Truth 281
    Students experience the World of Higher Spirituality 283
    Students experience Principles of Morality through Music Performance 288
    Performance based Music Education aids in developing Character . . . 293
    Performance based Music Education aids in developing Manners 303

About the Author 311

About the Editor 315

Books by David Whitwell 317

Part I

The Enigma of American Music Education

All American adults value Music.

American adults do not value Music Education.

Introduction

Music Education is the oldest form of education known to man, dating before any other kind of education, before any written language and even before the use of the vertical scratch on some surface to represent *one*. Plato testifies to established formal music education in ancient Egypt 10,000 years before his own time, which would put its date near or during the period of the cave paintings in France and Spain.

The oldest names known to history are music educators in ancient Egypt, Nikaure, instructor of the singers of the pyramid of King Userkaf, and Rewer, teacher of the royal singers, both of the Fifth Dynasty, c. 2,500 BC. It is only to be expected that their educational practice was centered in performance, as there was yet no concept of notation. Neither was there music notation in ancient Egypt nor in ancient Greece at the time of the "Golden Age" of that culture. During the period of Plato and Aristotle the individual notes did not even have names.

There was, however, an understanding from a very ancient time of the importance of the use of only the highest quality music in education. In his famous play, *The Clouds,* by Aristophanes (446–386 BC), where we have a portrait of a boys' music school, the playwright makes a point of mentioning that only more lofty music is used in their education. These highly disciplined young students are marching to a music class, thinly clad in spite of a snow storm and we read,

Brested the storm uncloak'd: their lyres were strung
Not to ignoble melodies, for they were taught
A loftier key ...[1]

[1] Lines 961ff.

Polybius, the ancient Greek historian (2nd century BC), makes a similar distinction when he asks why the Cynaethans were so known by their savage character?

> My own opinion is that they were the first and indeed the only people among the Arcadians to have abandoned an institution which had been nobly conceived by their ancestors, and was studied by all the inhabitants of Arcadia in their relation to their natural conditions. I am referring here to the special attention given to music, and by this I mean true music.[2]

[2] Polybius, *The Rise of the Roman Empire*, IV, 20.

One of the earliest treatises specifically devoted to education was by the most enlightened of sixteenth century Spanish philosophers, Juan Vives (1492–1540). His experience as a student at the University of Paris turned him against Scholasticism and his attacks on this old Church view of philosophy brought him to the attention of Erasmus and Henry VIII, who invited him to England. In his *Introduction to Wisdom*, seventeen centuries after Polybius, we find the same qualification, "Only let the pupil practice pure and good music."[3]

[3] *Vives: On Education*, trans. Foster Watson (Cambridge: University Press, 1913), IV, V.

In his music education treatise, *Maxims for Young Musicians*, Robert Schumann mentions several times the critical issue of the choice of literature. One instance reads,

> You ought not help to spread bad compositions, but, on the contrary, help to suppress them with all your force.

However obvious the relationship of the quality of the repertoire is to the quality of the education, it must be said that since the beginning of the twentieth century this fundamental issue has been largely ignored. Due to the significant amount of genetic musical information which is included in the birth of all people, together with the common experience of modern people, it should be no surprise when one finds that the issue of the poor quality of music used in music education is widely recognized by the common population. In the novel *Steppenwolf* (1929) the famous writer Hermann Hesse has his central character reflecting on hearing some jazz and observing,

> It was repugnant to me, and yet ten times preferable to all the academic music of the day.[4]

[4] Hermann Hesse, *Steppenwolf* (New York: Henry Holt, 1963), 43.

The famous conductor of the Harvard Glee Club, Archibald T. Davison, was so concerned with this problem that by 1945 he called for a revolution in music education. He would be very surprised if he could have known that by 2017 the revolution had not yet taken hold.

> The most serious demand is for teachers whose knowledge and experience of music is wide enough to guarantee a sound musical taste. Only when there is intelligent revolt against much educational material that now passes for music will there be hope for a productive music education in this country.[5]

[5] Quoted in Willi Apel, *Harvard Dictionary of Music* (Cambridge: Harvard University Press, 1947), 472.

Clearly the cultural level of the people of the United States has been affected by the generations of students who have been deprived of higher musical experience by the failure of their conductor/teachers to understand the deep significance of the role played by the quality of the music presented the students. One who did understand this, Richard Wagner, very clearly warned of the price to be paid.

> The acceptance of the empty for the sound is stunting everything we posses in the way of schools, tuition, academies and so on, by ruining the most natural feelings and misguiding the faculties of the rising generation ... But that we should pay for all this and have nothing left when we come to our senses—that, to be frank, is abominable![6]

[6] Richard Wagner, "On Poetry and Composition," in *Richard Wagner's Prose Works*, trans. William Ashton Ellis (New York: Broude Brothers, 1966), VI, 146ff.

The above impediment to high quality music education brings to mind another problem which is closely related and one nicely symbolized by a conversation I had recently with a gentleman on an Austin golf course. This man had recently retired as a rancher and as a retirement present for himself he bought a new truck. Like all new vehicles this one came with a CD player installed, something the old rancher had never seen before and whose purpose he could not imagine. A friend explained this new playback system and loaned him a CD of Mozart piano concerti. The next time the rancher went off in his truck he put the CD in and was so immediately taken that he pulled off the road to listen for fifteen minutes. He described this fifteen minutes as completely changing his life and the beginning of an obsession with classical music. In view of the enthusiasm with which he described his feelings, I asked about his earlier education. It turned out he was educated entirely in Austin and he swore that during the entirety of his public education he had never once been exposed to even fifteen minutes of "good music," as he put it. When I considered that Austin describes itself as a liberal, above average educated and affluent city it reminded me of how changed the environment had become since my youth. He did volunteer that he had been a member of the college marching band, but he appeared to have never considered that a musical activity. Needless to say, had this man been introduced to "good music" early in his life he would have become a man who regularly donated money to support the local orchestra, opera or ballet. It would seem to me that the quality of music used in music education in Austin should be given serious thought by those older citizens who are currently worried about the survival of these institutions.

Activities, of course, are the first thing which comes to mind when one reflects on high school music in this country. Any wholesome activity has value, but the question is how does one connect these values with education in the classroom? For instance, I have a granddaughter who is now a member of a junior high cheer leading team. There is no question that the amount of hours she spends rehearsing with this team far exceeds the number of hours a student would be required to devote to a middle school musical activity. And this does not include the many weeks of affiliated gymnastic classes she was obligated to take. My granddaughter loves this activity, she has made new friends and it is healthy. For all its apparent value, nevertheless, no one would attempt to correlate this activity to anything inside the classroom.

Sports bands and street marching bands are very similar. This week the local Austin paper published a brief interview with a local high school drum major. The young man described the countless hours of rehearsal involved, including "all of August," and identifies the purpose of the marching band as entertainment, with a repertoire consisting of "classic hits to today's pop tunes."[7]

All youth activities require private support from the parents to cover a host of costs associated with affiliated commercial businesses who provide uniforms, special teaching coaches, travel, etc. I spoke this past summer with a high school band conductor who has to organize a parent fund raising effort to meet the Fall budget of more than $100,000 in costs not supported by the public schools, the accomplishment of which leads to further ties to the world of private business.

The marching band, like cheer leading, is a fine activity, but how does it relate to *music* education? If you ask this very question of any adult associated with such musical ensembles you will hear an immediate list of things which have nothing to do with music—opportunities for leadership training, good posture, good citizenship and the teaching of basic musicianship such as rhythm, tone and attack. But the latter is only the grammar of music and not music at all. Further, in most parts of the US many full-time music conductors who are assigned this activity will admit to preferring to have the students inside sitting in chairs experiencing aesthetic music. However, there have been some educators who question this entire scene, among whom was the late, great Director of Bands at the University of Illinois, Dr. Mark Hindsley.

> We ourselves are the principal creators of public demand in our own field, and in nearly every case we are doing what we want to do rather than what we think or say we are forced to do.[8]

[7] *Austin American-Statesman*, September 13, 2015, C8.

[8] Mark Hindsley, "The Concert Band Conductor and the Marching Band," in *The College and University Band* (Reston, VA: Music Educators National Conference, 1977), 118.

Those loyal and helpful parents who had to raise $100,000 for the band program must ask themselves, if this is an activity made up entirely of students from this particular school why does not the school pay these costs? And with that thought the parents encounter the fundamental enigma of American music education. All students love music and they love to play music. The parents and public know this and they also all love music. But they do not support the costs of music education inside the schools. Yet they will not hesitate for a second to support the costs of teaching calculus, something hardly anyone will ever use the rest of their lives.

The purpose of this book is to provide the thoughtful reader with the background information which is fundamental for understanding the nature of music and its role in society and to thus be able to be in a position to formulate his own attitude regarding this enigma. Our views on music and its role in society are the product of a very long history of intellectual church and secular philosophy, natural science, philology, physiology and a tradition of thousands of years in the practice of music itself.

Following the subsequent four chapters which present this long and complex background of how we have arrived at our understanding of music and its role in society today, I shall conclude with my personal recommendation of what would be required to return music education to its original values, specifically what these values are and how they benefit the development and education of the child.

Tracing the Roots of the Enigma

1
What is Music?

> Music does not exist.
> *Sextus Empiricus (2nd c. AD)*

> I saw in some paper or other
> a charming remark by Theophile Gautier:
> "Music doesn't exist; it's just a sound going around."
> *Franz Liszt, 1878*[1]

> Sounds ... cannot become, in the literal sense, *things*.
> *George Santayana, 1896*

MOST READERS will undoubtedly find the above assertions that music does not exist to be quite inexplicable, in view of the fact that we find ourselves surrounded by music all day long and because music of some sort or other is loved by people all over the world. The root of such a seemingly absurd statement lies in one of the most mysterious and powerful characteristics of music itself: Music is the only Art you cannot see! A significant part of our individual belief system is based on our dependence on the most dominant of our senses, the eyes. "Seeing," we often hear, "is believing."

---

[1] Franz Liszt, letter to Olga von Meyendorff, Rome, September 12, 1878.

Ancient Descriptions of Music

On the Myths and Muses

IN THE ANCIENT WORLD before writing became part of knowledge, myth served as one means of contemplating the past. What was the origin of this mysterious art of music? In some of these ancient myths there may yet be embedded in these stories small nuggets of historical possibilities. Consider, for example, the myth of the sea god, Triton, and his "invention" of the trumpet. He, we are told, in the war against the giants, blew into a sea conch producing sounds so new and frightening that the giants, thinking they had encountered a terrible and ferocious monster, took flight. Well, if we leave out the part about the giants, it certainly is easy to imagine this as a possible scenario for the discovery of the trumpet-type instrument. That is to say, some distant man walking along the shore, picking up a large conch and blowing through it to remove the water and sand, may have produced a frightening sound.

Similarly, when Ovid relates a mythical musical contest between Pan with his panpipes and Apollo with his lyre,[2] a contest which the latter won, could not this be viewed as an allegorical testament to the transformation of Greek music from more ancient rural roots to the much more sophisticated music of the lyric poets?[3]

The lyric poets of the seventh and sixth centuries BC felt a particular relationship to the mythical figures we call the "Muses." Bacchylides (sixth century BC), for example, defined his music as a gift of the Muses,

> ... a monument not made with hands, [that it] might be a common joy for mankind.[4]

Mercury, son to Jupiter and Maia, was said to be of sweet voice and persuasive in speech, inventor of the lyre and aulos and forerunner of mathematicians and astronomers. Mercury is said to have invented, a few hours after birth, the lyre by

---

[2] *Metamorphoses*, Bk. XI. The reader will find a great deal more information on the ancient myths in David Whitwell, *Ancient Views on What is Music,* ed. Craig Dabelstein (Austin: Whitwell Publishing, 2013).

[3] Athenaeus, in *Deipnosophistae*, IX, 390, quotes Chamaeleon of Pontus, a disciple of Aristotle, as saying, "The men of old devised the invention of music from the birds singing in solitary places; by way of imitating them, men instituted the art of music."

[4] *Ode for an Athenian*, Winner of the Foot Races at Isthmus.

stretching sheep-gut strings over the hollow of a tortoise shell.

Plato (427–347 BC) mentioned Calliope, the Muse of Epic Poetry, in relating a discussion by Socrates which centered on an ancient fable about a grasshopper which illustrates the power of music to carry away the listener. We are pleased to find Socrates' assurance here that the Muses know who among us honors them!

> SOCRATES. A lover of music like yourself ought surely to have heard the story of the grasshoppers, who are said to have been human beings in an age before the Muses. And when the Muses came and song appeared the grasshoppers were ravished with delight; and singing always, never thought of eating and drinking, until at last in their forgetfulness they died. And now they live again in the grasshoppers, who, as a special gift from the Muses, require no nourishment, but from the hour of their birth are always singing, and ever eating and drinking; and when they die they go and inform the Muses in heaven which of us honors one or other of the Muses.[5]

[5] *Phdaerus*, 259c.

With Apollo, son to Jupiter, the supreme ruler of the universe, we find the beginning of the long association between music and medicine. He is also associated with the use of music in prophesy, as we see in an interesting poem by Tibullus (54–19 BC).

> His long robes hid the hallowed form from sight,
> and the hem seemed to ripple round his feet.
> At his left side a lyre hung, worked with skill
> that made it gleam with gold and tortoise-shell,
> and while he sang, he plucked it with a quill.
>
> But O the warning sung at that song's end!
> "Gods love all poets," he said, "and such men find
> Bacchus, Apollo, and each Muse a friend."
> Yet those wise sisters and the god of wine—
> they lack the power to see the future plain.
> Jove's gift of foresight is not theirs but mine.
> To me, inevitable fate is clear.[6]

[6] Tibullus, *Poems* III, iv.

Orpheus was considered the chief representative of song and the lyre. Taught by Apollo to play the lyre, Orpheus journeyed to Egypt to study the gods and their rites. In the most familiar myth of Orpheus, he goes to Hades to look for Eurydice, who has been killed by a snake. Orpheus is killed there, but his ghost remains with his beloved Eurydice. Seneca (3 BC – 65 AD) mentions Phoebus [Apollo] with his "unequal pipes" [panpipes, as opposed to the aulos][7] and the frequently told tale of Orpheus using music to conquer nature, which is also a symbol of the importance of the listener.

[7] Seneca, Hippolytus.

> Orpheus born of the melodious Muse, whose plectrum evoked chords at which torrents halted and winds fell silent, at whose music the birds left off their song and with the whole woodland attending followed the singer ... [8]

[8] Seneca, *Medea*, 620, also 350.

Pan, said to be a son to Mercury and a wood-nymph, was god of woods and fields, flocks and shepherds. Pan lived in caves and danced and made love to the Dryads. Fond of music, he invented the *syrinx* (panpipe) and was a master performer on this instrument. The unreasonable fear of Pan by travelers at night caused his name to be used in coining of the word "panic."

Pliny the elder (23–79 AD) gives the following history of the invention of music instruments, information he has gathered from unnamed sources available to him.

> The bronze trumpet [was invented] by Pysaeus son of Tyrrhenus ... Amphion [was responsible for the invention of] music, Pan son of Mercury the flute and single aulos, Midas in Phrygia the slanted flute, Marsyas in the same nation the double aulos, Amphion the Lydian modes, Thracian Thamyras the Dorian, Marsyas of Phrygia the Phrygian, Amphion, or others say Orpheus and others Linus, the harp. Terpander first sang with seven strings, adding three to the original four, Simonides added an eighth, Timotheus a ninth. Thamyris first played the harp without using the voice, Amphion, or according to others Linus, accompanied the harp with singing; Terpander composed songs for harp and voice. Ardalus of Troezen instituted singing to the aulos.[9]

[9] Pliny the Elder, *Natural History* VII, lxi, 204ff.

Finally, one of our favorite Greek myths concerns the use of music at the time of one's death. Philetaerus, in the fourth century BC, cites a myth that if one goes to Hades, but is a recognized lover of good music, one is permitted "to revel in love affairs," whereas "those whose manners are sordid, having no knowledge of music," are condemned to spend eternity carrying water in a fruitless effort to fill "the leaky jar."[10] Thus Philetaerus exclaims, "Zeus, it is indeed a fine thing to die to the music of the aulos!" By this he meant arranging to have these musicians playing as one dies so as to demonstrate to the gods that one truly appreciated good music. And this myth is why we find in the New Testament, before Jesus could perform one of his miracles, that of raising a girl from the dead, he had to first chase the flute players out of the house, saying, "Depart, for the girl is not dead but sleeping."[11]

[10] Philetaerus, *The Aulos Lover*, quoted in Athenaeus, *Deipnosophistae*, XIV, 633.

[11] Matthew 9:24. English translations always incorrectly translate aulos as "flute."

On Ancient Gods of Music

THE ANCIENT PHILOSOPHERS who contemplated the fact that Music cannot be seen did not fail to also observe the impact on the listeners of this mysterious invisible music. Together this made for an immediate association with Religion, which also could not be seen but the results of which were clearly visible in the people.[12]

The area of the Near East which we call Mesopotamia consisted first of isolated city-states, among the oldest of which were Ur, Susa and Kish. The area known as Babylonia consisted of Sumeria to the south and Akkad to the north. During the third millennium BC these peoples were united by the Semitic king, Sargon I. Based on the surviving evidence, Sumeria, c. 3,000 BC, is the oldest civilization we know which developed a sophisticated tradition of music. Since they believed music was of divine origin, they created temples for a number of gods, all of whom they believed had to be entertained, to keep them in good spirits, by singing and playing of instruments. Among these gods was one called *Enlil*, the father of humanity, who governed with a musical instrument called *al*.

[12] The reader can find a great deal of additional information on divine inspiration in David Whitwell, *Ancient Views on What is Music*, ed. Craig Dabelstein (Austin: Whitwell Publishing, 2013)

Soon after the beginning of the second millennium the Amorites invaded Sumeria, ending the Sumerian Empire. From the Sumerian capital, Babylon, we take the name of the people of the next period. The Babylonians (2,000–562 BC) were extraordinary people, excelling in mathematics, astronomy, geography and medicine. They founded schools in which they taught cuneiform writing and they first introduced the 354-day calendar with 12-hour days. With respect to culture, the Babylonians seemed to have little of their own and we can therefore understand that they absorbed completely that of the Sumerians, including their musical traditions. We find a new god, however, *Ea*, who was god of the mysteries and arts, especially associated with the flutist-psalmist.

The Assyrians (750–606 BC), who took their name from the god *Ashur*, were a fierce and warlike collection of tribes who conquered Babylonia. They built the great capital city of Nineveh and began to develop unusual skills in the art of sculpture.[13] But, if it were not for the great stone-reliefs now in the British Museum this empire would probably never be mentioned today, for after their defeat in 612 BC they disappeared from history. Aside from the stone-reliefs, we can see these feared warriors had also some appreciation for music in the fact that whenever they put a city to the sword, they spared the musicians who, with the rest of the valuable booty, were sent back to Nineveh.[14]

In Egypt (2,686–52 BC) as in other ancient civilizations, the spiritual nature of music caused it to be linked in myth with the gods. We find this especially interesting with respect to the limited hieroglyphic language of Egypt. For example, the symbol which represents the god who created earth is also used to represent the god *Hesu*, who created music. Another dual god, *Hathor*, was both the goddess of love and the goddess of music. A hymn to Hathor found in the temple of Dandera, seems to refer to the "music of the spheres," a familiar notion among the ancient philosophers, most notably Pythagoras.[15]

[13] Carl Engel, *The Music of The Most Ancient Nations* (London: Reeves, 1909), 24ff.

[14] Henry G. Farmer, "The Music of Ancient Mesopotamia," in *The New Oxford History of Music* (London: Oxford University Press, 1966), 237.

[15] The reader can find an extensive essay on the historical views on the Music of the Spheres, as well as on Pythagoras, in David Whitwell, *Ancient Views of the Natural World*, ed. Craig Dabelstein (Austin: Whitwell Publishing, 2013).

To thee, the heaven and its stars make music,
Sun and moon sing praises to thee,
The whole earth is making music for thee.[16]

[16] Quoted in Lise Manniche, *Music and Musicians in Ancient Egypt* (London: British Museum Press, 1991), 12.

There is an extraordinary painting from the more recent Graeco-Roman temple at Medamund, north of Thebes, which includes a complete hymn to the god Hathor. We see a group of female musicians, with harp, drum, and lute, beneath a hieroglyph description:

> The members of the choir take up their instruments and play them. The songstreses in full number adore the Golden Goddess and make music to the Golden Goddess: they never cease their chanting.

The text of the hymn is written behind the lutanist and a singer. We take notice especially of the aim of this music, "nourishment for the heart."

> Come, O Golden Goddess, the singers chant
> for it is nourishment for the heart to dance the *iba*,
> to shine over the feast at the hour of retiring
> and to enjoy dance at night.[17]

[17] Ibid., 61.

In yet another painting celebrating Hathor, no fewer than twenty-nine female musicians are pictured with percussion instruments.

Another goddess, *Merit*, was considered to be the personification of music. And then there was the strange dwarf god *Bes*, usually associated with childbirth but who, nevertheless, is usually pictured playing a variety of musical instruments. All in all, what we see in these myths is a special significance given to Music from the earliest of times.

In the oldest tomb paintings of the Old Kingdom (2,686–2,181 BC) we can see musicians included in scenes associated with the worship of the gods. In later periods we learn the names of such musicians who are also identified as having positions related to the worship of these gods. One of these, Amenemhab, who appears several times in the 18th Dynasty is described in a stela as having "followed the king's footsteps in foreign lands." He is identified as holding a very high office, "overseer of the singers of the North and South," and he describes his role as a performer in the temple:

> I purify my mouth. I adore the gods. I exalt *Horus* who is in the sky. I adore him. The *Ennead* listens, the inhabitants of the Underworld rejoice. They appear at my voice.

Plutarch (46–127 AD) wrote that "some have thought that God himself played upon the aulos."[18] He was probably referring to Apollo, into whose rites he had been initiated. In the Old Testament we are told that the Hebrew god was also a musician. Zechariah 9:14 tells us God was a trumpet player, although Psalm 105 describes him as a choral conductor.[19]

Although not among the ancient gods or muses, one of the Christian saints, St. Cecilia, has become in the English-speaking world, in effect, a modern goddess of Music. The oldest account of St. Cecilia is found in the "Martyrologium Hieronymianum" and her feast day has been celebrated since the fourth century. By an early date this celebration fell on November 22, on which it is still commemorated today. Since the fourteenth century she has been pictured with an organ as an attribute, or is represented as playing on the organ, evidently based on an incorrect translation of *organis*, "instruments." In any case this began the association with music and this has resulted in many poems and compositions in her honor.

For modern readers, of course, these tales of the association of music with various ancient gods can only be viewed as another type of myth. For earlier people, however, there were views taken quite seriously which were based on these ancient beliefs. Roger Ascham, a widely known intellectual and the private tutor of Queen Elizabeth I in England, in his *Toxophilus*, quotes the famous medieval medical writer, Galen, as observing that the lower crafts man learned by observing animals, such as learning weaving by watching spiders. However, the higher arts man learned from the gods, such as shooting and music from Apollo.[20]

---

[18] "Concerning Music." In "The Banquet of the Seven Wise Men," he points out that "the Gods are better pleased with the sounds of panpipes and the aulos than with the voice of men."

[19] The early Church father, Clement of Alexandria, also referred to "the Choirmaster, the Lord," in "The Miscellanies," trans. William Wilson (Edinburgh: T & T Clark, 1884), VI, xi.

[20] *Toxophilus*, in *The Whole Works of Roger Ascham*, ed. Rev. Giles (London: John Russell Smith, 1864), II, 25ff. Ascham explains at length why shooting is the ideal exercise for the student—such things as tennis and bowling being too "vehement."

On Natural Science and the Listener

AS MENTIONED ABOVE, for ancient writers the most mysterious aspect of music was that it could not be seen. But furthermore you cannot smell it, nor reach out and touch it. What is it, then? One might suppose that an early step toward discovering the correct answer to that question came when observers noticed that when on a string instrument you set the highest string in motion with the plectrum, the lowest string also begins to vibrate all on its own, without being touched. In the early years, when the Church made faith and not science the basis of knowledge, the descriptions of elements of natural science were sometimes sought in the supernatural. We see an example of this in a passage written by Agathias Scholasticus (536–594 AD) in which he quotes a musician named Androtion, who in turn quotes Aristotle's student, Aristoxenus (fourth century BC.)

> "When you set the highest string on the right in motion with the plectron, the lowest on the left quivers of its own accord with a slight twang, and is made to whisper reciprocally when its own highest string is struck; so that I marvel how nature made sympathetic to each other lifeless strings in a state of tension." But he swore that Aristoxenus, with his admirable knowledge of plectra, did not know the theoretical explanation of this. "The solution," he said, "is as follows. The strings are all made of sheep's gut dried all together. So they are sisters and sound together as if related, sharing each other's family voice. For they are all legitimate children, being the issue of one belly, and they inherit those reciprocal noises."[21]

It was from such logic that we find the following from an otherwise great writer, 1193–1280 AD:

> The animosity between the wolf and sheep is so strong its influence extends to all of their anatomical parts; thus, musical strings made of sheep gut do not resonate in harmony with strings made of wolf gut.[22]

Some early thinkers focused not on the vibrations in themselves, but rather on the air. We find this, for example,

[21] *The Greek Anthology*, trans. W. R. Paton (Cambridge: Harvard University Press, 1939), IV, 352.

[22] *De Animalibus*, trans. James Scanlan (Binghamton, NY: Medieval & Renaissance Texts, 1987), 158.

in some observations by the early Renaissance composer and writer, Chaucer (1343–1400 AD), in his poem, "The House of Fame." Sound, he says, is nothing but broken air, thus all speech is nothing but air.[23] Similarly, when a player strikes the harp strings, whether hard or lightly, "the air breaks apart with the stroke." When a pipe is blown "sharp" [strongly?], what we hear is the air "twisted and rent with violence."

Supernatural references also came to the early writers aid in accounting for the overtone series. No one knows how distant was the man who first heard overtones, but even with our diminished capacity if you can hear the fourth overtone you hear the major third, which may give us a clue why bone flutes thousands of years old have holes punched in them to form a diatonic scale. But for Plotinus (204–270 AD), the purpose of the overtones were to "wake the Soul to the consciousness of beauty."[24]

Marin Mersenne (1588–1648) could not offer the correct explanation for what the overtones were, physically, so he found in them a metaphor for moral action.

> If the tone of each string is more harmonious and agreeable as it makes a greater number of different tones heard in the same time, and if one may be permitted to compare moral actions to natural, and to translate Physics into human actions, one can say that each action is as much more agreeable and harmonious to God, as it is accompanied by a greater number of motives, provided that they all be good.[25]

From the perspective of the performance of music today the most important consideration of the overtone series, apart from intonation, is the relationship of the fundamental to the ear.

> As in musical concords, when the upper strings are so tuned as exactly to accord, the base always gives the tone; so in well-regulated and well-ordered families, all things are carried on with the harmonious consent and agreement of both parties, but the conduct and contrivance chiefly redounds to the reputation and management of the husband.[26]

[23] "The House of Fame," II, 765ff.

[24] *The Enneads*, trans. Stephen MacKenna (London: Farber and Farber, 1962), 59.

[25] *Harmonie universelle* V, iv, 10.

[26] "Of the Procreation of the Soul."

By the time Plutarch (46–127 AD), a great early philosopher and historian, wrote the lines above, the relationships of at least the lower portion of the overtone series had been understood for about five centuries. The analogy between marriage and harmony by Plutarch, therefore, is one in which the lowest, fundamental pitch governs music as should the husband govern the family. But there is another basic principle he may well have been thinking of, which relates to how we hear music. In the case of music which lies approximately in the octave above third-space C in the treble clef, our brain seems to alter what we hear by making these tones seem to us louder than they really are. This is almost surely a result of adaptation, the purpose being to make more distinct the higher pitched sounds of consonants used in ordinary speech.

We don't read about this phenomenon until the Renaissance, but then immediately one notices that conductors have learned how to overcome this phenomenon. We call this technique by a name given it in the nineteenth century, the "pyramid principle." In practical terms it means ensemble music, both vocal and instrumental, must be artificially balanced by making the lowest tones louder and the highest tones softer. If done carefully the result is that what the listener hears corresponds with what the composer wrote on paper. In a word, we fool the brain of the listener into thinking they hear what the composer wrote.

An early reference to the pyramid principle is found in an important early treatise on singing, the *De modo bene cantandi* (1474) by Conrad von Zabern, who was associated with Heidelberg University. The following discussion by Conrad, on the subject of singing too loud in the upper register, is a clear discussion of the problem and its correct accommodation.

> Another fault which is more obvious than the others is singing high notes with an unstintingly full and powerful voice. This is even more careless than what we have cited above, as will soon become evident. When this shouting is done by individuals with resonant and trumpet-like voices it

disturbs and confuses the singing of the entire choir, just as if the voices of cattle were heard among the singers. In a certain eminent collegiate establishment I once heard singers with these trumpet-like voices singing with all their strength in the highest register as if they wished to break the windows of the choir, or at least to shake them. As I marveled not a little at their coarseness, I was moved to make up this rhyme:

*In choir you bellow
Like cows in the meadow!*

I use this jingle in an informal fashion in my efforts and teaching regarding the art of good singing in order to ridicule all those presuming to sing loudly in the high register, to the end that they might recognize their careless crudeness and, after recognizing, zealously desist from it.

In order to recognize this error completely it must be realized that whoever wishes to sing well and clearly must employ his voice in three ways: resonantly and trumpet-like for low notes, moderately in the middle range and more delicately for the high notes—the more so the higher the chant ascends.

In the great early book on performance practice, the third volume of Michael Praetorius' *Syntagma Musicum* [1619], this composer and conductor makes an interesting recommendation regarding creating a third dimension of this principle in performing cadences.

As a piece is brought to a close, all the remaining voices should stop simultaneously at the sign of the conductor or choir master. The tenors should not prolong their tone, a fifth above the bass or lowest voice ... after the bass has stopped. But if the bass continues to sound a little longer, for another two or four *tactus*, it lends charm and beauty to the music [*Cantilenae*], which no one can deny.

Rene Descartes (1596–1650) also appears to have been aware of the necessary pyramid restructuring necessary to overcome the brain's tendency to hear the highest voices as the most important. In a comment regarding the bass voice he writes, "it must strike the ear more forcibly in order to be heard distinctly."[27]

In the early nineteenth century we have a clear presentation of the accommodation of this hearing problem by the

[27] "Compendium of Music," trans. Walter Robert (American Institute of Musicology, 1961), 48.

man who coined the term, "acoustic pyramid," Wilhelm Wieprecht, the most influential man in the reorganization of Prussian military music.

The first person who began to understand correctly the role of vibrations in the physical production of music was Francis Bacon (1561–1626), whom Will Durant called "the greatest and proudest intellect of the age."[28] Bacon came close, but was not entirely accurate when he concluded, "The sound is not created between the bow and the string; but between the string and the air." He believed the musical instrument set in motion something he called "local motion," and it was here the sound was created. His clearest explanation reads,

> It would be extreme grossness to think that the sound in strings is made or produced between the hand and the strings, or the quill and the string, or the bow and the string, for those are but *vehicula motus*, passages to the creation of the sound; the sound being produced between the string and the air; and that not by any impulsion of the air from the first motion of the string, by the return or result of the string, which was strained by the touch, to his former place; which motion of result is quick and sharp; whereas the first motion is soft and dull. So the bow tortures the string continually, and therefore holds it in a continual trepidation.[29]

He believed that a certain force was necessary to set this air in motion, which he believed was documented in the face of trumpet and horn players, as one could clearly see in wind players, "which appeareth by the blown cheeks of him that windeth them.[30] This explosion of air which he associates with tone production leads him to observe,

> It hath been anciently reported, and is still received, that extreme applause and shouting of people assembled in great multitudes, have so rarefied and broken the air, that birds flying over have fallen down, the air being not able to support them.[31]

Since Bacon understood music to be created in the air, and not in the vibrations, he was at a loss to explain why vibrating tongs set in water seem to produce sounds under

[28] Will Durant, *The Age of Reason Begins* (New York: Simon and Schuster, 1961), 169, 183.

[29] *Natural History* in *The Works of Francis Bacon* (Cambridge: Cambridge University Press, 1869), V, Section 137.

[30] Ibid., Section 116.

[31] Ibid., Section 127.

water where there is no air present.³² The true function of the ear turning these vibrations into "Music," would not be clearly understood until the late sixteenth century, in particular in the works of John Locke.

Of course the importance of the ear with respect to hearing music was evident from an early period and given its due attention. For example, we find this in Cicero (106–43 BC):

> The organ of hearing … is always open, since we require this sense even when asleep, and when it receives a sound, we are aroused even from sleep. The auditory passage is winding, to prevent anything from being able to enter, as it might if the passage were clear and straight; it has further been provided that even the tiniest insect that may attempt to intrude may be caught in the sticky wax of the ears. On the outside project the organs which we call ears, which are constructed both to cover and protect the sense-organ and to prevent the sounds that reach them from sliding past and being lost before they strike the sense. The apertures of the ears are hard and gristly, and much convoluted, because things with these qualities reflect and amplify sound; this is why tortoise-shell or horn gives resonance to a lyre, and also why winding passages and enclosures have an echo which is louder than the original sound.³³

The phenomenon of the echo was a complete mystery for a very long time. Bacon, for example, thought the echo to be "a great argument for the spiritual essence of sounds."³⁴ Kircher (1601–1680) devoted considerable space in Book Nine of his *Musurgia Universalis* (Rome, 1650) to echoes and found a building in Pavia which he reported would return an echo thirty times. It would take a long time before someone realized that if there was no player present, and no instrument present, in the direction from which one heard an echo, then it must be related to the original source.

While the fact that music could not be seen was a focus of much philosophical discussion, it followed that there was a growing interest in the listener for without a listener music can have no purpose, as Erasmus pointed out, "Hidden music has no listeners (and is thus worthless)."³⁵ Mersenne noticed that the listener needed variety and that a single

---

³² Ibid., Section 133.

³³ Cicero, *De Natura Deorum*, II, lvi, 140ff.

³⁴ Bacon, Ibid., Section 287.

³⁵ *The Collected Works of Erasmus* (Toronto: University of Toronto Press, 1992), XXXII, 117ff.

long tone could be "amazing tiresome" and that preference for specific instruments might have as much to do with the temperament of the listener as with the instrument itself. He also noticed that the distance between the listener and the musicians affected the effectiveness of the music.

Some listeners began to notice that music sounds better at night. For Bacon it was because it was easier to concentrate on one sense.[36] The Reverend Joseph Hall (1574–1656) agreed, "All harmonious sounds are advanced by a silent darkness."[37]

By the seventeenth century there developed considerable interest in whether music is affected by geography and climate as is suggested in the following by Montesquieu (1689–1755), in his "Of the Difference of Men in different climates."[38]

> As climates are distinguished by degrees of latitude, we might distinguish them also in some measure by those of sensibility. I have been at the opera in England and in Italy, where I have seen the same pieces and the same performers: and yet the same music produces such different effects on the two nations: one is so cold and phlegmatic, and the other so lively and enraptured, that it seems almost inconceivable.

Our interest in this question is, of course, whether the physiological impact of climate affects national character and, in turn, national predilections in music. One can find many observations such as the following conclusion by Robert Greene (1560–1592), an important English playwright and observer of manners.

> In Crete you must learn to lie, in Paphos to be a lover, in Greece a dissembler, you must bring home pride from Spain, lasciviousness from Italy, gluttony from England and carousing from the Danes.[39]

This reminds us of a letter the young Mendelssohn wrote to his sister, Rebecca.

> In Italy I was lazy, in Switzerland a wild student, in Munich a consumer of cheese and beer and in Paris I must talk politics.[40]

[36] *Natural History*, Section 241.

[37] *The Works of Joseph Hall, D.D.*, ed. Philip Wynter (New York: AMS Press, 1969), X, 142.

[38] Charles de Secondat, Baron de Montesquieu, *The Spirit of Laws* (1748), trans. Thomas Nugent in *Great Books*, XXXVIII (Chicago: Encyclopedia Britannica, 1952), 102ff.

[39] Robert Greene, *Mourning Garment* (c. 1590), in *The Life and Complete Works of Robert Greene*, ed. Alexander Grosart (New York: Russell & Russell, 1964), IX, 136. His romance, *Pandosto* (1588) was the source of Shakespeare's *Winter's Tale*.

[40] Letter of December 20, 1831.

With respect to music, such generalizations are particularly prevalent when the subject is the vocal characteristics of different nations. Thus one finds these sweeping conclusions by two German philosophers of the Renaissance. First, Henry Agrippa (1486–1536), in his discussion of moral philosophy, provides amusing characterizations of the men of various nations. After with comparing them as lovers, in their speech and dress, he adds,

> We know moreover that the Italians do bleat in their singing, the Spaniards wail, the Germans howl and the French sing with pleasant tone and accent.[41]

[41] Henry Cornelius Agrippa, *Of the Vanitie and Uncertaintie of Arts and Sciences*, ed. Catherine Dunn (Northridge: California State University, Northridge Press, 1974), 161.

Similarly, Andreas Ornithoparchus, in his *Musice active micrologus* of 1517, observes,

> Various nations have diverse fashions and differ in clothes, diet, studies, speech and song. Hence it is that the English carol, the French sing, the Spaniards weep, the Italians caper with their voices and others bark. But the Germans, I am ashamed to say, howl like wolves.[42]

[42] *Ornithoparchus, Musicae active mirologus* and Dowland, *Introduction: Containing the Art of Singing* (New York: Dover, 1973), 208ff.

We are not immune today from this ear-based prejudice as we speak, for example, in the difference between the French oboe sound and the German oboe sound. And for those who have lived and worked in Europe, the very phrases "German orchestras," "French orchestras" and "Italian orchestras" bring to mind powerfully different memories.[43]

[43] Additional information on the perception of music can be found in David Whitwell, *Music Education of the Future*, ed. Craig Dabelstein (Austin: Whitwell Books, 2011).

Is Music a Branch of Mathematics?

> Music is the daughter of Arithmetic.
> Anonymous, *Scholia enchiriadis*, c. 900 AD

THIS ANONYMOUS TREATISE, written at the very dawn of the creation of our modern music notation system, also epitomizes the central problem which all earlier philosophers had with music and which confuses music educators today. In a word, how do you make music, whose essence and values are non-rational, fit into a rational world? The answer for modern music educators is to ignore the inherent values in music and focus instead on teaching *about* music. For the early philosophers the answer was to simply ignore the characteristics of music they couldn't explain and take what they could understand and declare music Rational.

> [Music is] the rational discipline of agreement and discrepancy of sounds according to numbers in their relation to those things which are found in sounds ... Because everything comprehended by these disciplines exists through reason formed of numbers and without numbers can be neither understood nor made known.[44]

Once the ancients discovered they could use numbers to represent musical sounds they were delighted, for now they could bring music into their world of Reason. The early Church was also delighted, for now it could admit music into the curriculum as a branch of mathematics and avoid entirely the discussion of the emotions in music, a very sensitive topic since they had for so long preached that the emotions were "the first step toward sin!"

The origin of the idea of using numbers to represent music tones is usually attributed to Pythagoras (580–500 BC). Like much of ancient Greek culture, however, perhaps some of his ideas came from the older society of Egypt. Iamblichus (c. 250–325 AD) tells us, for example, that Pythagoras spent twelve years in Egypt where he studied "arithmetic, music and all the other sciences."[45] Since nothing by his own hand has survived, and because of that there is a lot of nonsense attributed to Pythagoras, it is difficult to determine exactly his role in music history. He certainly was not the first to discover the overtone series, but he may have been the first to use numbers as symbols to represent the intervals between the lower pitches of the series.[46] One can see how the relationship between mathematics and music followed.

Aristotle found here a fundamental theory for looking at the world.

> The so-called Pythagoreans, who were the first to take up mathematics, not only advanced this study, but also having

[44] Anonymous, "Of Symphonies," in Oliver Strunk, *Source Readings in Music History* (New York: Norton, 1950), 135. The reader can find additional information on the subject of Music and Mathematics in David Whitwell, *Ancient Views on What is Music*, ed. Craig Dabelstein (Austin: Whitwell Publishing, 2013).

[45] Iamblichus, "The Life of Pythagoras."

[46] Thus his greatest contribution to mankind, the idea that numbers could represent abstract thought was the beginning of all higher mathematics.

been brought up in it they thought that its principles were the principles of all things. And since of these principles *numbers* are by nature the first, and in numbers they seemed to see many resemblances to the things that exist and come into being—more than in fire and earth and water ... since again, they saw that the modifications and the ratios of the musical scales were expressible in numbers—since, then, all other things seemed in their whole nature modeled on numbers, and numbers seemed to be the first things in the whole of nature, they supposed the elements of numbers to be the elements of all things, and the whole heaven to be a musical scale and a number.[47]

[47] *Metaphysics*.

Following this line of thought, one can understand how medieval philosophers could come to the hypothesis that perhaps the organization of the planets was related to the numerical order of the intervals of the overtone series and that one could therefore study astronomy (in a time with no adequate telescopes) through studying music. But we are perhaps more surprised to discover that some early philosophers found a connection between music and *grammar*, as Sextus Empiricus (second century AD) did:

> For this is a feature of arts which are conjectural and subject to accidents such as navigation and medicine; but Grammar is not a conjectural art but akin to Music and Philosophy.[48]

[48] Sextus Empiricus, "Against the Professors," trans. R. G. Bury (Cambridge: Harvard University Press, 1949), I, 72.

In Aristotle's observation, quoted above, that numbers were to be thought of as the basis of nature, we can see that by the sixth century AD virtually all of science was now incorporated into mathematics. This is clearly expressed in a letter by Cassiodorus (480–573 AD) to the famous mathematician, Boethius (475–524 AD). Boethius certainly considered that music was within his expertise as a mathematician, leaving his readers to choke on musical description such as this:

> But since the nete synemmenon to the mese (3,456 to 4,608) holds a sesquitertian ratio—that is, a diatessaron—whereas the trite synemmenon to the nete synemmenon (4,374 to 3,456) holds the ratio of two tones ...[49]

[49] Boethius, *Fundamentals of Music*, trans. Calvin Bower (New Haven: Yale University Press), IV, ix.

Aurelian of Reome, in his *Musica Disciplina* of c. 843 AD, treats the relationship of mathematics and music as if the *numbers* of the intervals were subject to weighing and not hearing.

> Music has the greatest correspondence to mathematics and encompasses that part of mathematics that compares one quantity with another.[50]

With the beginning of the Renaissance we find a representative treatise by one of the *ars antique*, Jacques de Liege. His treatise is called a "music treatise," *Speculum Musicae* (1313), but the first five of its seven books deal with mathematics. His contemporary, Jean de Muris (c. 1290–1350), points to the relationship of music and geometry when he observes that "the wiser ancients long ago agreed and conceded that geometrical figures should be the symbols of musical sounds."[51] This he follows with an extraordinary omission, which, had he filled it, would be more interesting to us today than the rest of his entire treatise. It also reminds us that theory and notation always follow the actual practice of music.

> For reasons which we shall pass over, their symbols did not adequately represent what they sang.

It is among the German writers of the Baroque that we find the first clear documentation of a new era of philosophy in music, a philosophy *not* based on mathematics. The most important discussion on this view that has come down to us is by Johann Mattheson, (1681–1764). In his *Neu-Eröffnete Orchestre* Mattheson attacks the old notion of mathematics-based theory in music by going directly to the elements upon which the older theorists had based their reasoning, in particular the nature of the intervals. In his discussion of whether the interval of the fourth should regarded as a consonance or dissonance, Mattheson concludes it is not a matter of mathematics, but rather a matter of the ear, that is how the fourth is used. The reader should particularly notice, as a hallmark of the Baroque's movement away from music based on concepts to music based on feeling, that Mattheson specifies here that music communicates with "the inner soul."

[50] Aurelian of Reome, *The Discipline of Music*, trans. Joseph Ponte (Colorado Springs: Colorado College Music Press, 1968), VI.

[51] Ibid., 175.

> Numbers in music do not govern but merely instruct. The Hearing is the only channel through which their force is communicated to the inner soul of the attentive listener ... The true aim of music is not its appeal to the eye, nor yet altogether to the so-called "Reason," but only to the Hearing, which communicates pleasure, as it is experienced, to the Soul and the "Reason." Hence, if the testimony of the ear is followed, it will be discovered that in its relation to the surrounding sounds and harmony, the fourth will be either consonant or dissonant.[52]

However there were some in Germany who still professed the old mathematical rules of polyphony. One, Johann Buttstedt, an organist in Erfurt, published a book attacking Mattheson. To defend himself, Mattheson published a new book, *Das Beschützte Orchestre*, in which he appealed to a number of distinguished German musicians to join in the debate over mathematics versus feelings, and some distinguished musicians came to the defense of Mattheson. Handel wrote Mattheson at this time, taking a very practical approach to the debate.

> The question seems to me to reduce itself to this: whether one should prefer an easy & most perfect Method to another that is accompanied by great difficulties capable not only of disgusting pupils with Music, but also making them waste much precious time that could better be employed in plunging deeper into this art & in the cultivation of one's genius?[53]

Johann Heinichen, in language much stronger than Mattheson's, ridiculed the old-fashioned theorists as having wasted their entire life in pursuit of *rudera antiquitatis*.

> All will be sheer Greek to those steeped in prejudices when nowadays they hear that a moving music composed for the ears requires even more subtle and skillful rules—to say nothing of lengthy practice—than the heavily oppressive music composed for the eyes which the cantors of even the tiniest towns maltreat on innocent paper according to all the venerable rules of counterpoint ... And we Germans alone are such fools as to jog on in the old groove and, absurdly and ridiculously, to make the appearance of the composition on paper, rather than the hearing of it, the aim of music.[54]

[52] Johann Mattheson, *Das Neu-Eröffnete Orchestre* (Hamburg, 1713), 126ff. Mattheson also writes at length in opposition to the old dogma that mathematics is the basis of music in his book, *Das Forschende Orchestre* of 1721.

[53] George Friedrich Handel, letter to Johann Mattheson, February 24, 1719, quoted in Piero Weiss, *Letters of Composers Through Six Centuries* (Philadelphia: Chilton, 1967), 63.

[54] Quoted in Cannon, Beekman, *Johann Mattheson, Spectator in Music* [New Haven], 141ff.

How then does one describe the role mathematics plays in music, together with its other elements? Mattheson offers the following metaphor:

> The human mind is the paper. Mathematics is the pen.
> Sounds are the ink; but Nature must be the writer.

The point, he says, is this: "music draws its water from the spring of Nature; and not from the puddles of arithmetic." The composer expresses something understood from Nature. Only then can this be mathematically expressed, but not the other way around. When Mattheson speaks here of Nature, he is also thinking of God.

> Mathematics is a human skill; nature, however, is a divine force ... Now the goal of music is to praise God in the highest, with word and deed, through singing and playing. All other arts besides theology and its daughter, music, are only mute priests. They do not move hearts and minds nearly so strongly, nor in so many ways ... Music is *above*, not in *opposition* to mathematics.

In conclusion, Mattheson cannot resist taking a shot at those remaining exponents of the old mathematics-based polyphony.

> I have occupied myself with music, practical as well as theoretical, with great earnestness and ardor for over half a century already: I have also met many very learned *Mathematici* in this not insubstantial time who thought they made new musical wonders out of their old, logical writings; but they have, God knows! always failed miserably. On the other hand, I have quite certainly and very often experienced that not a single famous actor, musician, nor composer, not only in my time but as far as I can remember having read or heard about, has been able to construct even a simple melody which was of any value on the feeble foundations of mathematics or geometry ... What will happen in the future is yet to be seen.

We might also add that in his biographical work, *Ehrenpforte* (Hamburg, 1740), in reference to a person who had claimed both a goal of making "music a scientific or scholarly pursuit" and in association with Bach, Johann Mattheson adds that Bach certainly did not teach this man "the supposed mathematical basis of composition." "This," Mattheson testifies, "I can guarantee."[55]

Nothing much more was heard of mathematics until the twentieth century when the serial composers appeared. The Twelve-Tone Era lasted about fifty years (the same length as the Classical Period) and is now dead.[56] It produced music the public did not want to hear and today it is difficult to think of even five compositions from this period which remain in the repertoire.

[55] Quoted in Hans T. David and Arthur Mendel, *The Bach Reader* (New York: Norton, 1966), 440.

[56] Francis McBeth, a musician we admired, told us, "Thank God I lived long enough to see the death of Communism and Twelve-Tone music!"

On the Physiology of Music

WHAT IS ON PAPER is *not* music. Music is something you hear with the ears. This fact alone means that music is, and has forever been, physiological in its very nature. The very fact that the physical existence of music is unseen vibrations in the air which are miraculously interpreted as "music" by the inner ear and brain is something which never occurs to most music students. On the other hand, for listeners some physiological characteristics of music are so familiar to everyone that we take them for granted and never pause to consider their physiological significance. As an illustration, I was once discussing the physiological aspects of music with a very distinguished physician on a Los Angeles golf course. While the doctor professed to know nothing about music, when I began the discussion of the physiological nature of music he immediately interjected, "Oh, but of course everyone knows you can change your mood by changing the music!" And yet, that which he describes as something "everyone knows," is in fact a very sophisticated mental process.

In February 2006, during a dinner with a top nuclear physicist from Los Alamos, I turned the conversation to work being done by physicists in Europe who are studying geometric formations in molecules which occur as a result of the sounding of a pitch. While he did not know of this research, he responded that he was in no way surprised because everything consists of moving molecules.

This work in Europe is only one example of numerous clinical studies in recent years which deal with the physiological nature of music. Consider the important research being done by Dr. Deutsch at the University of California, San Diego, which has proven, among other things, that we do not hear "stereophonically," but that one ear hears higher tones and the other ear lower tones which are then, no doubt because of adaptation needed by early man for survival, "mixed" by the brain.[57]

[57] She says the only way for an audience to correctly hear a symphony orchestra would be to hang the audience from the ceiling by their feet. The point being that the ear which hears the higher pitches is on the wrong side of our head to hear the violins seated to our left.

And, finally, consider the fact that the emotional impact which the listener experiences in hearing music is also physiological. This should be a focus of music education, helping the student learn "who he is," emotionally. It should be a vital concern among music educators because they can teach in this area and the rest of the teachers in the school cannot.

The fact that we ignore all these manifestations of the physiological nature of music, and more, in our music schools is like teaching astronomy, or geometry, without the underlying math. Not only do American music schools not discuss the physiological nature of music in depth, they are *afraid* to discuss some aspects of this subject—like the influence of music on character, for example.

We have just touched on some of the contemporary areas of study dealing with the physiological nature of music. But the subject is very ancient. Below we will present some ancient views on the relationship of emotion and music. All philologists believe that musical sounds were used as a means of communication by early man before there was language. One who discussed this very topic was Richard Wagner and he added the concept of early man combining gesture with his musical utterances. Eons later, when oratory became a discipline, early teachers of oratory all stressed the relationships between oratory, gesture and music. What they meant by that was that, like the musician, the orator must emotionally move his listeners. And so to this very day teachers of oratory discuss the broad subject of the emotional connection with the audience. This does not happen in music studies. The music teacher does *not* discuss how to move the feelings of the listener. That is, emotions in music are not taught as the natural purpose and object of music communication, but only as an element of individual technique. The central purpose of music is to communicate feeling to a listener, yet we do not teach this. We leave the irony of this fact to the imagination of the reader.

On Early Music Therapy

Apollo was the Greek god of both music and medicine.

AMONG THE ANCIENT PHILOSOPHERS one finds a great variety of physical illnesses reported to have been cured by music. Of these, no doubt the accounts most familiar to the contemporary reader are those dealing with the bite of the spider. Athanasius Kircher (16010–1680), a German born scholar who spent most of his adult life in Rome, was the author of the *Musurgia Universalis* (Rome, 1650), a virtual encyclopedia of music. In Book Nine of this massive work, "The Magic of Consonance and Dissonance," Kircher discusses the effects of music on the mind and the use of music therapy, including the use of music to cure the bite of the Tarantula spider. Kircher cites several histories of this phenomenon, including a girl who was bitten and was cured by the music of only a drum. In another case, however, he reports a volunteer allowed himself to be bitten by two Tarantulas, of different colors. As the bite of one responded to music and dance, but the bite of the other was made worse, the patient died. Kircher's technical medical explanation reads,

> The poison is sharp, gnawing, and bilious and is received and incorporated into the medullary substances of the fibers. The music has the power to rarefy the air to a certain harmonic pitch; the air thus rarefied, penetrating the pores of the patient's body, affects the muscles, arteries, and minute fibers, and incites him to dance, which begets a perspiration, in which the poison evaporates.

In an earlier book, *Magnes siue De arte magnetica opus tripartitum* (Rome, 1641), Kircher also discusses "the magnetic power and faculties of music" and "the affections of the mind which music excites." Here again, of particular interest is a special science which he calls "Tarantism," the study of the "magnetism and amazing sympathy with music" of the Tarantula.

The great German commentator on Baroque performance practice, Johann Mattheson, cites a publication, *Quintessence des Novelles*, 1727, Nr. 18,[58] which contains the music of a Rondo recommended for use as a cure for the bite of the Tarantula spider. Finally, we have a testimonial of a physician, the Jacobean English doctor, Sir Thomas Browne. He has no doubt that these ancient tales are true.

> Some doubt many have of the *tarantula*, or poisonous spider of Calabria, and that magical cure of the bit thereof by music. But since we observe that many attest it from experience; since the learned Kircher has positively averred it, and set down the songs and tunes solemnly used for it; since some also affirm the *tarantula* itself will dance upon certain strokes, whereby they set their instruments against its poison, we shall not at all question it.[59]

Curiously, of all the physical ailments for which music received credit as being able to cure, the one most often mentioned by ancient philosophers was madness. One can see how important this idea must have been in the early accounts, for while even the most objective person would have to conclude that our society is far from civilized, it is very possible that earlier societies were even less well mannered. This certainly seems a distinct possibility when one reads the famous medical authority, Galen (second century AD):

> Whenever a man becomes violently angry over little things and bites and kicks his servants, you are sure that this man is in a state of passion.
>
> .....
>
> I watched a man eagerly trying to open a door. When things did not work out as he would have them, I saw him bite the key, kick the door, blaspheme, glare wildly like a madman, and all but foam at the mouth like a wild boar.[60]

If Galen's descriptions here of a passionate man were typical, then perhaps we can understand how music could have been more important to earlier societies than ours—at least most of us have advanced to a point of cultivation where we do not bite each other or foam at the mouth like a wild boar!

---

[58] Johann Mattheson, *Der vollkommene Capellmeister* (1739), trans. Ernest Harriss (Ann Arbor: UMI Research Press, 1981), I, iii, 43. The reader can find additional readings on both Music Therapy and on Pythagoras in David Whitwell, *Ancient Views on the Natural World,* ed. Craig Dabelstein (Austin: Whitwell Books, 2013).

[59] "Enquiries into Vulgar and Common Errors," in *Sir Thomas Browne's Works*, ed. Simon Wilkin (London: Pickering, 1836), II, 536.

[60] Galen, "On the Passions and Errors of the Soul," trans. Paul W. Harkins (Columbus: Ohio State University Press), 29, 38.

An important early reference is found in the most important book on music of the fifth century, the allegorical description of "The Marriage of Philology and Mercury," by Martianus Capella. This work is a defense of the importance of the seven liberal arts, which were by this time established in the Roman schools. These were the *Trivium,* consisting of Grammar, Dialectic, and Rhetoric, and the *Quadrivium,* consisting of Geometry, Arithmetic, Astronomy, and Music [here called by an ancient synonym, "Harmony"]. The book was written at a time when Christianity had not yet won its final battle against the "pagans" and might well be thought of as an attempt to fight back against the efforts of the new Church to shut down traditional education and knowledge. This book represents one of the efforts which helped keep the liberal arts alive during the "Dark Ages." Regarding madness, in this book the allegorical character, Music, speaks:

> I have frequently recited chants that have had a therapeutic effect upon deranged minds and ailing bodies; I have restored the mad to health through consonance, a treatment which the physician Asclepiades learned from me.[61]

The thirteenth century philosopher Bartholomew Anglicus mentions the use of music in writing of the treatment of madness. Those suffering from madness must be tied up, so they will not hurt themselves or others, and then,

> be refreshed, and comforted, and withdrawn from cause and matter of dread and busy thoughts. And they must be gladded with instruments of music, and somewhat be occupied.[62]

The great Renaissance philosopher, Erasmus (1466–1536), attributed the discovery that music could cure madness to the famous ancient Greek philosopher, Pythagoras.

> Pythagoras, by playing spondees in the Phrygian mode, transformed a young man mad with love and restored his sanity. A similar story is told of Empedocles, who is said by the use of some particular musical modes to have recalled to his proper wits a young man already beside himself with rage and hell-bent on murder.[63]

[61] *Martianus Capella and the Seven Liberal Arts*, trans. William Harris Stahl and Richard Johnson (New York: Columbia University Press, 1977), 358.

[62] "Medieval Medicine," in *Medieval Lore*, trans. Robert Steele (London: Stock, 1893), 58.

[63] Letter to Adrian VI [1522], quoted in *The Collected Works of Erasmus* (Toronto: University of Toronto Press, 1992), IX, 145ff.

The sixteenth century Church philosopher, Jean Bodin, following the official Church view, arrives at a startling conclusion, that *improvisation* in music drives men mad!

> Harmony weakened and overdone by excessive elaboration exerts an influence, for while one both simple and natural is wont to cure serious illness of the mind, on the contrary one contrived from a medley of sounds and rapid rhythms usually drives a mind insane. This happens to men too anxious to please their ears, who dislike the Doric mode and dignified measures. They affect the Ionian, so that it ought not to seem remarkable if many become insane.[64]

[64] Jean Bodin, *Method for the Easy Comprehension of History*, trans. Beatrice Reynolds (New York: Columbia University Press, 1945), 31.

In another place, in writing of the "Humors," in particular the influence of blood and black bile, he reports how this cure is effected in Germany.

> In Lower Germany there are almost none who are mad from black bile, but rather from blood; this type of lunacy the common man calls the disease of St. Vitus, which impels them to exultation and senseless dancing. Musicians imitate this on the lyre; afterwards they make use of more serious rhythms and modes, doing this gradually until by the gravity of the mode and the rhythm the madmen are clearly soothed.[65]

[65] Ibid., 103.

Curiously, the only such reference in Shakespeare seems to suggest that music, instead, *causes* madness! In *Richard II*, (V, v) the imprisoned king, having heard some music, says,

> This music mads me. Let it sound no more,
> For though it have helped mad men to their wits,
> In me it seems it will make wise men mad ...

Robert Burton (1577–1640), in his famous book, *The Anatomy of Melancholy*, has an extended discussion regarding the use of music for the cure of madness. Here, however, like the cure of the spider bite, it is the combination of dance with music which he advocates. When he lists what he considers the basic "diseases of the mind," among "Dotage, Phrenzy, Madness, Hydrophobia, and Llycanthropia," we are surprised to find "St. Vitus' Dance." His discussion of this condition is rather interesting.

S. Vitus' Dance; the lascivious dance, Paracelsus calls it, because they that are taken with it, can do nothing but dance till they be dead, or cured. It is so called, for that the parties so troubled were wont to go to S. Vitus for help, & after they had danced there a while, they were certainly freed. It is strange to hear how long they will dance, & in what manner, over stools, forms, tables; even great-bellied women sometimes (and yet never hurt their children) will dance so long that they can stir neither hand nor foot, but seem to be quite dead. Only in red clothes they cannot abide. Musick above all things they love, & therefore Magistrates in Germany will hire Musicians to play to them, and some lusty sturdy companions to dance with them. This disease hath been very common in Germany, as appears by those relations of Sckenkius, and Paracelsus in his book of Madness, who brags how many several persons he hath cured of it. Felix Platerus reports of a woman in Basle whom he saw, that danced a whole month together.[66]

Cassiodorus (480–573 AD), in a famous letter to Boethius, describes the process by which music heals. He then points to the effect of music on a host of mental illnesses, beginning with melancholy.

> The artist changes men's hearts as they listen; and, when this artful pleasure issues from the secret place of nature as the queen of the senses, in all the glory of its tones, our remaining thoughts take to flight, and it expels all else, that it may delight itself simply in being heard. Harmful melancholy he turns to pleasure; he weakens swelling rage; he makes bloodthirsty cruelty kindly, arouses sleepy sloth from its torpor, restores to the sleepless their wholesome rest, recalls lust-corrupted chastity to its moral resolve, and heals boredom of spirit which is always the enemy of good thoughts. Dangerous hatreds he turns to helpful goodwill, and, in a blessed kind of healing, drives out the passions of the heart by means of sweetest pleasures.[67]

Beginning with the late Renaissance one reads more about those suffering from being melancholic. Robert Burton, in his chapter on music and melancholy,[68] recalled that there have been many means by which philosophers and physicians have attempted to "exhilarate a sorrowful heart," but for him there is nothing so powerful as "a cup of strong drink,

[66] Robert Burton, *The Anatomy of Melancholy*, ed. Floyd Dell (New York: Tudor Publishing Company, 1938), 124.

[67] Letter to Boethius, in *Variae*, trans. Thomas Hodgkin (London: Frowde, 1886), II, xl.

[68] Burton, *The Anatomy of Melancholy*, 478ff.

mirth, musick, and merry company."[69] After citing some high recommendations of music by ancient writers, Burton observes,

[69] Ibid., 478ff.

> Musick is a tonic to the saddened soul, a [powerful cannon] against melancholy, to rear and revive the languishing soul, affecting not only the ears, but the very arteries, the vital and animal spirits; it erects the mind, and makes it nimble. This it will effect in the most dull, severe, and sorrowful souls, expel grief with mirth, and if there be any clouds, dust, or dregs of cares yet lurking in our thoughts, most powerfully it wipes them all away, and that which is more, it will perform all this in an instant: cheer up the countenance, expel austerity, bring in hilarity, inform our manners, mitigate anger … Our divine Musick, not only to expel the greatest griefs, but it doth extenuate fears and furies, appeases cruelty, abates heaviness, and to such as are watchful it causes quiet rest; it takes away spleen and hatred, be it instrumental, vocal, with strings, or wind; it leads us by the spirit, it cures all irksomeness and heaviness of the soul.

Aside from the more conspicuous madness and melancholy, the early philosophers write of music's ability to help with a wide variety of other mental illnesses. Iamblichus (c. 250–325 AD), records the techniques of Pythagoras in using music to alleviate a number of primarily emotional disorders. It is no doubt this passage which has caused some more recent scholars to regard Pythagoras as "the Father of Music Therapy."[70]

[70] Iamblichus, in Kenneth Guthrie, *The Pythagorean Sourcebook* (Grand Rapids: Phanes Press, 1987).

> Pythagoras conceived the first attention that should be given to men should be addressed to the senses, as when one perceives beautiful figures and forms, or hears beautiful rhythms and melodies. Consequently he laid down that the first erudition was that which subsists through music's melodies and rhythms, and from these he obtained remedies of human manners and passions, and restored the pristine harmony of the faculties of the soul. Moreover, he devised medicines calculated to repress and cure the diseases of both bodies and souls. Here is also by Zeus, something which deserves to be mentioned above all: namely, that for his disciples he arranged and adjusted what might be called "preparations" and "touchings," divinely contriving

mingling of certain diatonic, chromatic and enharmonic melodies, through which he easily switched and circulated the passions of the soul in a contrary direction, whenever they had accumulated recently, irrationally, or clandestinely—such as sorrow, rage, pity, over-emulation, fear, manifold desires, angers, appetites, pride, collapse or spasms. Each of these he corrected by the rule of virtue, attempting them through appropriate melodies, as through some salutary medicine.

Capella (fifth century), whom we have mentioned above, in addition to examples of using music to work with mentally disturbed and insane patients, mentions an extraordinarily diverse list of other kinds of patients.

> Have not I myself brought healing to diseased bodies by prolonged therapy? The ancients were able to cure fever and wounds by incantation. Asclepiades healed with the trumpet patients who were stone deaf, and Theophrastus used the flute with mentally disturbed patients. Is anyone unaware that gout in the hip is removed by the sweet tones of the aulos? Xenocrates cured insane patients by playing on musical instruments. Thales of Crete is known to have dispelled diseases and pestilence by the sweetness of his cithara playing. Herophilus checked the pulse of his patients by comparing rhythms.[71]

This calls to mind Theophrastus of Eresus (372–287 BC), a disciple of Aristotle, who wrote that a person suffering from sciatica would always be free from attacks if one played the aulos in the Phrygian mode over the part of the body affected?[72]

Johann Mattheson mentions two accounts of pain being treated by music. One of these regards a professor at Göttingen who attributed the alleviation of pain in limbs with the effect music has on muscles. A particularly interesting report is that the seventeenth century native Americans (Indians),

> use no other means than their somewhat coarse method of playing, by means of which they occasionally suppress and alleviate difficult infirmities and pains if not heal them.[73]

While some of these accounts may seem extraordinary to the reader, the fact is that music therapy works. We know,

---

[71] *Martianus Capella and the Seven Liberal Arts,* 358. Marchetto of Padua (fourteenth century), in his *Lucidarium*, also mentions that physicians judge the pulse by the aid of music.

[72] *On Inspiration*, quoted in Athenaeus, *Deipnosophistae*, XIV, 624. Plutarch, in "Concerning the Virtues of Women," also tells of a sickly woman who was healed by the study of music.

[73] Mattheson, *Der volkommene Capellmeister*, I, iii, 47. He quotes François La Mothe le Vayer, *Oeuvres de François de la Mothe le Vayer* (Paris, 1656), I, 521.

first-hand, of some medical conditions in which a music therapist accomplished what a medical doctor could not. We must expend more effort in identifying the physical basis for the role music plays in such cases. This would certainly result in greater recognition among doctors. One only has to reflect, for example, that music understanding is not only entirely physiological, but much of it is genetic. There must be some common links with medical understanding, for the body and everything about it is also physiological and genetic. But the research which identifies and explains medically what role music actually plays in healing is unlikely to be done by the medical community. Instead, the field of music therapy itself must be much more active in the basic research which explains scientifically how music cures. Music therapists must not only continue beating doctors at their own game, that is effecting healing where the medical profession cannot, but these cases must be vigorously reported and the practitioners honored. Music therapy must argue its own case, for only in this way will music therapy ever become fully recognized by the medical profession. After all, the other branches of medicine also had, at some earlier time, to make their own case. If the discipline of surgery had not done this, for example, then surgery would still be conducted by barbers.

Is Music Genetic?

> Infants before age one can distinguish whether particular chords contain a wrong note.[74]

> Infants two days old demonstrate specific behavioral responses to music heard as fetuses.[75]

> "Why," asks Aristotle, "do all men love music?"

> Is it because we naturally rejoice in natural movements? This is shown by the fact that children rejoice in [rhythm and melody] as soon as they are born.[76]

A number of early philosophers have also observed the response of newly born infants to lullabies. From this observation alone the first century AD philosopher, Philodemus of Gadara, concluded music was both universal and genetic.

> We have an innate affinity with the Muses, one which does not have to be learned. This is clearly shown by the way infants are lulled to sleep with wordless singing.[77]

Erasmus (1469–1536) also observed this response and, as a very rational man, was particularly fascinated that a lullaby could have this effect when the infants "have no idea what music is."[78]

These early ideas are found again in a famous treatise, "On the Sublime," by the first century AD philosopher, Longinus, a man of whom otherwise virtually nothing is known. In addition, he contends that the genetic elements of music which we arrive with at birth also prepare man for understanding more complex communications, such as that of the orator.

> For does not the flute instill certain emotions into its hearers and as it were make them beside themselves and full of frenzy, and supplying a rhythmical movement constrain the listener to move rhythmically in accordance therewith and to conform himself to the melody, although he may be utterly ignorant of music? ...
> Are we not, then, to hold that composition (being a harmony of that language which is implanted by nature in man and which appeals not to the hearing only but to the soul

[74] Research by Sandra Trehub, University of Toronto.

[75] Research by Peter Hepper, *Irish Journal of Psychology* (1991, 12, pp. 95–107).

[76] *Problemata*, 920b.28.

[77] Quoted in Warren D. Anderson, *Ethos and Education in Greek Music* (Cambridge: Harvard University Press, 1966), 173. The reader can find additional information on this subject in David Whitwell, *Ancient Views on the Natural World,* ed. Craig Dabelstein (Austin: Whitwell Books, 2013).

[78] "Adages," in *The Complete Works of Erasmus* (Toronto: University of Toronto Press, 1992), XXXI, 167.

itself), since it calls forth manifold shapes of words, thoughts, deeds, beauty, melody, all of them born at our birth and growing with our growth, and since by means of the blending and variation of its own tones it seeks to introduce into the minds of those who are present the emotion which affects the speaker and since it always brings the audience to share in it and by the building of phrase upon phrase raises a sublime and harmonious structure: are we not, I say, to hold that harmony by these selfsame means allures us and invariably disposes us to stateliness and dignity and elevation and every emotion which it contains within itself, gaining absolute mastery over our minds? But it is folly to dispute concerning matters which are generally admitted, since experience is proof sufficient.[79]

[79] Longinus, *On the Sublime*, trans. W. Rhys Roberts (Cambridge: University Press, 1935), XXXIX, 2.

Several of the early Christian fathers also commented on the fact that music must be genetic. St. John Chrysostom (c. 345–407 AD) wrote that music "is thoroughly innate to our mind."[80] His younger contemporary, St. Augustine (354–430 AD), observed that the appreciation of fine performance is genetically present in the listener, not just the musician.

[80] "Exposition of Psalm XLI."

AUGUSTINE. How do you explain the fact that an ignorant crowd hisses off a flute player letting out futile sounds, and on the other hand applauds one who sings well, and finally that the more agreeably one sings the more fully and intensely it is moved? For it isn't possible to believe the crowd does all this by the art of music, is it?
STUDENT. No.
AUGUSTINE. How then?
STUDENT. I think it is done by nature giving everyone a sense of hearing by which such things are judged.
AUGUSTINE. You are right.[81]

[81] *On Music*, trans. Robert Taliaferro in *Writings of Saint Augustine* (New York: Fathers of the Church), v.

Marsilio Ficino, the fifteenth century founder of the Florentine Academy, was a philosopher who was an active musician in his leisure, playing the lyre for his own relaxation, but also in concerts in the Medici palace.[82] His combined interests in music and philosophy resulted in some very interesting conclusions on the virtues of music. Music, he believed, served man's "spirit" in the same way medicine serves the body and theology the soul. In his view, what we call the genetic aspects of music were to him a memory in the

[82] Paul Kristeller, "Music and Learning in the Early Italian Renaissance," *The Journal of Renaissance and Baroque Music* (1947), I, Nr. 4, 269ff.

soul of the divine music found in the mind of God and in the music of the spheres.[83] The great Italian Renaissance theorist, Zarlino, agreed and thought it was the genetic memory of the music of angels which impels man to sing as a means of easing labor.

> Many were of the opinion that in this life every soul is won by music, and, although the soul is imprisoned by the body, it still remembers and is conscious of the music of the heavens, forgetting every hard and annoying labor.[84]

The brilliant composer and theorist, Jean-Philippe Rameau (1683–1764), was absorbed for years with the idea that man is born with a genetic pitch template. He was pondering observations which he had made along these lines in 1734, when he wrote,

> In music the ear obeys only nature. It takes account of neither measure nor range. Instinct alone leads it.
>
> .....
>
> Whether a novice or the most experienced person in music, the moment one sings an improvisation, one ordinarily places the first tone in the middle register of the voice and then continues up, even though the voice range above or below this first tone is about equal; this is completely consistent with the resonance of any sounding body from which all emanating overtones are above its fundamental tone which one thinks one is hearing alone.
>
> .....
>
> On the other hand, inexperienced as one may be, one hardly ever fails, when improvising on an instrument, immediately to play, ever ascending, the perfect chord made up of the overtones of the sounding body, the major form of which is always preferred to the minor, unless the latter is suggested by some reminiscence.[85]

Twenty-five years later he was still struggling with this idea. He begins by discounting the ancient explanations based on faith and wonders why these early philosophers did not pursue natural rules, that is, understanding based on Nature.

[83] Ficino carries his belief in the "music of the spheres" to an association of the signs of the zodiac with the tones of the scale.

[84] "Le Istitutioni harmoniche," quoted in Claude V. Palisca, *Humanism in Italian Renaissance Musical Thought* (New Haven: Yale University Press, 1985), 179.

[85] Jean Philippe Rameau, *Observations sur notre instinct pour la musique et sur son principe* [1734], quoted in Sam Morgenstern, *Composers on Music* (New York: Pantheon, 1956), 44.

[The ancient writers] found the relationships between sounds in divinely inspired order; they discoursed a great deal on that subject, and every reason they were able to advance evaporated like a wisp of smoke. Finally the geometricians and the philosophers became disheartened. Can it be true that up to the present time man has always been so enthralled by this single inspiration that it never occurred to anyone to seek the reason why, despite ourselves, we should be compelled to prefer certain intervals to others after certain sounds, especially after the first sound? Allow your natural feelings to operate in yourself with no preconceived expectation and then try to see if you can ever ascend a semitone after a given semitone, and whether you can do the same thing after two successive tones. Why was this suggested to me in this way?[86]

The French musician, Michel de Saint-Lambert, in his *Les Principes du Clavecin* of 1702, was certain that we carry genetically into birth specific information of a musical nature, in particular rhythm. After briefly mentioning some of the abilities needed in performance, he says,

Though this at first sight may appear a large order, it is nevertheless sure that this extreme accuracy in intonation and rhythm is a gift given to almost all men, like sight and speech. There are very few who do not sing and dance naturally; if it is not with the delicacy and correctness that Art has sought, it is at least with the correctness which Art dictates and which Art itself has derived from Nature. It is already a great asset for those who want to learn music or to play some instrument that they know they have discernment of the ear by nature, that is, the first and most important of these aptitudes.[87]

The French philosopher, Charles Batteaux (1713–1780), in reference to the innate character of music, believed it was melody which was genetic, quoting, without source, a Latin expression, "We are led to melody by natural instinct."[88]

Gottfried Wilhelm Leibniz (1646–1716) was reared in a highly educated family, his father being a professor at Leipzig University. Leibniz also entered Leipzig University, receiving a bachelor's degree in philosophy at age sixteen and two doctorates by age twenty-one. Leibniz was a bril-

[86] Letter to A. M. Beguillet, October 6, 1762, quoted in Gertrude Norman and Miriam Shrifte, *Letters of Composers*, 20.

[87] Michel de Saint-Lambert, *Les Principes du Clavecin* [1702], quoted in Carol MacClintock, *Readings in the History of Music in Performance* (Bloomington: Indiana University Press, 1979), 212.

[88] *Les beaux-arts reduits a un meme principe* [Paris 1746], quoted in Peter le Huray and James Day, *Music and Aesthetics in the Eighteenth and Early-Nineteenth Centuries* (Cambridge: Cambridge University Press, 1981), 50ff.

liant mathematician, having discovered the foundations of differential and integral calculus.

Leibniz was a great believer of genetic knowledge in general, writing, for example,

> Nothing can be taught us the idea of which is not already in our minds, as the matter out of which our thought is formed.[89]

Leibniz's most extensive writings on the general subject of genetic knowledge is found in his *New Essays on Human Understanding* (1704) which was written in refutation of John Locke's (1632–1704) *Essay Concerning Human Understanding* (1690). Locke had gone to some length to contend that man is born with no innate ideas.[90] For him it was sufficient proof that there is no such thing as universal, genetic knowledge that one found no such things in children and idiots.[91]

In the preface to his own work, Leibniz associates Locke with those who believed man is born a "blank slate," whereas he finds a passage in the New Testament to prove this is not true.[92] In this same preface, Leibniz also points to some inconsistencies in Locke, for the purpose of suggesting that perhaps Locke believed in some form of genetic knowledge but did not recognize it as such.

> Perhaps our clever author will not wholly differ from my view. For after having employed the whole of his first book in rejecting innate intelligence, taken in a certain sense, then nevertheless, at the beginning of the second and in the sequel, admits that ideas, which do not originate in sensation, come from reflection. Now reflection is nothing else than attention to what is in us, and the senses do not give us what we already carry with us.

Since Leibniz was a great believer of genetic knowledge in general, we notice two passages which seem to suggest that perhaps he was thinking of this with respect to music as well. In the first passage he speaks of the unconscious memory of music, in the context of a discussion of genetic knowledge.

> It seems that our clever author claims that there is nothing *virtual* in us, and indeed nothing of which we are not always

[89] Leibniz, "Discourse on Metaphysics" (1686), xxvi, in "A New Method for Learning and Teaching Jurisprudence" (1667), I, xxxiv, in Leroy Loemker, *Philosophical Papers and Letters* (Dordrecht: Reidel, 1956), 320.

[90] "Essay on Human Understanding," in *The Works of John Locke* (London, 1823; reprinted in Aalen: Scientia Verlag, 1963), I, ii, 1ff.

[91] Ibid., I, ii, 5.

[92] Leibniz, *New Essays Concerning Human Understanding* [1704], trans. Alfred Langley (La Salle: The Open Court Publishing Company, 1949), Preface. The St. Paul reference is found in Romans 2:15,

> They show that what the law requires is written on their hearts, while their conscience also bears witness and their conflicting thoughts accuse or perhaps excuse them on that day when, according to my gospel, God judges the secrets of men by Christ Jesus.

actually conscious; but he cannot take this rigorously, otherwise his opinion would be too paradoxical; since, moreover, acquired habits and the stores of our memory are not always perceived and do not even always come to our aid at need, although we often easily recall them to the mind upon some slight occasion which makes us remember them, just as we need only the beginning of a song to remember it.[93]

Leibniz also believed that the average man often dreamed of music,[94] and that perhaps that music heard live creates a "sympathetic echo in us."[95]

David Hume (1711–1776), born into a Scottish Presbyterian family, studied at the University of Edinburgh, but left before graduation to pursue philosophy and indeed wrote his great *Treatise on Human Nature* at age twenty-six. He raised the entire subject of the emotions to a higher level than any former philosopher, even going so far as to make feeling dominant over rational ideas. No one had ever before written anything so extraordinary as the following:

> All probable reasoning is nothing but a species of sensation. It is not solely in poetry and music, we must follow our taste and sentiment, but likewise in philosophy. When I am convinced of any principle, it is only an idea, which strikes more strongly upon me. When I give the preference to one set of arguments above another, I do nothing but decide from my feeling concerning the superiority of their influence.[96]

As we pointed out above, earlier philosophers, beginning with Aristotle, probably felt inclined to assume there was something genetic about music simply on the basis of its universality. But it has only been during the past fifty years that breakthroughs in medical research have for the first time thrown some genuine light on this subject, offering physical proof to support earlier philosophical speculation. In particular the research by Dr. Sperry on the bicameral brain and the work of Dr. Hans Jenny in Switzerland on the impact of vibrations on the body in particular have introduced a new era of research. Thus far we have seen many individual scientists studying a wide variety of aspects of music perception which seem to point toward genetic

[93] Leibniz, *New Essays Concerning Human Understanding*.

[94] Leibniz, "A Fragment on Dreams" (c. 1666–1676), in Loemker, *Philosophical Papers and Letters*, 115.

[95] "On Wisdom" (c. 1690–1698), in Loemker, *Philosophical Papers and Letters*, 425ff.

[96] *A Treatise of Human Nature*, I, iii, 8.

foundations. It is too early for a unified theory, but these individual findings are remarkable. Consider the following:

- Dennis Molfese of the University of Pennsylvania has found an affinity for musical language in infants less than forty-eight hours after birth.[97]
- Psychologist Jerome Kagan of Harvard University in a study for infants four months old found an apparent genetic predilection to consonance over dissonance.[98]
- University of California researchers believe that infants are born with a genetic ability to recognize and respond to music, even before language.[99]
- Research at UCLA with newborns before they left the hospital establish bicameral patterns for speech versus musical sounds. Furthermore the brain adds amplification: to the left ear for music (right brain) and to the right ear for speech.[100]
- Psychologists have found that even before age one infants can detect errors in music.[101]
- There is evidence that almost all musicians who began their training before the age of six possess absolute pitch, compared with none of those who began after the age of eleven.[102] Some believe absolute pitch may be a vestigial talent of our primate ancestors.
- Research by Dr. Jamshed Bharucha, of Dartmouth College, has found that we have a genetic preference for certain kinds of melodic patterns.
- A study by Stewart Hulse of Johns Hopkins University found that starlings have the ability to recognize a simple melody in different keys. In another experiment, pigeons were trained to distinguish random excerpts of music by J.S. Bach from excerpts by Stravinsky and were able to correctly categorize music by other composers as being either "Bach-like" or "Stravinsky-like."[103]
- Jay Dowling, of the University of Texas at Dallas, has found clinical evidence to suggest that ordinary people

[97] Reported in Craig Buck, "Knowing the LEFT from the RIGHT," *Human Behavior*, June, 1976.

[98] Reported in the *Los Angeles Times*, Dec. 2, 1996.

[99] Reported in the *Associated Press*, January 23, 1992.

[100] UCLA Press Release, Sept. 10, 2004.

[101] Reported in "The Musical Brain," *U. S. News & World Report*, June 11, 1990.

[102] D. Sergeant, "Experimental Investigation of Absolute Pitch," in *Journal of Research in Musical Education*, 9169, 17, 135–143.

[103] Reported in "The Musical Brain," *U. S. News & World Report*, June 11, 1990.

perceive melodic patterns on the basis of the relationship between the notes themselves, and not on the basis of precise pitches. Hence almost everybody can sing "Happy Birthday" beginning from any note on the piano.[104]

- John Pierce of Stanford has demonstrated that the brain has little ability to recognize melodic patterns played backwards. For example, most people do not realize that the sound of the word *we* is the reverse of the sound of the word *you*.[105]

- In 1974, physician and researcher, Dr. Thomas wrote, "The need to make music, and to listen to it, is universally expressed by human beings ... It is like speech, a dominant aspect of human biology."[106]

A great deal of additional research has been done in recent years which seems to suggest we come into this world with some elements of music. It is because the basic emotions and elements of music are universal and genetic in character that the expression about music being the international language is true. Indeed, music is the only activity that 100% of the people on the globe are drawn to as listeners or participants, not soccer, gardening or even religion. That fact alone is strong evidence for a genetic background.

Music teachers therefore have an unbelievable advantage. Suppose you were a geology teacher and someone told you, "every student loves geology and every student has the basics of geology implanted genetically before he enters the school." Would that not be a happy geology teacher, who would suddenly feel his teaching area was fundamental and important to mankind?

Music teachers have not capitalized on this unique relationship between music and the child. Our grandchildren will be hard pressed to explain why the music educators of today have failed to base music education on the actual performance of music and have instead constructed an educational edifice built on conceptual information *about* music, an edifice no child has any interest in visiting.

[104] Reported in Ibid.

[105] Reported in Buck, "Knowing the Left from the Right." This is unwelcome news for twelve-tone composers.

[106] Jacqueline Schmidt Peters, *Music Therapy, an Introduction* (Springfield: Charles Thomas, 1987), 49.

Suppose you were a young person who wanted to learn to play golf and so you take a course called, "Introduction to Golf." What do you do when you find it is not a course in playing golf at all, but only a course of conceptual information *about* golf? You don't return and you go off and teach yourself golf. And this is the reason why the majority of school children are not in our music classes. And all those students who are *not* in our classes, every single one of them, are involved in music on their own, utterly unsupervised.

No one should be surprised when parents and governing bodies look at this reality and see little reason to increase funding on music education.

On Movement and Music

> All these things—language, harmony, dance and ornament—are imitations one of another, and each accommodates and resembles each other, but all are made similar to a prime cause and are imitations of it: the life of men, happy or wretched, their actions and morals, and thoughts of the mind.[107]
>
> Agnolo Segni, 1573

IT SEEMS REASONABLE to assume that one of the very earliest physiological manifestations of music was dance. We know from the footprints and instruments left in the caves of Spain that very ancient man danced to music. The ancient physiological connection between movement and music is easily understood if one, once again, reminds oneself that *real* music is something that occurs *live*. That is, live music travels through time, linking the listener with the performer lock-step in present tense. It is in this experience of music moving through time where you will find the ancient origin for musicians and listeners experiencing the urge to express themselves by physical movement while hearing the music. It was a form of acknowledgement of their being connected with their experience in the present tense.

The fundamental relationship between music and movement is the expression of feeling. Movement is also a kind of *visual* emotion and thus only a single alphabet letter separates "motion" from "emotion" in our language. It is because of this relationship that the ancients often thought of dance as the part of music that you could see. It is for this reason that Socrates, in a discussion of the knowledge necessary to be a good musician,[108] maintains that a musician must understand how emotions are reflected in movement and that this movement ought to be called music.

> ... when you have learned also how similar emotions appear and come to be in the movements of bodies, which when measured by numbers ought, as they say, to be called rhythms and measures ...

[107] "Lezioni intorno alla poesia," quoted in Claude V. Palisca, *Humanism in Italian Renaissance Musical Thought* (New Haven: Yale University Press, 1985), 401.

[108] Plato, *Philebus*, 17c.

Similarly, the important early philosopher, Roger Bacon (b. c. 1214), also included dance within his definition of music.

> Music, moreover, consisting in what is visible, is necessary; and that it is such is evident from the book on the *Origin of the Sciences*. For whatever can be conformed to sound in similar movements and in corresponding formations, so that our delight may be made complete not only by hearing, but by seeing, belongs to music. Therefore dances and all bendings of bodies are reduced to gesture, which is a branch of music, since these are conformed to sound in similar movements and corresponding formations, as the author of the aforesaid book maintains. Therefore Aristotle says in the seventh book of the Metaphysics that the art of dancing is not complete without another art, that is, without another kind of music to which the art of dancing is conformed.[109]

The Renaissance philosopher and mathematician, Girolamo Cardano (1501–1576), made the same point, observing,

> In antiquity dancing was called a sixth part of music.[110]

This again seems to imply that dance was a visible from of music. This has been an idea slow to die. Jean Paul Richter, the writer who so influenced nineteenth century Romantic composers, once wrote that "music is invisible dance, as dancing is silent music."[111]

There is one more important point to be made along these lines. First, the sole purpose of music is to communicate feeling and emotion; every listener understands that. Thus, it follows that it is because of this mirror-like relationship between music and dance, movements themselves are capable of communicating powerful emotions. It is because this understanding is also very ancient that we have one of the most frequently retold tales of ancient Greece. Herodotus, the great fifth century BC historian, tells this story of a great banquet during which a final group of suitors for the daughter of Cleisthenes were to compete with each other "in music and in talking in company."

> In both these accomplishments, it was Hippocleides who proved by far the doughtiest champion, until at last, as more

[109] *Opus Majus*, "Causes of Error," XVI, in *The Opus Majus of Roger Bacon*, trans. Robert Burke (New York: Russell & Russell, 1962), I, 259ff.

[110] Clement Miller, *Hieronymus Cardanus, Writings on Music* (American Institute of Musicology, 1973), 117.

[111] *Levana* (1807).

and more wine was drunk, he asked the flute player to play him a tune and began to dance to it. Now it may well be that he danced to his own satisfaction; Cleisthenes, however, who was watching the performance, began to have serious doubts about the whole business. Presently, after a brief pause, Hippocleides sent for a table; the table was brought, and Hippocleides, climbing on to it, danced first some Laconian dances, next some Attic ones, and ended by standing on his head and beating time with his legs in the air. The Laconian and Attic dances were bad enough; but Cleisthenes, though he already loathed the thought of having a son-in-law like that, nevertheless restrained himself and managed to avoid an outburst; but when he saw Hippocleides beating time with his legs, he could bear it no longer. "Son of Tisander," he cried, "you have danced away your marriage."[112]

[112] Herodotus, *The Histories*, VI, 128.

We know that dance and movement were very much part of the ancient Greek choral performances, but we know little about the specific movements. Cardano added a curious note on the origin of these movements.

Dancing and gesticulation express the ample movements that were left from antique statues, and the movements were then transferred from the figures to choral dances, and from choral dances to wrestling schools.[113]

[113] Ibid., 119.

Thucydides, the fifth century BC historian, wrote of a tradition of the festival accompanying the Delian games which was already centuries old.

The cities brought choirs of dancers. Nothing can be clearer on this point than the following verses of Homer, taken from a hymn to Apollo:

> Phoebus, where'er thou strayest, far or near,
> Delos was still of all thy haunts most dear,
> Thiter the robed Ionians take their way
> With wife and child to keep they holiday,
> Invoke thy favor on each manly game,
> And dance and sing in honor of thy name.[114]

[114] Thucydides, *The Peloponnesian War*, III, 103.

Another ancient tradition which we wish we knew more about, dating from the eighth century BC, is recorded by Livy. He writes of these choirs in processionals "chanting their hymns to the triple beat of their ritual dance."[115]

[115] Livy, *The History of Rome*, I, 20.

Based on the little literature which survives, it appears the use of movement by the ancient Greek choirs (*khoros*) was already common by the time of the lyric poets, seventh century BC. According to Athenaeus, at this time the singers used few facial expressions, but were active with the feet, "both in marching and in dance steps."[116] Pindar's (b. c. 518 BC) "Ode for Hieron of Aetna, Winner of the Chariot Race," clearly implies the steps of the feet were specifically based on the music itself.

> O glorious lyre, joint treasure of Apollo
> And of the Muses violet-tressed,
> Your notes the dancers' step obeys ...[117]

We understand the importance of the movements and that they were done by the singers themselves, for in one of the poems of Alkman a singer complains that he is too old and weak to dance with the chorus.[118]

When the period of the ancient Greek drama arrives (fifth century BC), the chorus which functions in these plays also used movement. According to Athenaeus, Thespis, Pratinas, Cratinus, and Phrynichus among older playwrights "not only relied upon the dancing of the chorus for the interpretation of their plays, but, quite apart from their own compositions, they taught dancing to all who wanted instruction."[119] Athenaeus also notes that the first great playwright, Aeschylus, took a very personal interest in the movements of the chorus.

> Aeschylus was the first to give poses to his choruses, employing no dancing masters, but devising for himself the figures of the dance, and in general taking upon himself the entire management of the piece.[120]

Athenaeus also tells us that the great playwright, Sophocles, himself, was expert in both music and dancing.

> Sophocles, besides being handsome in his youth, became proficient in dancing and music, while still a lad, under the instruction of Lamprus. After the battle of Salamis, at any rate, he danced to the accompaniment of his lyre around the

---

[116] *Deipnosophistae*, I, 22. One of these early poets, Alkman (c. 640–600 BC), was a choral conductor.

[117] Geoffrey S. Conway, *The Odes of Pindar* (London: Dent, 1972), 81.

[118] Nr. 42, in. Guy Davenport, *Archilochos, Sappho, Alkman* (Berkeley: University of California Press, 1980).

[119] Athenaeus, *Deipnosophistae*, I, 22.

[120] Ibid.

trophy, naked and anointed with oil. Others say he danced with his cloak on. And when he brought out the *Thamyris* he played the lyre himself.[121]

[121] Athenaeus, *Deipnosophistae*, I, 20.

Although we know little about the specific movements the ancient Greek choral groups used in their performances, or how they were specifically intended to underwrite the emotions of the song, it seems safe to say they were probably continuing very ancient traditions. Dance to music, of course, must be ancient far before literature. There are early pictures of dancers and music, such as a fragment of a Sumerian vase which dates from 3,200 BC, which shows two lyre players accompanying a dance. But this may be considered relatively modern if one recalls the evidence of music and dancing in the cave paintings.

Among the tomb paintings of ancient Egypt we are attracted to an extraordinary painting from the more recent Greco-Roman temple at Medamund, north of Thebes, which includes a complete hymn to the god Hathor. We see a group of female musicians, with harp, drum, and lute, beneath an hieroglyph description:

> The members of the choir take up their instruments and play them. The songstresses in full number adore the Golden Goddess and make music to the Golden Goddess: they never cease their chanting.

The lyrics of the hymn are written behind the lutanist and a singer. We take notice especially of the emotional aim of this music and movement, "nourishment for the heart."

> Come, O Golden Goddess, the singers chant
> for it is nourishment for the heart to dance the *iba*,
> to shine over the feast at the hour of retiring
> and to enjoy dance at night.[122]

[122] Quoted in Lise Manniche, *Music and Musicians in Ancient Egypt* (London: British Museum Press, 1991), 61.

We should also point out that there is one extraordinary hieroglyph from Amarna, dating 1,580 BC, which pictures a music school. In addition to illustrating various scenes of music instruction and store rooms for instruments, we see in one classroom a harpist and instructor teaching movement.

There is another important form of movement captured in the tomb paintings, and that is the early conductor. He was first named a *chironomist*, "one who gestures with his hands," by Marcus Fabius Quintilinus. One hieroglyph representation of him we particularly like for he is identified through two hieroglyph symbols as one who "sings with the arm." A perfect definition, it seems to us, of a good conductor's movements.

Before we leave this brief survey of movement and music in the ancient worlds, there are two other rather interesting examples. First, while examples of a dancer who sings at the same time are not rare,[123] there are some early illustrations of a much more rare practice of instrumentalists who dance while they play. The most interesting of these, an ancient Assyrian stone-relief, shows a reception for Ashur-Idanni-Pal (668–626 BC), by the city of Susiana, in Elam. Here we see three male harp players, two of whom are dancing while playing; a man playing a kind of dulcimer, who is also dancing; a male aulos player; four female harp players; female players of an aulos and a drum; together with thirteen singers.

Finally, we should not forget that the ancient Greeks used music to train the movements necessary to be a good soldier. The reader will no doubt recall the often quoted comment by Socrates that "the best dancer makes the best soldier."[124] One illustration of the use of music by the ancient Greeks to train military movements was in the performance of the dance known as the *pyrrhiche*. This was danced to the aulos and the first part consisted of very fast feet movement, needed to chase the enemy, or escape its pursuit. The second part was a simulated combat and the third part consisted of leaping movements, as might be needed to leap over walls and ditches, etc.[125]

One who shared no enthusiasm for this long observed connection between movement and music was Pope John XXII (1324–1325). In his bull, "Docta Sanctorum," the pope outlaws a number of performance practices which he finds an embarrassment to the Church. Among these he includes

[123] In *Euphues' Shadowe* (1592) by the Elizabethan playwright, Thomas Lodge, Philamis commands the cornets to play a "Barginet," to which he sings and dances. Similarly, in Moliere's *The Affected Ladies* (scene xiii) Mascarille sings and dances.

[124] Athenaeus, *Deipnosophistae*, XIV, 628. In nineteenth century Hungary army recruitment was done in part through the use of music and dance. The theory being that the best dancer was likely to be the best coordinated and hence was made captain of the village troops.

[125] Georges Kastner, *Manuel Général de Musique Militaire* (Paris, 1848), 9ff.

those singers who "endeavor to convey by their gestures the sentiment of the music which they utter." Since we assume he really did not want church music sung with no feeling, he must have observed gestures which he associated with popular music.

We have somewhat of a summary of the state of views on movement and music in 1588 in the famous dancing manual, *Orchesography*, by Thoinot Arbeau. First, we note that in spite of the objections of the Church, such as the one just mentioned, Arbeau reports,

> In the primitive church there was a custom, which has survived into our own times, of dancing and swaying while chanting the hymns of our faith, and it may still be seen in several places.

He regrets that knowledge of the dances of the ancient Greeks has been lost.

> As regards ancient dances all I can tell you is that the passage of time, the indolence of man or the difficulty of describing them has robbed us of any knowledge thereof.

His admitted lack of information on the views of the ancient Greeks perhaps explains why he associates dance movements more with oratory than music.

> Most of the authorities hold that dancing is a kind of mute rhetoric by which the orator, without uttering a word, can make himself understood by his movements and persuade the spectators that he is gallant or worthy to be acclaimed, admired and loved.

During the sixteenth century a fundamentalist religious sentiment began to appear in many parts of Europe, best known in England for the resultant Quakers and Puritans. For many of these people, dance became a new symbol of sin and music was not left untouched due to its association. The German philosopher Henry Agrippa (1486–1536) is a typical example.

> To Music, moreover, belongs the Art of Dancing, very acceptable to maidens and lovers, which they learn with great care,

and without tediousness do prolong it until midnight, and with great diligence do devise to dance with framed gestures, and with measurable passes to the sound of the cymbal, harp, or flute, and do, as they think very wisely, and subtly, the fondest thing of all and, little differing from madness, which except that it is tempered with the sound of instruments ... There is no sight more ridiculous, taken out of context, than dancing: this is a liberty to wantonness, a friend to wickedness, a provocation to fleshly lust, enemy to chastity, and a pastime unworthy of all honest persons.[126]

In England the literature of the religious right is almost unbelievable. We will quote one as representative of the entire school, Philip Stubbs's *Anatomy of the Abuses in England* (1583).

Wherefore, if you would have your son become womanish, unclean, smooth mouthed, affected to bawdy, scurrility, filthy rhymes, and unseemly talking; briefly, if you would have him, as it were, transformed into a woman, or worse, and inclined to all kinds of whordom and abomination, send him to dancing school, and to learn music, and then shall you not fail of your purpose. And if you would have your daughter whorish, bawdy, and unclean and a filthy speaker, and such like, bring her up in music and dancing, and, my life for your's, you have won the goal.[127]

Even in France, the country we associate with dance, in Voltaire's play, *The Prude* (I, v), when the character Mme Dorfise is asked about music and dancing, she answers, "they are the devil's inventions."

In Zurich, under the influence of the strict Protestant, Zwingli, public dancing was actually forbidden. A civic ordinance of 1519 reads,

Let it be announced in the pulpits of the city and written notice sent into the country that since dancing has been forbidden, it is also forbidden to musicians or anyone else to provide dances in courts or other places, whether it be at public weddings or church festivals.[128]

At the beginning of the twentieth century, a remarkable educator named Emile Jaques-Dalcroze attempted to create

---

[126] Henry Cornelius Agrippa, *Of the Vanitie and Uncertaintie of Arts and Sciences*, ed. Catherine Dunn (Northridge: California State University, Northridge Press, 1974), 69. Interestingly enough, he associates the origin of dance to the movement of the planets and the "music of the spheres." See footnote 112, above.

[127] Philip Stubbs, *The Anatomy of the Abuses in England* [1583], ed. Frederick Furnivall (London: The New Shakespeare Society, n.d.), 169ff.

[128] Quoted in Jackson, *Huldreich Zwingli* (New York: Putham, 1901), 24.

a Renaissance in music education with a new system of education called "Eurhythmics." While main-stream American music educators pay only token recognition to his ideas, he has had to the present day many fervent individual supporters. It will strike the reader, in the following excerpts of his writings,[129] that Dalcroze attempted to take education full circle back to the beliefs of the ancient Greeks in the unity of music, movement and the emotions.

[129] "Rhythm, Time, and Temperament" (1919), 63, 107, 119, 139.

> The aim of eurhythmics is to enable pupils, at the end of their course, to say, not "I know," but "I have experienced," and so to create in them the desire to express themselves; for the deep impression of an emotion inspires a longing to communicate it, to the extent of one's powers, to others.
>
> .....
>
> Rhythm is the live essence of feeling, the fundamental impulse of a movement in the form impressed on it by the first emotional reaction.
>
> .....
>
> Gesture must define musical emotion and call up its image.
>
> .....
>
> Gesture itself is nothing—its whole value depends on the emotion that inspires it.

The Location of Music (and us) in our Bicameral Brain

> We all speak well of our hearts, we none of us dare speak well of our minds.[130]
> La Rochefoucauld (1613–1680)
>
> But though I distrust my head, I am always sure of my heart.[131]
> Voltaire (1694–1778)

[130] *The Maxims of La Rochefoucauld*, trans. Louis Kronenberger (New York: Random House, 1959), Nr. 98.

[131] Letter to abbe Chaulieu, July 26, 1717.

IN 1981, FOLLOWING TWO DECADES of surgical experimentation, Dr. Roger Sperry, one of America's most famous and decorated neurobiologists of the twentieth century, was awarded the Nobel Prize in Medicine for his discovery that severing the corpus callosum resulted in a normal person having, in effect and reality, two separate brains. The bottom line is that we possess two different kinds of thinking. We have a rational side of our personality, found in the left hemisphere of the brain, and an experiential side of our personality, found in the right hemisphere of the brain. These two brains operate the body, including the eyes, in a crossover fashion, the left hemisphere controls the right side of the body and the right hemisphere the left side.

The subsequent thirty years of research proved that most brain activity in a normal person has some connections in both sides, causing these later researchers to distain the use of the terms "left" and "right," although the official medical names remain "left brain" and "right brain." None of this more recent research has altered the basic fact that we are at once a rational and an experiential person.

The discovery, physically, of our bicameral mind has enormous consequences. Our rational side, the left hemisphere, contains entirely information we have read or which has been told us by someone else. We are told "two plus two equals four; memorize that." We are told "this animal's name is spelled 'C–A–T'; memorize that." Consequently, everyone in the world has the same answers in the left hemisphere; no one has a different answer for "how much is two plus two?"

The information contained in our right hemisphere is experiential, information which is the result of our own personal experiences. A word like "pain," for example exists as a dictionary word in the left hemisphere, but it is understood in the right hemisphere as the result of all of our own personal experiences with pain. Since the vital experiential fields such as love, music and the emotions are understood in the right hemisphere, one can say that the right hemisphere is the *real* us, the "us" who is an individual, differing with everyone else on earth.

This new knowledge answers many questions, such as these found in the two quotations above. It is now evident why we can have a very profound and vivid feeling of love for someone, but when we attempt to write a love letter it comes out stupid and childlike. This is because we are calling upon the left hemisphere, where the language vocabulary resides,[132] to write a letter on a subject it knows absolutely nothing about. We should not fail to mention that the right hemisphere of the brain is mute, it cannot write nor speak. Music is, in fact, the most powerful voice of the right hemisphere. It was for this reason that Guillaume de Machaut (1300–1377), when he desired to send a love letter to a lady, instead sent a song.

> And if it please you, my dear lady, to consider the last little song I sang, of which I composed both words and music, you can easily tell whether I'm lying or speaking the truth.[133]

He did not know how accurate he was; only the left hemisphere can lie.

The fact that Machaut would trust a melody to accomplish what he feared his words could not, echoes something which happens in our ordinary speech. The right hemisphere supplies to our speech the emotional tone, the melodic rise and fall of our sentences which makes the meaning of the particular words clear to the listener. Try speaking "I love you," emphasizing the first word and once again emphasizing the third word—the difference is significant. The famous actor, Kirk Douglas, mentioned something similar:

[132] Since the corpus callosum is not fully connected until about age six or seven, there resides in the right hemisphere the vocabulary of a child but without the ability to form a sentence with these words.

[133] "Remede de Fortune."

It's as if there are two brains in your head, two different personalities, and one is watching the other. The one that's playing the role is completely in the part, with all the warmth and feeling, while the other is watching and guiding it.[134]

It follows that the implications for the world of education are quite astounding. The great majority of traditional school teaching is aimed at the left hemisphere, where everyone can be expected to be the same, and not to the right side where the real individual student is found. Furthermore, all information in the left hemisphere is past tense, while the student sits there in the present tense! We are teaching the wrong side, in the wrong tense.

Dr. Sperry has given music educators the long sought argument for making music a core subject in the schools, for the experiential nature of music[135] is found in the same hemisphere as the experiential nature of the emotions. Through music, teachers can help students understand their own emotions and their consequences. Here music teachers can perform a service for society which no other teacher can do. It is the ultimate "core subject." But here is the supreme irony: the music education establishment has, save some token articles here and there, never understood the importance of this medical gift. The music education establishment tries to take "Music," which is a verb, "to make music," and turn it into a noun, sending it to the left hemisphere where it can be graded and the only location where it can be said all music is equal. The music education establishment takes the present tense experience of music, which children love, and turns it into past tense verbal concepts which can be of little interest to anyone.

This subject is the most important fundamental issue with regard to the future of music education. It is for this reason that the following discussions are provided, to help give the complete historical and psychological background necessary for the reader to feel comfortable with a new kind of music education.

[134] Kirk Douglas, *The Ragman's Son*, 1988, p. 76. This reminds me of an occasion in 1966 when I was playing French horn recitals throughout South America for the State Department. I found myself in a situation in Bolivia where the only piano tuner was on strike and the instrument was further flat than my tuning slide could accommodate. Since it was unreasonable to ask the pianist to transpose the entire difficult program (Hindemith, Strauss, Mozart, etc.) I had no choice but to transpose the horn part on the spur of the moment. I did it, but the curious thing was that during the recital the part of myself I call "me" felt that I was listening to someone else playing the recital—a clear illustration of the "many minds" hypothesis.

[135] The notation system of music, with its attendant forms of grammar is found in the left hemisphere, but this is not properly "music." It is more properly another symbolic language, which, indeed, is why it is found in the left hemisphere. No one should ever hold up a piece of paper with music written on it and say, "This is music."

The Debates on Reason versus Emotion

Is Man Ruled by Reason or Emotion?

> *Truth can be grasped through pure reason rather than by a reliance on subjective sense impressions.* DESCARTE
>
> *Few people still read Descartes, whose works have in fact become totally useless.*[136] VOLTAIRE

[136] Stuart Isacoff, *Temperament* (New York: Vintage Books, 2001), 173, 176.

THE ANCIENT PHILOSOPHERS lacked our clinical medical research which establishes that we are clearly bicameral in mind. Because we now know only the left hemisphere can write or speak, it is easy for us to see how they concluded that Reason, among all our potentialities, must rule. Of course it is precisely because of our bicameral mind's dual-composition that they had such difficulty in discussing our emotions, even though they never hesitated to acknowledge their power over us. The strongest testimonial to this difficulty are the repeated warnings, apparently unheeded generation after generation, that Reason must rule.[137]

Heeded or not, centuries of philosophical writing, strongly seconded by the new Christian Church, could not be answered in kind by the right hemisphere of our brain because it is mute. As a consequence, today society has endless difficulties in dealing with emotions. The most frequent choice, and the worst, is to try to deal with them in the terms of the left hemisphere of the brain, the rational and intellectual side of us. A case in point is contemporary music education in America, where the professors have attempted to recast the nature of music into the world of reason and intelligence. But this does not work now, just as it never worked in the ancient world.

In general those ancient philosophers who had such difficulty in dealing with the emotions left descriptions of the emotional side of us which are, for the modern reader, often quite extraordinarily negative. Cicero (106–43 BC), as a case in point, could accept the idea that our senses were a natural part of nature, but he found the emotions were something quite different and clearly something to be avoided!

[137] A much more extensive discussion of the debate between Reason and the Emotions can be found in David Whitwell, *Ancient Views on What is Music,* ed. Craig Dabelstein (Austin: Whitwell Books, 2013).

WHAT IS MUSIC?

The emotions of the mind, which harass and embitter the life of the foolish (the Greek term for these is *pathos*, and I might have rendered this literally and styled them "diseases," but the word "disease" would not suit all instances; for example, no one speaks of pity, nor yet anger, as a disease though the Greeks term these pathos. Let us then accept the term "emotion," the very sound of which seems to denote something vicious, and these emotions are not excited by any natural influence. The list of the emotions is divided into four classes, with numerous subdivisions, namely sorrow, fear, lust, and that mental emotion which the Stoics call by a name that also denotes a bodily feeling, *hedone*, "pleasure," but which I prefer to style "delight," meaning the sensuous elation of the mind when in a state of exultation), these emotions, I say, are not excited by any influence of nature; they are all of them mere fancies and frivolous opinions. Therefore the Wise Man will always be free from them.[138]

[138] Cicero, *De Finibus*, III, x, 35.

And again, in his treatise *On Duties*, sounding like an early Church father or later Puritan, he emphasizes that any display of emotions suggests that we are not in control of ourselves. The more highly developed person, he with a "greater soul," must especially observe this warning. In spite of the strong warning he proposes to give here, we cannot help noticing the indication that he had some awareness, no doubt through simple observation, that there are two sides of our being, those which here he calls thought and passion.

> We must be careful that the movements of our soul do not diverge from nature, and the care must be all the greater as the soul is greater. We shall achieve this if we are careful not to reach states of extreme excitement or alarm and if we keep our minds intent on the preservation of *decorum*. The movements of our souls are of two kinds: some involve thought, others involve passion. Thought is mostly expended in seeking out the truth, passion urges men to action. Therefore we must take care to expend thought on the best objects and to make clear that our passions are obedient to our intellect.[139]

[139] Cicero, *De Officiis*, 131ff.

And since Cicero probably anticipated that his warning, that "passions must be obedient to our intellect," would fall on deaf ears, as a last desperate effort he now paints for us contrasting pictures of the man under the influence of emotion and the man who has succeeded in subjecting his emotions to Reason.

> The man whom we see on fire and raging with lusts frantically pursuing everything with insatiable desire, and the more lavishly he swallows down pleasure from all quarters, the worse and more burning his thirst—would you not be entitled to call him most unhappy? The man who is carried away with frivolity and empty euphoria and uncontrolled desires, is he not the more wretched the happier he *thinks* he is?
>
> So just as these people are wretched, so are those happy whom no fears alarm, no distresses gnaw, no lusts arouse, no pointless euphoria dissolves in languorous pleasure. Just as the sea is recognized as calm when not even the slightest breeze ruffles the waves, so a state of mind can be accounted calm and peaceful, when there is no disturbance by which it can be agitated.[140]

[140] Cicero, *Tusculan Disputations*, V, 15ff.

Aristides Quintilianus, who lived between the first and fourth centuries AD and was one of the last of the ancient Greek philosophers, looked back and confessed that Reason was incapable of controlling the emotions.

> No cure could be found in Reason alone for those who were burdened by these emotions; for pleasure is a very powerful temptation, captivating even the animals that lack reason, and grief which remains unsolaced casts many people into incurable illnesses.[141]

[141] The Aristides quotations are quoted in Andrew Barker, *Greek Musical Writings* (Cambridge: Cambridge University Press, 1989), II, 457ff.

He is one of many witnesses who speak of the ancient Greeks' using music to mold character and he also points out that it was their belief that music could do what Reason could not, with respect to the control of the emotions. He tells us that the ancients made everyone cultivate music from childhood throughout their lives in order that the proper kind of music would have a positive impact on the soul. The effectiveness of music in doing this he compares to the "diverting of a stream, which was rushing through impassable crags or dispersing itself in marshy places, into an easily trodden and fertile plain." One of the chief concerns of the ancients, he tells us, was with regard to the misuse of music.

> Those who neglected music, melody and unaccompanied poetry alike, were utterly crude and foolish; those who had

involved themselves in it in the wrong way fell into serious errors, and through their passion for worthless melodies and poetry stamped upon themselves ugly idiosyncrasies of character.

It was this concern, he recalls, which caused the authorities to assign "educational music" to as many as a one hundred days, and the "relaxing kind of music" to no more than 30.

He does not entirely condemn entertainment music, but in granting its place he still does not waver from the principal value of music, to form character.

> We should not avoid song altogether just because it gives pleasure. Not all delight is to be condemned, but neither is delight itself the objective of music. Amusement may come as it will, but the aim set for music is to help us toward virtue.

He points to the success of the Greeks in doing just that and concludes, "Music is the most powerful agent of education, rivaled by no other, [and it can be shown where music education was missing] that our characters commonly deteriorate if they are left undisciplined, lapsing into base or brutal passions."

During the Renaissance there are a number of fictional works which focus on this same theme, the struggle between Reason and the emotions. In fifteenth century England we actually find a work by John Lydgate called, "Reson and Sensuallyte." A similar contemporary work, one of our favorites, is by Henry Medwall (b. 1461). It is entitled "Nature," but has the same theme. Here we find Nature warning man once again to "Let Reason govern you in every situation."

But now Sensuality enters and protests to Nature that she should have equal status with Reason. She contends, "I am the chief perfection of his nature! Without me, man would have no feeling, he might as well be made of wood or stone."

> And now you have put me out of his service,
> And have assigned Reason to be his guide
> With Innocence his nurse; thus am I set aside!

> You made him lord of all beasts living,
> And nothing worthy, as far as I can see;
> For if there be in him no manner of feeling
> No lively quickness, what kind of lord is he?
> A lord made of rags! or carved from a tree!
> And fares as an image carved from stone
> That can do nothing but stand alone!

"Allow me to have influence with him," Sensuality pleas with Nature, "and I will make him governor of the world."

"No," says Nature, "Reason must be preferred," reminding Sensuality, "You have brought many men to a wretched end." "You should obey me," Reason says to Sensuality, "wherever I go." Sensuality answers, "No, that I shall never do!"

At length Man decides to subjugate his Sensuality to Reason.

> Reason, Sir, my chief counselor.
> And this, Innocence, my previous nurse,
> And Sensuality, that other, by whom I have power
> To do as all sensuous beasts do.
> But Reason and Innocence, chiefly these two,
> Have the whole rule and governance of me,
> To whom is subdued my Sensuality.

Later another character, Pride, suggests that a "wild worm" has come into man's head if he thinks he will always be led only be Reason. He doubts that Reason will always endure with man, pointing out that, "Sensuality ... is chief ruler, when Reason is away."

In Sir Philip Sidney's *The Countesse of Pembrokes Arcadia*, there is an internal masque performed by a group of shepherds under the title, "The Battle between Reason and Passion." Here we find such dialog as,

> REASON. Who Passion doth ensue, lives in annoy.
> PASSION. Who Passion doth forsake, lives void of joy ...
>
>   .....
>
> REASON. Yet Passion, yield at length to Reason's stroke.
> PASSION. What shall we win by taking Reason's yoke?

There were still important philosophers who continued to argue that Reason must rule. The great Dante (1265–1321), for example, made the rather extraordinary statement that the senses "exist for reason's sake alone."[142] In one of his poems he even suggests that a sensation such as pain cannot be understood by mere experience, but must be understood by reason as well.[143] His strongest statement supporting the supremacy of Reason comes in another place in his "Banquet."

> Anyone who sets reason aside and uses only his sensitive part lives not as a man but as a beast.[144]

Dante uses this expression again in his *Divine Comedy*.

> You were not made to live like beasts, but for
> The pursuit of virtue and of knowledge.[145]

The great Francesco Petrarch (1304–1374), in spite of being a musician as well as a poet of much love poetry, in the Preface to his *Remedies for Fortune Fair and Foul*, gives us this colorful description of Reason defending us against emotions:

> You should read the book *as if* those four most famous, twin-born passions of the mind, HOPE or DESIRE and JOY, FEAR and SORROW, brought forth at the same time by the two sisters Prosperity and Adversity, fiercely assaulted from all sides the mind of man, and REASON, who governs this citadel, took on all of them at once. In her buckler and helmet, by stratagem and proper force, and, more so, with God's help, she fends off the weapons of the roaring enemies around her.[146]

In one place Petrarch calls love a "poison to sound judgment"[147] and he gives many examples of love interfering with Reason.

> If to love another more than oneself—if to be always sighing and
> weeping, feeding on sorrow and anger and trouble—
> If to burn from afar and freeze close by—if these are the causes

[142] *The Banquet*, trans. Christopher Ryan (Stanford University: Anma Libri, 1989), III, xv, 4.

[143] Dante, "Donne ch'avete intelletto d'armore," in *Dante's Lyric Poetry*, trans. K. Foster and P. Boyde (Oxford: Clarendon Press, 1967), 11.

[144] *The Banquet*, II, vii, 3.

[145] *Inferno*, XXVI.

[146] *Remedies for Fortune Fair and Foul*, trans. Conrad Rawski (Bloomington: Indiana University Press, 1991), I, Preface, 10.

[147] Second letter to Cicero, in *Letters from Petrarch*, trans. Morris Bishop (Bloomington: Indiana University Press, 1966), 18.

that I untune [*distempre*] myself with love, yours will be the blame,
Lady, mine the loss.[148]

We find a similar stance in his great contemporary, Guillaume de Machaut (1300–1377). While he offers token tribute to the idea that Reason must rule,[149] his more personal illustrations point to the contrary. After a debate over love and its consequences, the character, Loyalty, stipulates, "A lover would be a fool to listen to you, Reason."[150] Similarly, in complimenting good speech, Machaut describes it as "moderate, well-chosen, and appropriate, based wholly on Reason."[151] But, what happens to Reason-dominated speech when Love is present? It can, Machaut observes, force one,

> to cut short his words and interrupt them with sighs, drawn from the depths of his being, that render him mute and silent, and he has no choice but to remain speechless.

The fourteenth century English theologian and poet, Richard Rolle, recommends that if we concentrate on spiritual things, meditations, sermons and reading holy books, then we experience a form of delight which has none of the "inordinate stirrings."[152] For the Spaniard, St. John of the Cross (1542–1591), the solution was simply to erase from the mind all memory of pleasure deriving from appetites, for "When all things are forgotten, nothing disturbs the peace or stirs the appetites."[153] Needless to say, he does not recommend any expression of the emotions.

> Never allow yourself to pour out your heart, even though it be but for the space of a creed.[154]

Desiderius Erasmus (1469–1536), in his advice to a young prince, recommended he follow God's example and ignore the emotions. This same passage also reveals Erasmus' level of respect for the common man.

> Although God is swayed by no emotions, he nevertheless orders the world with the greatest good judgment. Following his example in all his actions, the prince must disregard emotional reactions and use only reason and judgment.

---

[148] "S' una fede amorosa, un cor non finto," in Ibid., 380.

[149] Especially in his poem, "The Tale of the Alerion."

[150] Guillaume de Machaut, "*Le Jugement du roy de Behaigne*,' trans. James Wimsatt and William Kibler (Athens: The University of Georgia Press, 1988), 154.

[151] Guillaume de Machaut, "*Remede de Fortune*," trans. James Wimsatt and William Kibler (Athens: The University of Georgia Press, 1988), 180.

[152] Richard Rolle, "Of the Vertu," in *English Prose Treatises of Richard Rolle* (London: Humphrey Milford, Oxford University Press, 1866, 1921), 14 and 16.

[153] "The Ascent of Mount Carmel," in *The Collected Works of St. John of the Cross*, trans. Kieran Kavanaugh and Otilio Rodriguez (Washington, D.C.: Institute of Carmelite Studies, 1979), 222.

[154] "Maxims and Counsels," in Ibid., 679.

Nothing is higher than God, and similarly the prince should be removed as far as possible from the low concerns and sordid emotions of the common people.[155]

Saint-Évremond (1610–1703), in a letter to the Mareschal de Crequi, seemed no longer burdened with the idea of making a choice.

> I can say one thing of myself, as extraordinary as true, that I never felt in myself any conflict between Passion and Reason. My Passion never opposed what I resolved out of duty; and my Reason readily complied with what a sense of pleasure inclined me to. I don't aim at praise on account of this easy agreement; on the contrary, I confess I have often been the more vicious for it. Not out of any perverse disposition to evil, but because the vice was entertained as a pleasure, instead of appearing as a crime.[156]

Eventually this accommodation was a matter of age, as he writes another correspondent,

> How unhappy is my condition! I have lost everything on the side of Reason, and I see nothing for me to pretend to on the side of Passion.[157]

The great Francis Bacon (1561–1626) accepts emotions and even admits they, like Reason, are capable of good. He finds, however, a third faculty, Imagination, independent of either, but through which both Reason and the emotions operate. Bacon finds Reason consisting of four separate faculties, those to invent, to seek, to judge and to communicate. He also writes of the danger which the affections represent to Reason and in fact suggests that man is only able to function rationally because imagination forms a "confederacy" with Reason against the affections.[158]

Another great philosopher of this period, David Hume (1711–1776), found the principal role of Reason to be one primarily of identification. No doubt set in motion by Bacon, he now finds seven forms of its activity: resemblance, identity, relations of time and place, proportion in quantity or number, degrees in any quality, contrariety and causation.[159]

[155] "The Education of a Christian Prince,' [1516] in *The Collected Works of Erasmus* (Toronto: University of Toronto Press, 1992), XXVII, 221. In his "A Complaint of Peace Spurned and Rejected by the Whole World," [Ibid., XXVII, 296], Erasmus again mentions "the common people, who are swayed by their passions like a stormy sea."

[156] *The Letters of Saint-Évremond*, ed. John Hayward (Freeport, NY: Books for Libraries Press, 1971), 114.

[157] Saint-Évremond, Letter to Duchesse Mazarin, 1676, Ibid.,168.

[158] *The Works of Francis Bacon* (Cambridge: Cambridge University Press, 1869), VI, 258ff. 299.

[159] *A Treatise of Human Nature*, I, iii, section 1.

Hume raises the entire subject of the emotions to a higher level than any former philosopher, even going so far as to make feeling dominant over ideas. No one had ever before written anything so extraordinary as the following:

> All probable reasoning is nothing but a species of sensation. It is not solely in poetry and music, we must follow our taste and sentiment, but likewise in philosophy. When I am convinced of any principle, it is only an idea, which strikes more strongly upon me. When I give the preference to one set of arguments above another, I do nothing but decide from my feeling concerning the superiority of their influence.[160]

[160] Ibid., I, iii, section 8.

Another who was inclined to raise the emotions to a level above Reason was Voltaire (1694–1778). First, he looked at the long history during which all philosophers, not to mention the Church, insisted that Reason must rule man and he found little to recommend this principle.

> When one considers that Newton, Locke, Clarke, and Leibniz would have been persecuted in France, imprisoned at Rome, and burned at Lisbon, what are we to think of human reason?[161]

[161] "Decartes and Newton," in *The Works of Voltaire* (New York: St. Hubert Guild, 1901), XXXVII, 174.

Further, under "Abuse of Words," in *his Philosophical Dictionary*, Voltaire goes to some lengths to demonstrate that language, and books, the traditional centers of Reason, "rarely give us any precise ideas" and are often taken by the listener in an incorrect sense. As an example he finds it curious that "the same word (Adoration) that is used both in addressing the Supreme Being and in addressing a mistress."

Voltaire was also keenly aware that there is more to man than Reason, that there is a feeling side which, in the course of daily actions, may be even more important.

> What will I gain from knowing the path of light and the gravitation of Saturn? These are sterile truths. One feeling is a thousand times more important.[162]

[162] Letter to Pierre-Robert Le Cornier de Cideville (February, 1737), in *The Selected Letters of Voltaire*, trans. Richard Brooks (New York: New York University Press, 1973), 63.

There were some in the Baroque Period who saw an inherent co-ordination between Reason and the emotions. One was Alexander Pope (1688–1744), who in his "Essay on Man," could pen this nice thought:

On life's vast ocean diversely we sail,
Reason is the [compass], but passion is the gale.

Another who wrote of the co-ordination of Reason and emotion was William Whycherley (1641–1715). His was a rather extraordinary observation for the time:

> It is very rare that Reason cures our passions, but one passion is cured by another. Reason generally places itself on the strongest side, and therefore there can be no violent passion, but has its Reason to authorize it.[163]

John Donne (1573–1631) arrived by intuition at an absolutely original idea for the time, that it is the heart which rules man. In a treatise known as "Meditation II," he calls the heart, and not the brain, the "Principalitie, and in the Throne, as King, the rest as Subjects … "[164] In another place, he suggests that if Nature explains how we differ in our "essence," we would all be alike, whether idiot or "Wizard," as we all have the same *kind* of Reason.[165]

For most Puritan philosophers, however, it was still a battle between Reason and the emotions. Joseph Hall (1574–1656), like nearly all clerics before him, warns that the affections can overwhelm Reason. The affections he calls the "secret factors of sin and Satan," which must be controlled by Reason and religion.

> If there be any exercise of Christian wisdom, it is in the managing of these unruly affections … Christianity gives not rules, but power, to avoid this short madness.[166]

Robert Burton (1577–1640) also acknowledges the great power, and danger, of the emotions in their capability to overwhelm Reason.

> Good discipline, education, philosophy, divinity, may mitigate and restrain these passions in some few men at some times, but for the most part they domineer, and are so violent, that as a torrent, bears down all before, and overflows his banks, lays bare the fields, lays waste the crops, they overwhelm reason, judgment & pervert the temperature of the body. The charioteer is run away with, nor does the chariot obey the reins.[167]

---

[163] *The Complete Works of William Wycherley* (New York: Russell & Russell, 1964), IV, 130.

[164] John Donne, *Devotions Upon Emergent Occasion*, ed. Anthony Raspa (Montreal: McGill-Queen's University Press, 1975), 56.

[165] John Donne, "Paradoxes and Problems," in *Selected Prose*, ed., Helen Gardner (Oxford: Clarendon Press, 1967), 13. Modern clinical findings tend to agree. All on the rational side of us is based on "spectator" information; everyone agrees 2 + 2 = 4, etc.

[166] "Heaven upon earth," in *The Works of Joseph Hall, D. D.*, ed. Philip Wynter (New York: AMS Press, 1969), VII, 14ff. Joseph Hall (1574–1656) was a bishop in the Church of England.

[167] Robert Burton, *The Anatomy of Melancholy*, 218.

Even John Milton (1608–1674), in his famous "Paradise Lost" warns, "Take heed least Passion sway thy Judgment," and,

> Sensual Appetite, who from beneath
> Usurping over sovereign Reason claimed
> Superior sway.[168]

In spite of the warnings of these Puritans of the seventeenth century, not to mention the centuries of similar warnings before, The Enlightenment made possible a new, less Church dominated perspective. Gradually more trust is found in the emotions, making possible such comments as the one written by George Washington to Lafayette, "Democratic States must always *feel* before they can *see*"[169] and the one by Robert Schumann, "The understanding may err, but not feelings."[170]

Finally we must mention Herbert Spencer, born in 1820 in England, who was the first important philosopher to discern what modern clinical research has now established, that in fact it is our emotions which determine all our major decisions, not Reason after all. He begins by making an observation which, if one considers the development of the earliest man, must be true, that intelligence and Reason could only have been built upon the earlier foundation stones of feelings and the senses.[171] In modern man, Spencer makes a finding that would have shocked, even offended 3,000 years of earlier philosophers, that "The chief component of mind is feeling."[172]

As we have indicated above, Spencer had the courage to conclude what modern research has now established: it is our emotions, not our reason, which drives our choices. Emotions, he says, is that element of thought,

> Which thus upon occasion shows itself supreme at all times; for the prevailing emotions, higher or lower, are those components of mind which determine the daily conduct, now dutiful now lax, now noble now base. That part which we ordinarily ignore when speaking of mind is its essential part.[173]

Thus, he concludes,

---

[168] "Paradise Lost," IX, 1129ff, in *The Works of John Milton*, ed. Frank Patterson (New York: Columbia University Press, 1931-1938), II, 300.

[169] Letter of July 25, 1785.

[170] Schumann's Diary of c. 1833.

[171] Hector Macpherson, *Spencer and Spencerism* (New York: Doubley, Page, & Co., 1900), 110ff.

[172] Herbert Spencer, *Facts and Comments* (New York: Appleton & Co., 1902), 36.

[173] Ibid.

The emotions are the masters, the intellect is the servant. The guidance of our acts through perception and reason has for its end the satisfaction of feelings, which at once prompt the acts and yield the energy for performance of the acts.[174]

[174] Ibid.

Early Intuitions on the Bicameral Mind

WHILE THE CLINICAL RESEARCH is new, the fact that man has competing intellectual and emotional faculties has long been a matter of common observation. Indeed the manifestations are everywhere. The French word for "Law," one of the most conceptual, logical and rational professions, is "droit" ("right" as in right hand[175]), the significance of which is obvious if the reader remembers that the hemispheres of the brain operative opposite sides of the body. Similarly, the Indians of the American Southwest distinguished between the functions of the hands, the right for writing and the left for music.[176]

The previous section concentrated on early commentary on the relative importance of Reason and Emotion, or the rational versus the non-rational sides of man. Here we provide the reader with a sampling of additional views of early philosophers who understood through observation or intuition the dual nature of our bicameral mind.

Among the early Greeks, Epictetus (55–135 AD) was well aware of the rational and non-rational nature of the person and observed, "by nothing is the rational creature so distressed as by the irrational." We are particularly impressed with the insight of Aristides Quintilianus (first to fourth century AD), who not only recognized the rational and non-rational division,

> These, then, are its two aspects, the rational, through which it accomplishes the works of wisdom, and the irrational, through which it engages in the business of the body.[177]

but he also stated that the "leader and high priest" of the first branch of learning is philosophy and the "ruler" of the second is music.

In one of the early music treatises, the *Musica Disciplina* of 843 AD, Aurelian of Reome not only finds that music joins "Reason to the body," but more surprising that it is music which connects the rational and non-rational part of us.

[175] The same association is true in Spanish.

[176] In David Whitwell, *Ancient Views on What is Music,* ed. Craig Dabelstein (Austin: Whitwell Books, 2013) the reader will find many examples of the curious prejudice in favor of the right-hand throughout history.

[177] Aristide's discussion begins Book II. Our quotations are from the translation by Andrew Barker, *Greek Musical Writings* (Cambridge: Cambridge University Press, 1989), II, 457ff.

What else is it that binds together the parts of the soul and body of man himself, who, as Aristotle is pleased to put it, has been joined together of the rational and the irrational.[178]

We find an extraordinary insight by the philosopher known as Pico in 1519.

> The intellect does not permit any lower faculty to function in collaboration with it. Rather, whenever anything comes near the intellect and arouses it, the intellect, like a roaring fire, burns it up, and converts it into itself.[179]

He was quite correct for in clinical experiments the left hemisphere of our brain tends to ignore the existence of the mute right hemisphere.

Early poets writing of love often found themselves having to sing of both hemispheres, as if they realized that the emotions were fundamentally apart from language. A striking example is found in Dante (1265–1321), who, in the introduction to one of his sonnets, clearly seems aware of the separation of faculties.

> In this sonnet I make two parts of myself in accordance with the way in which my thoughts were divided. One I call *heart*, that is desire; the other *soul*, that is reason; and I relate what one says to the other.[180]

And, when Reason does speak to Desire, it makes reference to the power of the emotions to shut down Reason.

> Who is this one
> that comes with consolation for our mind
> and who, possessing such outrageous strength,
> will not allow another thought to stay?[181]

This must have been impressive, if confusing, to Dante—that feeling could so overpower Reason. In one poem he observes that Love overcomes the intellect like a ray of sunlight overcoming eyes that are weak.[182] He returns to this idea in the *Divine Comedy* in a reference at the beginning of *Paradise* again using his terms of desire and intellect.

> As it approaches its desire,
> Our intellect submerges so profoundly
> That our memory is unable to go back.[183]

---

[178] Aurelian of Reome, *The Discipline of Music*, trans. Joseph Ponte (Colorado Springs: Colorado College Music Press, 1968), III. The Aristotle reference is apparently to the *Nicomachean Ethics*, I, 13.

[179] Giovanni Pico della Mirandola, *Commentary on a Canzone of Benivieni*, trans. Sears Jayne (New York: Peter Lang, 1984), 148.

[180] *Vita Nuova*, trans. Mark Musa (Oxford: Oxford University Press, 1992), 76.

[181] Ibid., 77.

[182] "Amor che ne la mente mi ragiona," lines 59–60, in Frederick Goldin, *German and Italian Lyrics of the Middle Ages* (Garden City: Anchor Books, 1973), 377.

[183] *Paradise*, I.

Another early example of one who was aware of the separate faculties was Geoffrey Chaucer (1340–1400), who, in his "The Romaunt of the Rose," observes,

> You must both perceive *and* feel that pride is a sin.[184]

Later in the Renaissance, Cervantes recognized love's difficulty in communication:

> Auristela finished her speech and began to weep tears that undid and erased everything she'd just said.[185]

Juan Vives, in his famous book, *On Education* of 1531, was not only clearly aware of the separate functions of Reason and emotions in the brain, but believed that Reason needed help and understanding in order to hold its own against the emotions.

> All the precepts of Moral Philosophy have been prepared, like an army, to bring support to Reason. Wherefore the whole man must be understood, from within and without. Within the mind are the intellect and the emotions. We must know by what things the emotions are aroused and developed; by what things on the other hand they are restrained, calmed, removed ... Our intellect is enveloped by too dense a darkness for it to see through, for the passions, aroused through sin, have spread a great and most obscuring mist before the eyes of Reason. Reason has need of being clear, and of being as little perturbed as possible.[186]

The problem in trying to have the left hemisphere speak about love (found in the right hemisphere), something it knows nothing about, of course reflects the independent nature of the two hemispheres.

One frequently finds references to the interference of one hemisphere or the other, such as one by Erasmus, who noticed that "when someone is chattering away, one cannot listen to the lute."[187] Similarly, Martin Luther used to complain about his little son, Hans, singing while he was trying to write.[188]

Here are some similar examples of recognition of the separate hemispheres found in English literature of the Renaissance.

[184] Lines

[185] Miguel de Cervantes, *The Trials of Persiles and Sigismunda,* trans. Celia Weller and Clark Colahan (Berkeley: University of California Press, 1989), II, v.

[186] *Vives: On Education,* trans. Foster Watson (Cambridge: University Press, 1913), V, iii.

[187] "The Tongue," in *The Collected Works of Erasmus* (Toronto: University of Toronto Press, 1992), XXIX, 279.

[188] In a conversation of 1532 reported by Veit Dietrich, in *Luther's Works* (St. Louis: Concordia, 1961), LIV, 21. A comment in the same conversation reveals that Luther understood the left hemisphere knew no emotions. See Ibid., 83.

Robert Greene (1560–1592):

Can wisdom win the field, when Love is Captain?[189]

John Lyly (1554–1606):

I cannot tell what reason it should be, But love and reason here do disagree.[190]

William Shakespeare:

Ask me no reason why I love you; for though Love use Reason for his physician, he admits him not for his counselor.[191]

The accumulation of centuries of such common observations resulted in a considerable increase in discussion of the bicameral mind during the Baroque. In addition to the difficulty of communication of feelings by the rational left hemisphere of the brain, the great German philosopher Gottfried Leibniz (1646–1716) added the problem the rational side often has in describing the senses themselves.

> Additional simple primitive terms are all those confused phenomena of the senses which we certainly perceive clearly, but which we cannot explain distinctly, neither define them through other concepts, nor designate them by words.[192]

He struggled with the problem of how the rational mind could have the "idea," that is, a rational understanding, of something like emotion.[193] In the end, being a highly rational person himself (a mathematician) he fell back on the old principle that the Reason must rule.

> The highest perfection of man consists not merely in that he acts freely but still more in that he acts with reason. Better, these are both the same thing, for the less anyone's use of reason is disturbed by the impulsion of the affections, the freer one is.[194]

His great contemporary, the French philosopher, Marin Mersenne (1588–1648), after much speculation concludes that the different voices which express "the passions of the soul" in men and animals are natural, but language itself

---

[189] *Arbasto: The Anatomy of Fortune* [1584], in *The Life and Complete Works of Robert Greene*, ed. Alexander Grosart (New York: Russell & Russell, 1964), III, 197.

[190] John Lyly, *The Maydes Metamorphosis*, IV, i.

[191] *The Merry Wives of Windsor*, II, i, 4.

[192] Leibniz, "An Analysis of the Elements of Language," in *General Investigations Concerning the Analysis of Concepts and Truths,* trans. Walter O'Briant (Athens: University of Georgia Press, 1968), 33.

[193] Leibniz, "What is an Idea?" [1678], in Leroy Loemker, *Philosophical Papers and Letters* (Dordrecht: Reidel, 1956), 207.

[194] Leibniz, "Criticala Thoughts on the General Part of the Principles of Descartes" [1692], "On Article 37," in Ibid., 388.

is artificial.[195] This eventually leads him, in Proposition 12, to wonder if "the musician can invent the best language of all those by which the conceptions of the mind can be expressed."[196]

The Frenchman, Blaise Pascal (1623–1662), a brilliant thinker and inventor, seems to have been clearly aware of a bicameral division in the mind and one of his expressions of this is a familiar and widely quoted maxim,

> The heart has its reason, which reason does not know. We feel it in a thousand things.[197]

We find some additional interesting reflections of our bicameral mind among French writers of the Baroque, first in Charles de Saint-Évremond, in a poem contained in a letter to the Duke of Buckingham (1678), quite correctly suggests that the two hemispheres are inclined to work separately and not together.

> Sometimes let Reason, with a sovereign sway,
> Control all your desires:
> Sometimes let Reason to your heart give way,
> And fan your warmest fires.[198]

Jean de La Bruyere (1645–1696) makes the same point by way of reference to separate famous French playwrights.

> The plays of Corneille occupy one's mind; those of Racine stir one's heart.[199]

At the beginning of the previous section we quoted one of La Rochefoucauld's famous maxims which reflects our bicameral mind. There are two more which perhaps should not be omitted:

> The mind is always the dupe of the heart.[200]
>
> .....
>
> Not all those who know their minds know their hearts as well.[201]

---

[195] Marin Mersenne, Treatise Three, Book One, *Traitez de la Voix, et des Chants,* trans. Edmund LeRoy (New York: Julliard School, unpublished dissertation, 1978), III, i, 10.

[196] One who had some success using music as a language was François Sudre, see David Whitwell, *La Téléphonie and the Universal Musical Language,* 2nd edn. (Austin: Whitwell Books, 2012), available from amazon.com.

[197] Blaise Pascal, *Pensées* (New York: Modern Library, 1941), III, 277.

[198] Quoted in *The Letters of Saint-Évremond,* ed. John Hayward (Freeport, NY: Books for Libraries Press, 1971), 205.

[199] La Bruyere, *Characters,* trans, Jean Stewart (Baltimore: Penguin Books, 1970), 38.

[200] *The Maxims of La Rochefoucauld,* Nr. 102.

[201] Ibid., Nr. 103.

There are two other maxims of his which have a different focus and impress us very much. These two are relevant to the fact that the right hemisphere of our brain is mute and has no language to express itself (except through music). The first of these maxims pictures a right hemisphere communicating in a manner other than through language.

> Tone of voice, look and manner can prove no less eloquent than choice of words.[202]

More extraordinary is his insight that there are forms of understanding unique to the right hemisphere. This is a very correct and valid truth and represent a fundamental part of us that is never approached by the field of education, since society has made the emotions "off-limits" to teachers.

> Nature would seem to have hidden deep within us talents and abilities we know nothing about; only strong emotion is able to bring them to light, and to give us at times insights beyond the reach of [rational] thought.[203]

We only find one original idea of importance on our subject by the famous Descartes. This is found at the very beginning of his "Rules for the Direction of the Mind," where he contends that the hand trained for harp playing, cannot be used for other pursuits, such as agriculture. All this is by way of introducing his observation that it was the arts which convinced the other intellectual disciplines that one must be a specialist in only one subject, devoting his entire life to that alone. Otherwise, he was rather a "left-brained man," which we can see clearly in a letter of 1641 to Henricus Regius, a professor of medicine at Utrecht.

> There is only one soul in man, the rational soul; for no actions can be reckoned human unless they depend on reason.

Montesquieu (1689–1755) lets the air out of this balloon with a wonderful story about a man who had been unable to sleep for thirty-five days. Ordinary physicians, at a loss, proposed to give him opium, but a friend took him to an holistic doctor (a man who "does not practice medicine, but has a

---

[202] Ibid., Nr. 249. Either hemisphere can work the face.

[203] Ibid., Nr. 404.

multitude of remedies") who gave him a six-volume study of law. After reading a few pages, the man fell asleep.[204] This reminds us of another wonderful story, this one by Voltaire. His "Zadig" (1747) is a tale about a Babylonian philosopher and a wise man who "knew as much of metaphysics as hath ever been known in any age, that is, little or nothing at all." This story reflects another aspect of our bicameral mind, the fact that, as each hemisphere controls the opposite side of the body, so each eye feeds into the opposite hemisphere. Thus we must think of the right eye as the rational eye and the left as the eye dealing with our emotional life. With this in mind we return to the beginning of this story when a young man, Zadig, is wounded in the eye. A messenger is sent to Memphis for the famous physician, Hermes, who came with his large retinue. After his examination of Zadig, the doctor observed,

[204] Montesquieu, *The Persian Letters* (London: Athenaeum, 1901), 269.

> Had it been the right eye, I could have cured it; but the wounds of the left eye are incurable.

In the English Baroque we find many references to our bicameral brain. Indeed, the great philosopher, David Hume (1711–1776) once noted,

> Everyone of himself will readily perceive the difference between feeling and thinking.[205]

[205] *A Treatise of Human Nature*, I, i, section 1.

A poem by Thomas Sheridan (1687–1738), a priest and schoolmaster, is a remarkable example of someone who had arrived at a very accurate understanding of the bicameral division of the brain purely by intuition. He is absolutely, and astonishingly, correct in his assigning of right or left eye and ear functions vis-a-vis their actual relationship with the brain hemispheres. Indeed, it is difficult to believe this was written before the availability of the results of clinical brain research.

> With my left eye, I see you sit snug in your stall,
> With my right I'm attending the lawyers that scrawl.
> With my left I behold your bellower a cur chase;
> With my right I'm reading my deeds for a purchase.

My left ear's attending the hymns of the choir,
My right ear is stunned with the noise of the crier.[206]

Since, as most readers know today, our two hemispheres tend to work separately, and not together, according to which side is best equipped for a particular problem, we should like to include two examples of English writers complaining about the interference of one side or the other. Charles Avison (1709–1770), in one place, observes that people sing with more emotion when they visit foreign churches and cannot read the words to the hymns. His point, of course, is that in this case the right hemisphere is not hampered by the left at all.[207]

On the other hand, so to speak, Richard Steele, in the *Spectator* for September 24, 1712, published a fictitious complaint that our emotions carry us away, whereas the sermon is soon forgotten.

> A loose trivial song gains the affections, when a wise Homily is not attended to.

For the nineteenth century we need only point to the experience of the great composers, who also made observations which reflect the recognition of the conflict between the two hemispheres of our brain. Mendelssohn, for example, once noticed that sometimes he became so emotionally involved while he was conducting that he had difficulty in maintaining the beat. In this case, we know conductors use the right hand to give the beat, as it is controlled by the left hemisphere which knows the notation and the numbers of music. When Mendelssohn became emotionally involved, his right hemisphere was interfering with the left hemisphere function. Similarly, Schumann once remarked that when he was absorbed in music he found that he had difficulty remembering his German language!

The musician who wrote most extensively on the subject of our bicameral selves was Richard Wagner and his writings are worthy of thoughtful contemplation, certainly by all musicians. Instead of using terms like left and right (which he had no knowledge of) or rational versus non-rational,

[206] Quoted in *The Poetical Works of Jonathan Swift* (London: Bell and Daldy, n.d.), III, 245.

[207] Charles Avison, *An Essay on Musical Expression* [London, 1753] (New York: Broude Reprint, 1967), 88.

he used the terms Understanding versus Feeling, which, of course, match perfectly the primary functions of the two hemispheres of our brain. He makes a number of contentions, beginning with the statement that the musician "addresses himself to Feeling, and not to Understanding."[208] And he says if the musician is answered in terms of Understanding, you might as well say he was not understood.

He also wrote in this regard on the subject of the development of modern languages, pointing out that language must have been based on feeling but that it has developed in such a manner that today, "we speak a language we do not understand with the Feeling [side]."[209] On the other hand, he contends that poetry is impossible unless it passes "from the Understanding to the Feeling."[210]

Wagner also attempts to write of music theory in terms of feeling,[211] certainly a foreign concept in modern classrooms. In our view his explanation is not so successful here, but in making the effort he creates a wonderfully romantic discussion of this left-brain topic which is very refreshing. It also reminds us that Galileo once described the interval of a perfect fifth as "like a gentle kiss and bite."

[208] *Richard Wagner's Prose Works,* trans. William Ashton Ellis (New York: Broude, I, 270ff.

[209] Ibid., II, 230.

[210] Ibid., II, 232.

[211] Ibid., II, 291.

On the Importance of the Experiential

> Experience does not err.[212]
> Leonardo da Vinci
>
> We know nothing in the world but by experience.[213]
> Voltaire

[212] Jean Paul Richter, ed., *The Literary Works of Leonardo da Vinci* (London: Phaidon, 1970), II, 240.

[213] Voltaire, "The Ignorant Philosopher."

THE REAL PROBLEM for any philosophy which generalizes that Reason must rule is that in the end the rational side of ourselves is not the real *us*. Everything understood by the rational areas of our brain is second-hand information. This fact has been recognized for a very long time. Aristotle (b. 384 BC) states this in the very first sentence of his "Posterior Analytics."

> All teaching and learning that involves the use of reason proceeds from pre-existent knowledge.[214]

[214] Trans. Hugh Tredennick (Cambridge: Harvard University Press, 1960).

Toward the end of the sixth century BC, several philosophers began to isolate the separate natures of reason and experience. Gorgias, in particular, was on the correct path in coming to understand that we cannot really know something unless we experience it ourselves. This same philosopher was also the author of one of the most frequently quoted statements of the fifth century:

> He who deceives is more honest than he who does not deceive and he who is deceived is wiser than he who is not.

Plutarch pointed out that sometimes even Reason grows out of experience, and he provided an example from his own life.[215]

[215] "Life of Demosthenes."

> Upon which that which happened to me, may seem strange, though it be true; for it was not so much by the knowledge of words, that I came to understanding of things, as by my experience of things I was enabled to follow the meaning of words.

The Roman philosopher Lucretius (99–55 BC) focused on the dependence of Reason on the senses, asking in one place,

> Can anyone
> Explain what bodily sensation is
> Unless he trusts his own experience of it?[216]

[216] *The Way Things Are*, III, 351.

This philosopher also noticed the curious characteristic of the feeling sense that we call today "phantom limb." This is the perception that one can feel a leg, for example, in that case where the leg in fact no longer exists. Reason, of course, had no explanation for this phenomenon so vividly illustrated by Lucretius:

> It is said scythe-bearing battle chariots,
> Red-steaming from their killing course, can cut
> Limbs off so quickly you can see them tremble
> Or quiver on the ground, before their soldier
> Has any inkling what has happened to him.
> His fighting spirit pushes his attack
> With what equipment he still has; he'll charge
> And never know his left arm and his shield
> Are swept off with marauding chariot-wheels
> And scythes and horses, while nearby, a comrade
> Lifts his right arm to scale a wall, and sees
> His right arm isn't there, or attempts to rise
> While his leg is kicking at him from the ground.[217]

[217] Ibid., III, 641.

We find one extraordinary argument that experience gives meaning to that most rational representative of Reason, grammar. In his treatise on "Mathematics," Roger Bacon (b. c. 1214 AD) contends that the theologian must have training in music in order to understand the Scriptures.[218] One reason, of course, is simply to be able to fully understand the many references to music in the Old Testament. The second reason is relative to the many kinds of meters found in the old Hebrew text. Here he notes that while the grammarian may teach the practical rules, only music gives "the reasons and theories" for these meters. In the same manner, he points to the issue of pronunciation, as the Scripture is filled with "accents, longs, shorts, colons, commas, and periods."

[218] This entire discussion is found in "Mathematics," in *The Opus Majus of Roger Bacon*, trans. Robert Burke (New York: Russell & Russell, 1962), I, 259.

> All these belong causally to music, because of all these matters the musician states the reason, but the grammarian merely the fact.

This idea is worthy of thought when one remembers that all philologists today believe that music preceded speech in early man.

Bacon, by the way, is sometimes credited as being the first to clearly point to the separate hemispherical functions of the brain. He does this in a passage where he argues that Reason is never certain until it tests its contentions by experience.

> For there are two modes of acquiring knowledge, namely, by reasoning and experience. Reasoning draws a conclusion and makes us grant the conclusion, but does not make the conclusion certain, or does it remove doubt so that the mind may rest on the intuition of truth, unless the mind discovers it by the path of experience.[219]

[219] Ibid., "Experimental Science," I.

This idea, that Reason cannot rest until it has been proven by experience, is one often used by those who doubted the primacy of Reason. This was a point made frequently by Leonardo da Vinci (1452–1519).

> No human investigation can be called true science without passing through mathematical tests; and if you say that the sciences which begin and end in the mind contain truth, this cannot be conceded, and must be denied for many reasons. First and foremost because in such mental discourses experience does not come in, without which nothing reveals itself with certainty.[220]

[220] *The Literary Works of Leonardo da Vinci*, ed. Jean Paul Richter (London: Phaidon, 1970), I, 31ff.

.....

> To me it seems that all sciences are vain and full or errors that are not born of experience, mother of all certainty, and that are not tested by experience, that is to say, that do not at their origin, middle or end pass through any of the five senses.[221]

[221] Ibid., I, 33ff.

Geoffrey Chaucer (1340–1400) went even further writing that we should trust Reason only in the absence of personal experience. "We should honor and believe these old books, where there is no test other than experience."[222] Indeed, in numerous places Chaucer clearly states that various kinds of knowledge is proven only by experience. For example, with regard to the fact that there is a limit to one's lifespan,

[222] "The Legend of Good Women," line 27.

Chaucer says we need no authority for this, as it is proven by experience.[223] Even, Chaucer says, where the Bible does not suffice, experience will teach you.

> And yf that hooly writ may nat suffyse,
> Experience shal the teche.[224]

Michel Montaigne (1533–1592), after first suggesting that it is only when reason fails us that we make use of experience, makes a comment similar to the previous one by Chaucer,

> Were I a good pupil there is enough, I find, in my own experience to make me wise.[225]

We must add that there were still some philosophers, especially Churchmen, who refused to recognize the importance of experience. A case in point is St. John of the Cross, an old style Church philosopher so severe that he seems to us to belong in the darkest of the Dark Ages. He begins his major treatise, "The Ascent of Mount Carmel," by declaring that in his writings he will not rely on his own experience or on science, "for these can deceive us." All answers will come from the Scriptures![226]

A more contemporary remark was made by Voltaire in a letter to Père Porée. Voltaire contends that the artist learns by experience, and not from books.

> No matter how many books are written on the technique of painting by those who know their subject, not one of them will afford as much instruction to the pupil as will the sight of a single head by Raphael.[227]

In particular, when it came to "doing" things, the actual exercises of one's life or profession, a number of early philosophers were quick to place more value on personal experience than on Reason or learning. Socrates, in taking this stand, pointed to the example of midwives. Speaking of the fact that only women who have had child-bearing experience should act as midwives, we read,

> SOCRATES. It is said that Artemis was responsible for this, because though she is the goddess of childbirth, she is not

[223] "The Knight's Tale," 3001.

[224] "L'Envoy de Chaucer a Bukton," 21. For additional references to understanding being proven by experience, see "The Wife of Bath's Tale," 468; "The Friar's Tale," 1517; "The Sumner's Tale," 2057; "The Merchant's Tale," 2238; "Troilus and Criseyde," III, 1283; "The House of Fame," II, 370; and "Romaunt of the Rose," 5553.

[225] Michel de Montaigne, *Essays*, trans. M. A. Screech (London: Penguin, 1993), III, xiii, 1218.

[226] "The Ascent of Mount Carmel," in *The Collected Works of St. John of the Cross*, trans. Kieran Kavanaugh and Otilio Rodriguez (Washington, D.C.: Institute of Carmelite Studies, 1979), 70. Juan de Yepes y Alverez (1542–1591), known as St. John of the Cross, was imprisoned for a time by the Inquisition for his liberal views, although the modern reader is hard pressed to find such views in his surviving works.

[227] Letter to Père Porée (1730), quoted in Barrett Clark, *European Theories of the Drama* (New York: Crown, 1959), 279.

herself a mother. She could not, indeed, allow the barren to be midwives, because human nature cannot know the mystery of an art without experience.[228]

[228] *Theaetetus*, 149c.

Aristotle took a more fundamental view, with respect to "doing" and he went on to contend that it is from these direct experiences that character is formed.

> Of all the things that come to us by nature we first acquire the potentiality and later exhibit the activity (this is plain in the case of the senses; for it was not by often seeing or often hearing that we got these senses, but on the contrary we had them before we used them, and did not come to have them by using them); but the virtues we get by first exercising them, as also happens in the case of the arts as well. For the things we have to learn before we can do them, we learn by doing them, e.g. men become builders by building and lyre players by playing the lyre; so too we become just by doing just acts, temperate by doing temperate acts, brave by doing brave acts . . .
>
> . . . . .
>
> It is from the same causes and by the same means that every virtue is both produced and destroyed, and similarly every art; for it is from playing the lyre that both good and bad lyre players are produced . . . For if this were not so, there would have been no need of a teacher, but all men would have been born good or bad at their craft. This, then, is the case with the virtues also . . . Thus, in one word, *states of character arise out of like activities*. This is why the activities we exhibit must be of a certain kind; it is because the states of character correspond to the differences between these. It makes no small difference, then, whether we form habits of one kind or another from our very youth; it makes a very great difference, or rather *all* the difference.[229]

[229] *Ethica Nicomachea* 1103a.25 and following.

Giovanni Boccaccio (1313–1375) would appear to agree completely with Aristotle when he maintains that it is a man's personal experience, not merely knowledge, which makes him productive. In this passage he seems to infer that experience and the man become one.

> It is difficult for anyone to accomplish anything in which he has not had any experience . . . This is the reason a worker is

able to use his tools—a man is known according to his inner nature.[230]

Girolamo Cardano (1501–1576), one of the most prolific philosophers of the Renaissance, testified,

> I have been more aided by experience than by my own wisdom or by the faith in the power of my art.[231]
>
> .....
>
> Perhaps someone will quite rightly ask whether the same people who know these rules also play well or not. For it seems to be a different thing to know and to execute ... The same question arises in other discussions. Is a learned physician also a skilled one? In those matters which give time for reflection, the same man is both learned and successful, as in mathematics, jurisprudence, and also medicine ...
>
> .....
>
> But in those matters in which no time is given and guile prevails, it is one thing to know and another to exercise one's knowledge successfully, as in gambling, war, dueling, and commerce. For although acumen depends on both knowledge and practice, still practice and experience can do more than knowledge.[232]

Cardano's suggestion above that a learned physician may or may not be a skilled one reminds us of a similar discussion by Montaigne, who recalled that Plato[233] once wrote that we should never submit ourselves to a doctor unless he himself had had the same illness and cured himself. This leads Montaigne to make the observation,

> If doctors want to know how to cure syphilis it is right that they should first catch it themselves![234]

To return to the subject of "doing," we might also point out that Izaak Walton, in his *The Compleat Angler*, mentions an author, a Mr. Hales, who was ridiculed for writing a book on fencing. This was, Walton points out, because "that art was not to be taught by words, but practice."[235] Leonardo da Vinci found that even writing, an essentially rational occupation, was based on experience.

[230] "A Warning against Credulousness," in *The Fates of Illustrious Men*, trans. Louis Hall (New York: Ungar, 1965), 25.

[231] Quoted in Oystein Ore, *Cardano The Gambling Scholar* (New York: Dover, 1953), 47.

[232] *The Book on Games of Chance*, trans. Sydney Gould (New York: Dover, 1953), 225.

[233] *Republic*, III, 408 D-E.

[234] Michel de Montaigne, *Essays*, trans. M. A. Screech (London: Penguin, 1993), III, xiii, 1218.

[235] Izaak Walton, *The Compleat Angler* (London: Oxford University Press, 1935), 6. Izaak Walton (1593–1683) is best known for his biographies of contemporary English writers.

They will say that I, having no literary skill, cannot properly express that which I desire to treat of; but they do not know that my subjects are to be dealt with by experience rather than by words; and experience has been the mistress of those who wrote well.[236]

The sixteenth century Spanish playwright, Fernando de Rojas, suggested that it was experience which made the difference in all professions, observing that "Experience makes men artists in their profession."[237] The most famous Spanish playwright of this period, Lope de Vega, pauses to remind his listeners that Love is something which can be understood *only* by experience.

Let no man speak Love's name that has not felt its power.[238]

The early philosophers also often point to music as something which must be learned by experience, not from books. We have seen, above, Aristotle observe, "lyre players learn by playing the lyre," and in a similar vein we find,

The art of music causes the man to be a musician.[239]
    Boethius (475–524)

For in any art those things which we know of ourselves are much more numerous than those which we learn from a master.[240]
    Guido of Arezzo, Micrologus (1026–1028)

For it seems impossible that anyone should become a builder who has not first built something; or that anyone should become a harpist who has not first played the harp.[241]
    Thomas Aquinas (1224–1274)

Practice is the best teacher of any subject. One learns music by playing.[242]
    Erasmus (1469–1536)

And in the case of composition one often finds writers who question the value of the written rules. Charpentier, the seventeenth century French composer, concludes his book on the rules of composition by admitting,

Practice teaches more about this than all the rules.

---

[236] Quoted in *The Literary Works of Leonardo da Vinci,* ed. Jean Paul Richter (London: Phaidon, 1970), I, 116.

[237] Fernando de Rojas, *Celestina,* trans. James Mabbe (New York: Applause Publishers, 1986), 37.

[238] Lope de Vega, *The Knight from Olmedo,* trans. Jill Booty, in *Lope de Vega, Five Plays* (New York: HIll and Wang, 1961), 179.

[239] Boethius, *Consolatione Philosophiae,* trans. Samuel Fox (London: George Bell, 1895), XVI, iii.

[240] Quoted in Oliver Strunk, *Source Readings in Music History* (New York: Norton, 1950), 117.

[241] *Commentary on the Metaphysics of Aristotle*, trans. John Rowan (Chicago: Henry Regnery, 1961), 684–685 (IX.L.7:C 1850).

[242] "Adages," in *The Collected Works of Erasmus* (Toronto: University of Toronto Press, 1992), XXXII, 25.

To which Voltaire added,

The composer of *Armide* and *Issé* [Lully], and the worst of composers, worked according to the same musical rules.[243]

[243] Letter to Père Porée (1730), quoted in Barrett Clark, *European Theories of the Drama* (New York: Crown, 1959), 279.

The Baroque: Emotion takes Precedence over Rules

> I never met with any man that suffered his passions to hurry him away so much whilst he was playing on the violin as the famous Arcangelo Corelli, whose eyes will sometimes turn as red as fire; his countenance will be distorted, his eyeballs roll as in an agony, and he gives in so much to what he is doing that he doth not look like the same man.[244]

[244] O. Strunk, "François Raguenet, *Comparison between the French and Italian Music* (1702)," *The Musical Quarterly* XXXII (1946), 419fn.

NOTHING, IN OUR VIEW, so clearly defines the Baroque as the above eye-witness description of Corelli. How far removed is this understanding of music from the old Catholic Scholastic dogma which held that music was a branch of mathematics! Between these two poles stands the Renaissance which, in music, symbolizes the rediscovery of the ancient truth that the purpose of music is to communicate feeling. The real story of the Baroque, in music, is an enthusiastic embrace of emotions in music and a fervent search for how this happens through music.

One is tempted to suppose that, after the extraordinary leadership of Italy in the arts during the Renaissance, she needed a period of rest. A more objective view might see the influence of a colder intellectual climate caused by the Church after the Council of Trent.[245] This is most apparent in painting, where nudes were no longer allowed and only the fervent pleas of a group of artists prevented the Pope Clement VIII from having Michelangelo's *Last Judgment* completely painted over. In music, the noble patrons turned to entertainment and great numbers of distinguished musicians left for other countries, making Italian music important everywhere except in Italy.

[245] The Inquisition remained a fearful part of the conservative Church climate. Monteverdi, in his letters, writes of having to go to great lengths to have his son (a doctor of medicine!) released from prison for having read a book which he did not realize was on the prohibited list.

It is in Germany, in particular, where one finds the most enthusiastic and dedicated search for studying the role of the emotions in music, a study which has been sometimes called, "The Doctrine of the Affections." The belief in this was strongly believed, as we seen in the declaration by F. W. Marpurg in 1749, "All musical expression has an emotion for its foundation."[246]

[246] F. W. Marpurg, *Der critische Musicus an der Spree* (Berlin), September 2, 1749.

In the Renaissance the most frequently given purpose for music was to "soothe" the listener's feelings. During the Baroque, as we approach the modern concept of a concert, this purpose is transformed into something with a more Aristotelian ring to it, more like the description of a catharsis, "to refresh the spirit." Georg Muffat, in the Foreword to his *Auserlesene Instrumental-Music* (1701) explains that in his previous collections he has sought to draw "liveliness and grace" from the "Lullian well." But, in the present collection he now presents "certain profound and unusual affects of the Italian manner, various capricious and artful conceits, and alternations of many sorts, interspersed with special diligence between the [ripieno] and [concertino]." The purpose of this music, as he makes very clear, is to listen to, it is concert music. It is also important to notice the variety of situations which he equates with "concert music," considering how limited a definition we acknowledge today (concert hall, lights off, white tie, programs, etc.).

> These concerti, suited neither to the church (because of the ballet airs and airs of other sorts which they include) nor for dancing (because of other interwoven conceits, now slow and serious, now gay and nimble, and composed only for the express refreshment of the ear), may be performed most appropriately in connection with entertainments given by great princes and lords, for receptions of distinguished guests, and at state banquets, serenades, and assemblies of musical amateurs and virtuosi.[247]

[247] Quoted in Oliver Strunk, *Source Readings in Music History* (New York: Norton, 1950), 449.

In the title pages of Bach's *Clavier Ubung*, Part III, and the "Goldberg Variations," he gives the purpose to "refresh the spirits." Similarly, when he was looking at a position in Halle, he was sent a contract which specified that the church music should have the result that "the members of the Congregation shall be the more inspired and refreshed in worship."[248]

[248] Quoted in Hans T. David and Arthur Mendel, *The Bach Reader* (New York: Norton, 1966), 65.

As we all understand today, the most important purpose of music is to communicate feelings, a purpose to which Johann Scheibe paid tribute in 1739.

> Music which does not penetrate the heart nor the soul

Does indeed consist of tones yet only is compelling to the ears,
Which nature and art have not given sound, grace, strength,
Is quite dead, and lacks spirit and vitality.²⁴⁹

A more typical expression of this purpose during the Baroque is given by Georg Muffat, in his *Florilegia* (1695). He writes that he has given each suite the name of "some state of the affections which I have experienced," namely, Piety, The Joys of the Hopeful, Gratitude, Impatience, Solicitude, Flatteries, and Constancy.

The most accurate testimonial of the view of the Baroque composer may be the one inadvertently expressed in 1711 by Heinichen. He means to complain that no theorist has really written the definitive work on the "doctrine of affections." But he was describing musicians at large, including composers, when he admits that no one is interested in this topic. For this is how it has nearly always been: composers compose and the theorists come along later, and not before.

> What a bottomless ocean we still have before us merely in the expression of words and the affections in music. And how delighted is the ear, if we perceive in a refined church composition or other music how a skilled virtuoso has attempted here and there to move the feelings of an audience through his *galanterie* and other devices that express the text, and in this way to find successfully the true purpose of music. Nevertheless, no one wants to search deeper into this beautiful musical *Rhetorica* and to invent good rules. What could one not write about musical taste, invention, accompaniment, and their nature, differences, and effects? But no one wants to investigate the matters aiming at this lofty practice or to give even the slightest introduction to it.²⁵⁰

In the end, no matter what emotions the composer was feeling and attempting to notate, a great responsibility remains to the performer if these emotions are to be perceived by the listener. A student of Bach relates that the latter had this foremost in mind even in the performance of the most simple music.

> As concerns the playing of chorales, I was instructed by my teacher Kapellmeister Bach, who is still living, not to play the

[249] Poem in honor of the publication of Johann Mattheson, *Der vollkommene Capellmeister* [1739], trans. Ernest Harriss (Ann Arbor: UMI Research Press, 1981), 74.

[250] Johann David Heinichen, *Anweisung zum Generalbass* (1711) in George J. Buelow, *Thorough-Bass Accompaniment According to Johann David Heinichen* (Berkeley and Los Angeles: University of California Press, 1992), 326.

songs merely offhand but according to the sense [*Affect*] of the words.[251]

Heinichen concurs that the notes alone are not sufficient for this purpose.

It is impossible to find the tenderness of the soul of music with mere numeric changes of dead notes.[252]

The German writer, Christoph Bernhard (1627–1692), in a treatise on singing, has left a remarkable description, in 1649, of the singer's range of emotion in the new Florentine opera style.

In the recitative style, one should take care that the voice is raised in moments of anger, and to the contrary dropped in moments of grief. Pain makes it pause; impatience hastens it. Happiness enlivens it. Desire emboldens it. Love renders it alert. Bashfulness holds it back. Hope strengthens it. Despair diminishes it. Fear keeps it down. Danger is fled with screams. If, however, a person faces up to danger, then his voice must reflect his daring and bravery.[253]

Marpurg confirms a wide variety of emotions in performance and provides an interesting discussion of the integrity of the performer.

All musical expression has an affect or emotion for its foundation. A philosopher when expounding or demonstrating will try to enlighten our understanding, to bring it lucidity and order. The orator, the poet, the musician attempt rather to inflame than to enlighten. The philosopher deals in combustible matter capable of glowing or yielding a temperate and moderate warmth. But in music there is only the distilled essence of this matter, the most refined part of it, which throws out thousands of the most beautiful flames, always with rapidity, sometimes with violence. The musician has therefore a thousand parts to play, a thousand characters to assume at the composer's bidding. To what extraordinary undertakings our passions carry us! He who has the good fortune at all to experience the inspiration which lends greatness to poets, orators, artists, will be aware how vehemently and diversely our soul responds when it is given over to the emotions. Thus to interpret rightly every composition which is put in front of him a musician needs the utmost sensibility and the most felicitous powers of intuition.[254]

[251] Johann Ziegler (1746), quoted in Hans T. David and Arthur Mendel, *The Bach Reader* (New York: Norton, 1966), 237.

[252] Johann David Heinichen, *Anweisung zum Generalbass* (1711) in George J. Buelow, *Thorough-Bass Accompaniment According to Johann David Heinichen* (Berkeley and Los Angeles: University of California Press, 1992), 330.

[253] Quoted in Ellen Harris, "Voices" in *Performance Practice: Music after 1600* (New York: Norton, 1989), 110.

[254] F. W. Marpurg, *Der critische Musicus an der Spree* (Berlin), September 2, 1749.

Finally, from Forkel we have the interesting insight that even the instrument was a consideration for Bach in this regard.

> Bach preferred the Clavichord to the Harpsichord, which, though susceptible of great variety of tone, seemed to him lacking in soul.[255]

[255] Quoted in Robert Donnington, *The Interpretation of Early Music* (New York, 1964), 576.

One of the clearest harbingers of the new galant style was the appreciation of *Gout*, or taste itself. The most famous Baroque discussion of this among musicians is found in Heinichen, who contends that taste can only be acquired through personal experience.

> If experience is necessary in any art or science, it is certainly necessary in music. In this *Scientia practica*, first of all, we must gain experience … either at home, provided opportunities are sufficient, or through traveling. But what is it that one believes one must seek in the experience? I will give a single word … *Gout*. Through diligence, talent, and experience, a composer must achieve above all else an exquisite sense of good taste in music … The definition of *Gout, Gusto* or *guter Geschmack* is unnecessary for the experienced musician; and it is as difficult to describe in its essentials as the true essence of the soul. One could say that good taste was in itself the soul of music, which so to speak it doubly enlivens and brings pleasure to the senses. The *Proprium 4ti modi* of a composer with good taste is contained solely in the skill with which he makes his music pleasing to and beloved by the general, educated public, or which in the same way pleases our ear by experienced artifices and moves the senses … In general, this can be brought about through a good well-cultivated, and natural invention or through the beautiful expression of words. In particular, through an ever dominating *cantabile*, through suitable and affecting accompaniments, through a change of harmonies recommended for the sake of the ears, and through other methods gained from experience and frequently looking poor on paper, which in our times we only label with the obscure name of "rules of experience …" An exceptional sense of good taste is so to say the musical *Lapis philisophorum* and the principal key to musical mysteries through which human souls are unlocked and moved and by which the senses are won over … For even the natural gift or talent endowed with most invention resembles only crude

gold and silver dross that must be purified first by the fire of experience before it can be shaped into a solid mass—I mean into a finely cultivated and steadfast sense of good taste.[256]

We would like to think that it was this view of the future which Bach had in mind in a note to the Leipzig town council in 1730:

> The present *status musices* is quite different to what it used to be formerly—the art being much advanced and taste marvelously changed, so that the old-fashioned kind of music no longer sounds well in our ears.[257]

What Bach is referring to is the old mathematics-based polyphonic style of the Roman Church. One can find numerous statements by composers and even theorists who now condemn the older practice. Nevertheless it is somewhat surprising to find Agostino Agazzari implying as early as 1607 that this style is "no longer in use," for as we know some composers would in fact continue to compose this older style of polyphonic church music until well into the eighteenth century.

> That kind of music is no longer in use, both because of the confusion and babel of the words, arising from the long and intricate imitations, and because it has no grace, for, with all the voices singing, one hears neither period nor sense, these being interfered with and covered up by imitations; indeed, at every moment, each voice has different words, a thing displeasing to men of competence and judgment ... Such compositions are good according to the rules of counterpoint, but they are at the same time faulty according to the rules of music that is true and good.[258]

The most far-reaching accomplishment by the late sixteenth century Italian humanists was the reestablishment of music's most natural purpose, the expression of feeling. They affected this also through their philosophical criticism of the old mathematics-based polyphony and by creating modern opera as a demonstration of their aims. This purpose is clearly expressed, in 1600, by Emilio de' Cavalieri in the preface to his *Rappresentazione di Anima, et di Corpo*, where he

---

[256] Johann David Heinichen, *Anweisung zum Generalbass* (1711) in George J. Buelow, *Thorough-Bass Accompaniment According to Johann David Heinichen* (Berkeley and Los Angeles: University of California Press, 1992), 285ff.

[257] Quoted in Robert Donnington, *The Interpretation of Early Music* (New York, 1964), 99.

[258] Agostino Agazzari, *On Playing upon a Bass in ... Consort*, quoted in Oliver Strunk, *Source Readings in Music History* (New York: Norton, 1950), 430.

states that his purpose is to "move the listener to different emotions, as pity, joy, tears, and laughter, and other similar emotions."[259] Caccini, in his *Le Nuove Musiche*, writes that the goal was "to move the emotions of the soul."[260]

The most fundamental performance principle in early opera was the addition of improvisation for the purpose of expression of the emotions of the text, something the written notes could not yet do, as they tended to follow the rhythms of the text.

For the famous singing teacher, Tosi, the obligation to improvise was nowhere more expected, even required, than in the da capo aria. In one of his most often quoted lines, after explaining the basic form of the aria, Tosi observes that "in repeating the Aria, he that does not vary it for the better, is no great Master."[261] He adds that a moderate singer with good improvisation gets more esteem that a better singer who does not employ it. Indeed, the reason for varied improvisation on the da capo, in Tosi's view, had much to do with judging singers.

> Without varying the Aria, the knowledge of the singers could never be discovered; but from the nature and quality of the variations, it will be easily discerned in two of the greatest singers which is the best.

He is one of many who also document improvisation by all the members of an ensemble, although here he cautions the players of the orchestra to take turn in their ornamentation, for,

> Each must regard the other, giving it room and not conflicting with it; if there are many, they must each await their turn and not, chirping all at once like sparrows, try to shout one another down.[262]

The most important, and thorough, observer of German Baroque performance practice was the conductor and composer, Johann Mattheson (1681–1764). He believed the central purpose of music, after praising God, was the communication of emotion. The whole question of the "passions," Mattheson suggests, is perhaps more the province of the

[259] Emilio de' Cavalieri, *Rappresentazione di Anima, et di Corpo*, Preface, quoted in Carol MacClintock, *Readings in the History of Music in Performance* (Bloomington: Indiana University Press, 1979), 183.

[260] *Le Nuove Musiche*, 45.

[261] P. F. Tosi, *Observations on the Florid Song* (London: Wilcox, 1743), VII, ivff.

[262] Agostino Agazzari, quoted in Oliver Strunk, *Source Readings in Music History* (New York: Norton, 1950), 429.

philosopher than the Kapellmeister, but on a practical level it is fundamental to composer and performer if they are to communicate with the listener.[263]

In reflecting on the emotions in general, he observes that "most are not the best, and certainly must be curtailed or kept in check." Love is an emotion frequently represented by music and in these cases the composer should "consult his own experience." Sadness is second only to love in its use by composers, no doubt, he observes, "because almost everybody is unhappy." It is for this reason that sacred music employs this emotion so effectively, because it represents the "penance and remorse, sorrow, contrition, lamentation and the recognition of our misery."

Regarding the expression of emotions through music, Mattheson first gives several obvious illustrations which we might recognize today as simple text-painting: Joy, being an expansion of our soul, represented by large and expanded intervals; Sadness, being a "contraction of these subtle parts of our body," represented by small intervals and Hope and Depression through obvious melodic direction. Mattheson then turns to more specific prescriptions for representing emotions through music.[264] Pride, Haughtiness and Arrogance are represented by a "bold, pompous style ... majestic musical figures which require a special seriousness and grandiloquent motion." For these, the melodic line must invariably ascend. The opposite emotions of Humility, Patience, etc., are represented by humble music with descending melody.

Stubbornness, he writes, "deserves a special place among the affects that are appropriate to musical rhetoric," and is represented by "so-called capricci ... namely when one writes such peculiar passages in one or another voice which one is resolved not to change, cost what it may." For Anger, Ardor, Vengeance, Rage, Fury and other such "violent affections" it is not enough,

> that one rumbles along strongly, makes a lot of noise and boldly rages: notes with many tails will simply not suffice, as many things; but each of these violent qualities requires its

[263] Johann Mattheson, *Der vollkommene Capellmeister* [1739], trans. Ernest Harriss (Ann Arbor: UMI Research Press, 1981), I, iii, 52ff.

[264] Ibid., I, iii, 72ff.

own particular characteristics, and, despite forceful expression, must still have a becoming singing quality.

Hope, "is a pleasant and soothing thing, consisting of a joyful longing which fills the spirit with a certain courage." This, therefore, "demands the loveliest use of the voice and the sweetest combination of sounds in the world." Mattheson assigns dissonance to the expression of the unpleasant, disagreeable, frightening and horrible, although interestingly enough "the spirit even occasionally derives some peculiar sort of comfort from these." Despair should be represented by "unusual passages and strange, mad, disordered sequences of notes." In contrast, Composure is best represented by a "soft unison."

He suspects most composers who fail to effectively express emotions in music do so because they do not know their own desires or what they actually wanted to achieve. But failure in this has significant implications for the listener. He says here, in effect, that whatever is written which represents only the "theory" of music communicates nothing to the listener. It is a fundamental lesson which is rarely taught in music schools.

> Is it then astonishing that with pieces thus formed, where true natural theory of sound together with the pertaining science of human affections are completely absent, merely the ears of the poor, simple, and self-righteous listeners are tickled, but their hearts and minds are not aroused in proper measure.[265]

Now Mattheson attempts to address the emotions with the purpose of establishing some correlation with style.[266] His discussion is so interesting, from the perspective of illuminating late Baroque thought on the "affections," we will quote it at length.

> Among those affections which one commonly attributes to the high style are many which do not deserve to be called high at all, in the good sense. For, what can be lower than anger, fear, vengeance, despair, etc. Beating, boasting, snoring is indeed not true nobility. Arrogance is itself only an inflating of the soul, and actually requires more bombast than nobility

[265] Ibid., I, iii, 89.

[266] Ibid., I, x, 22ff.

for expression: now the most haughty are again unfailingly the most angry, in their feelings one debility after another takes the helm. For, though anger will have the *appearance* of being action of a great spirit, still it springs in *fact* from an effeminate heart: one would have to consider it then a special, holy, and just bureaucratic wrath, which nevertheless should punish and discipline, without any indignation.

Great and valiant spirits are forbearing; but small and timid souls can endure nothing. Frivolous people are easily provoked and are as quickly moved to anger, as is the turning around of weather-cocks or weather vanes on the roofs. In short, anger is a ridiculous affection. It sounds quite base and does not entail an elevated presentation.

Fear and fright are indeed probably the most foolish emotions in the world, and really deserve nothing so little as something of the elevated in their expression. Alas! One finds these unfortunate impulses in all creatures, even in those which seem to have no other emotion and are scorned. Nothing can however be lower than miserable human vengeance, which has so little noble in it that it finds a place only in the most depraved hearts.

If we come to despair, then that is the extreme to which fear can lead: hence one would have to set it on the highest peak of sadness if it really is to have something of nobility. The Italians therefore rightly call all malicious and dangerous people, whose spirit is dejected and lost, *Huomini tristi*.

I will meanwhile not deny that something of strength, turbulence, passion and ecstasy is required if one desires to express properly these and similar passions in music; just as the affections of impetuosity, vengeance, etc., are so constituted that they, according to the difference in station, have the appearance of a high proud quality, although they deny its strength. Here one must also admit that this presumptuous arrogance occasionally requires something of the stately in oratory and music (yet greatly different from the true type); but which is not at all of the mighty, majestic, etc.

Shrieking and grumbling is suitable in anger and quarreling; an uneven, broken, shocking, trembling style in fright; something of daring with vengeance; something frantic with despair; something turgid with arrogance; as long as it did not come out too naturally and arouse disgust: but all of this has nothing to do with the elevated style.

But whoever would want to relegate devotion, patience, diligence, desire, etc., to the middle style might be considered only as moderately devout, moral, patient, diligent and desirous. Indeed, desire corresponds in very many ways with the highest and most emphatic affection in and outside of the world, namely love, how then can it be relegated to the middle of the road? It is true that desire is according to the nature of the desired object also small or large, high or low, and so on; yet it is the same with almost all emotions.

On the one hand diligence can have much of nobleness, on the other it can have something trifling as the goal. In the last case it would be a work in the dark so to speak (*obscura diligentia*) and would not even deserve to stand in the middle, but rather at the low end. There is nothing at all high-flown about patience, though always something noble: and everyone knows that devotion serves to lift the spirit.

Finally, common dance songs either all, or at least most of them, would indeed have to embody something of the beggarly, slavish, cowardly, disconsolate, base, boorish, stupid, and clumsy, if these qualities of the low style were to be found in them. Low and base are again very different, and if we indeed should exclude from this the most nonsensical peasant dances, though not the clever *Land-Tanze, Country Dances*, then for all of that there probably would be no one who would expect beggars in a spirited minuet, slaves in a happy rigaudon, cowards in an heroic entree, despair in a lusty gavotte, or base spirits in a magnificent chaconne.

Drinking songs and lullabies, amorous little pieces, etc., must not always be indiscriminately called trifling: if they are done quite naturally they are often more pleasing and have greater impact than high and mighty concerti and stately overtures. The former no less require their master in their own way than the latter. Yet, what am I to say? Our composers are all kings; or of royal descent ... They do not fret over trivialities.

Among Mattheson's discussion of the major instrumental forms,[267] his comments on the Sonata are most enlightening. The Sonata, he says, is a form,

> whose aim is principally towards complaisance or kindness, since a certain Complaisance must predominate in sonatas, which is accommodating to everyone, and which serves each listener. A melancholy person will find something pitiful and compassionate, a sensuous person something pretty, an angry person something violent, and so on, in different varieties

[267] *Der vollkommene Capellmeister*, II, xiii, 137ff.

of sonatas ... For some years rudimentary sonatas for the clavier have been composed with good success ... [but] they aim more toward movement of the fingers than the heart. Yet amazement over uncommon dexterity is also a type of affection, which often gives rise to envy; although it is said, its true mother is ignorance.

He does not find as much variety in emotions in the *Concerto grosso*, but rather curiously a tendency toward "sensuous pleasure." To this he adds a fascinating reference to the concerto *style* of the late sixteenth century definition.

Most [concerti] depend upon the full elaboration, indeed, one even overdoes it, so that it resembles a rich table which is set not for hunger but for show. Once can easily guess that in such a contest, from which all concerti get their name, there is no lack of jealousy and vengeance, or envy and hate, as well as other such passions.[268]

[268] Ibid., II, xiii, 139.

It is very interesting and revealing that Mattheson defines the traditional Baroque instrumental forms not so much by tempo, as by their subjective styles. For example he finds.[269]

[269] Ibid., II, xiii, 81ff.

Minuet moderate cheerfulness

Govotta true jubilation

Bourree contentment and pleasantness, not so degenerate as the gavotte

Rigaudon somewhat trifling joking

La Marche somewhat heroic and fearless, yet not wild and running

Entree noble and majestic

Gigue [270] ardent and fleeting zeal

Polonaise frank and free

Angloise stubbornness

Hornpipe frivolity

Sarabanda to express ambition

Courante sweet hopefulness

Allemanda a content or satisfied spirit

Chaccone more satiating than tasteful

Intrada to arouse longing

[270] Mattheson associates with the Gigue the French *Loure*, which he identifies with "a proud, arrogant nature"; the Spanish *Canarie*, "eagerness, swiftness and simplicity"; and the Italian *Gige*, used for "fiddling, ... extreme speed and volatility."

With the absence of text, the performer of instrumental must take even more careful note of the Italian expressions at the beginning of the composition for clues to the emotions. Here the reader will be surprised by Mattheson's understanding of the characters and emotions associated with the familiar "tempo" terms.

> An *Adagio* indicates distress; a *Lamento* lamentation; a *Lento* relief; an *Andante* hope; an *Affetuoso* love; an *Allegro* comfort; a *Presto* eagerness . . .[271]

[271] Ibid., II, xii, 34ff.

That instrumental music can indeed express emotions is obvious in practice, he observes, but "never in theory." By this he means it is a subject difficult to write about, although he himself makes an admirable summary.

> The proper goal of all music [melody] can be nothing other than the sort of diversion of the hearing through which the passions of the soul are stirred: thus no one at all will obtain this goal who is not aiming at it, who feels no affection, indeed who scarcely thinks at all of a passion; unless it is one which is involuntarily felt deeply. But if he is stirred in a more noble way and wants to move others with harmony, then he must know how without the words to express sincerely all the emotions of the heart through selected sounds and their skillful combination in such a way that the listener might fully grasp and clearly understand therefrom, as if it were actual speech, the impetus, the sense, the meaning, and the expression, as well as all the pertaining divisions and caesuras. It is then a joy! Much more art and a better imagination is required if one wants to achieve this without, rather than with words.[272]

[272] Ibid., II, xii, 31.

Music as a Language

THE IDEA OF CREATING one universal language for all mankind has been discussed for a long time. Several of the early commentators pointed to a line in Genesis 11:1, "Now the whole earth had one language and few words." One early philosopher, Anne-Pierre-Devisme, who wrote a book, *Pasilogie, Consideration of an Universal Language,* in 1806 seemed to believe that this sentence from the bible referred to music.

> As music is the most simple way to express one's ideas, it is for this reason that human beings at the beginning of creation, and everywhere on the globe must have, before the creation of letters, used sounds as the unique way that they had to manifest to express their emotions, and that is why music became the primitive language and consequently the universal language of the people of the globe.
>
> This sentence of the bible confirms our opinion, and is remarkable, because Moses used and preferred the word *labii* (for lips) instead of *lingua,* as for us to learn that then the sounds were the only way that humans could express themselves, since they needed then only the movement of their lips to make a sound and to produce more or less low sounds, more or less high sounds, and there were then no languages as we know them now ...

The famous J.-J. Rousseau, in his *On the Origin of Languages,* seemed to be thinking along these lines and quoted Strabo (c. 64 BC – 24 AD), an ancient Greek geographer and philosopher to this effect.

> The first languages were singing and passionate: all the notes of music were as so many accents. In the first times, we spoke as well with the sounds and rhythm than with the articulations and the voice. Speaking and singing were once the same thing, says Strabo.

And it was probably with this in mind that Michel de Chabanon (1730–1792), a French violinist, composer and music theorist, observed,

> Languages, idioms and dialects differ so much that often one cannot understand the peasant of one's own village, while music is one for all earth.

One of the most perceptive discussions of this subject is found in the *Dictionnaire philosophique* by Voltaire.

> There is no complete language which has the power to express all of our ideas and feelings, whose nuances are very numerous and imperceptible.
>
> No one can express precisely the degree of feeling that he feels. One is obliged, in consequence, to use a general name, such as love or hate, for thousands of different kinds of love and hate—everyone would be different. It is the same for pain and pleasure. All languages are imperfect, as we are ...
>
> The most beautiful language should be the one which can express the weakest and most impetuous movements of the soul. It will be the one which most resembles music.

Ideas such as these helped give birth to a remarkable Universal Musical Language created by François Sudre, a French school teacher, who died in 1862. He developed a French Dictionary which contained 11,000 words, all of which could be expressed by varying the order of the same five musical tones. He gave public demonstrations of this new language throughout Europe and England to the astonishment and praise of everyone. He wanted only recognition in the form of a gift of 50,000 francs from the French government which, after numerous trials before famous Parisian composers and their strong recommendations, never materialized. So, Sudre never revealed the key to his system and it remains impossible for anyone since to recreate it.[273]

One of Sudre's strong admirers was Hector Berlioz who, in a newspaper article in the *Journal de Dèbats* of 17 November 1849, wrote a poignant reflection of the fate which is faced by all new inventors.

> M. Sudre is offering to us at this moment a new and sad example of the fate of all the inventors in our inattentive, forgetful, and jealous society. For twenty years he has been fighting, swimming against the current, speaking, writing, demonstrating, proving that a discovery of the highest importance for armed forces of the earth and sea, and even also for

[273] This amazing story is presented at length, with original reviews of his performances, in David Whitwell, *La Téléphonie and the Universal Musical Language,* ed. Craig Dabelstein (Austin: Whitwell Books, 2012).

the rapid propagation of pacific ideas, is in his possession. He is demonstrating that this discovery is his, that he alone made it, that he then perfected and simplified it to the point of making its use extremely easy, and for twenty years they have sent him about his business, they scorn him in a thousand ways, they make him promises not kept, in his regard they commit unspeakable abuses of confidence, and meanwhile, the poor man is using, in order to exist, his last resources and those of his friends ...

But this is the fatal law to which the unfortunate, bent under the weight of a new idea, have, in all times and in all places, been subjected. Two years have not passed when they wrote before, here, very seriously to prove the impossibility of the use of the electric telegraph and the absurdity of the attempts made for its application. Yet, today human thought circulates lightening fast from one end of Europe to the other, and in the northern half of America, by means of this simple wire, so ridiculed, whose conduction power [they said] would be paralyzed by the simple contact with a magpie. Napoleon did not recognize the future of steam, and Fulton, in his eyes, was only a fool, whose claims and experiments obsessed him.

Shortly, we will have the repetition of the same spectacle for a discovery even more important, that of the directing of lighter-than-air craft by means of a combination of propellers and inclined planes. Obviously, the latter, once demonstrated and put into usage, the relations of the diverse peoples who make up the large human family will be entirely changed; an immense revolution will be accomplished whose fortunate consequences are incalculable. This is precisely why the audacious mechanic who wishes to give man wings capable of defying the winds and swooping over the storm, will experience a stronger and more obstinate resistance. He will be ruined, he will die in harness; he expects to, he is prepared for it. But navigation of the aerial ocean will nonetheless be opened to us sooner or later, and our descendants will be astonished then, because a corner of the veil had already been lifted, that their fathers, doubting for centuries the solution to the problem, should have been so seemingly determined to prowl the terrestrial crust like the most infirm animals.

Time is a great teacher, true, but man is a very stupid scholar.

Music is the Language of our Emotions

Music is a language of feelings without words.[274]
    Martin Luther (1483–1546)

All musical expression has an affect or emotion for its foundation.[275]
    F. W. Marpurg, 1749

Music is to me the perfect expression of the soul.[276]
.....
Schubert unburdened his heart on a sheet of music paper, just as others leave the impression of passing moods in their journals. His soul was so steeped in music that he wrote notes where others use words.[277]
    Robert Schumann

Music is the speech of Passion.[278]
.....
Music, who speaks to us solely through quickening into articulate life the most universal concept of the inherently speechless Feeling … [279]
    Richard Wagner

Music is the shorthand of emotion.[280]
    Leo Tolstoy

Music is an outburst of the soul.[281]
    Frederick Delius

Music is a distinct language which speaks clearly.[282]
.....
People usually complain that music is so ambiguous; that it is so doubtful what they ought to think when they hear it; whereas everyone understands words. With me it is entirely the reverse. And not only with regard to an entire speech, but also with individual words; these, too, seem to me to be so ambiguous, so vague, and so easily misunderstood in comparison with genuine music, which fills the soul with a thousand things better than words. The thoughts which are expressed to me by a piece of music which I love are not too indefinite to be put into words, but on the contrary too definite.[283]
    Felix Mendelssohn

---

[274] Preface, Rhau's *Symphoniae incundae*. The reader can find a great deal of additional information on this subject in David Whitwell, *Ancient Views on Music*, ed. Craig Dabelstein (Austin: Whitwell Books, 2013).

[275] F. W. Marpurg, *Der critische Mussicus an der Spree* [Berlin], September 2, 1749.

[276] Letter to his mother, Leipzig, May 8, 1832.

[277] Letter to Friedrich Wieck, Heidelberg, Nov. 6, 1829.

[278] Wagner, "Judaism in Music."

[279] *Richard Wagner's Prose Works* (New York: Broude Brothers), V, 77.

[280] Quoted in Nat Shapiro, *An Encyclopedia of Quotations About Music* (New York: Da Capo, 1978), 199.

[281] Ibid., 11.

[282] Letter to Carl Zelter, Rome, June 31, 1831.

[283] Letter to Marc Andre Souchay, October 5, 1842.

Music is a means of communicating with people, not an aim in itself.
Modeste Moussorgsky

Music ... is a language, but a language of the intangible, a kind of soul language.[284]
Edward MacDowell

[284] *Critical and Historical Essays* (1912).

Music is an idealization of the natural language of passion.[285]
Herbert Spencer (1820–1903)

[285] Herbert Spencer, *Essays on Education* (London: J. M. Dent & Sons, 1966), 320.

WE SHOULD BELIEVE that the basic purpose of music given in the above testimony by musicians, writers and philosophers would surprise no thinking person. Mendelssohn's observation is particularly interesting and valid, for it is true that ordinary language is often quite limited. It is for this reason that one finds a number of similar quotations from the perspective of the additional importance of music when traditional language fails.

When one is at a loss what to say or write, well—one tries to help oneself with music.[286]
Franz Liszt

[286] Letter to Adelheid von Schorn, Rome, Sept. 15, 1877.

It is a truth forever, that where the speech of man stops short, there Music's reign begins.[287]
Richard Wagner

[287] Wagner, "A Happy Evening."

Where words fail, music speaks.
Hans Christian Anderson

Music is the shorthand of emotion. Emotions which let themselves be described in words with such difficulty, are directly conveyed to man in music, and in that is its power and significance.[288]
Leo Tolstoy

[288] Quoted in Nat Shapiro, *An Encyclopeadia of Quotations about Music*, 199.

To sing seems a deliverance from bondage. Music expresses that which cannot be said, and which cannot be suppressed.
Victor Hugo

Language is not subtle enough, tender enough to express all we feel, and when language fails, the highest and deepest longings are translated into music.
Robert Ingersoll

Every person on the planet who has ever heard any kind of music understands what the above quotations bear witness to, that the principle purpose of music is to communicate feelings and emotions to the listener. The fact that the basic emotions are genetically implanted in all persons makes this possible and the process has often been compared to the way a magnet attracts a piece of iron in its vicinity. This, in turn, explains how even a person who "knows nothing about music" nevertheless falls under the power of music, as was pointed out by Longinus in his first century treatise, *On the Sublime.*

> Music is a language which is implanted by nature in man and which appeals not to the hearing only but to the soul itself ... For does not the flute instill certain emotions into its hearers and as it were make them beside themselves and full of frenzy, and supplying a rhythmical movement constrain the listener to move rhythmically in accordance therewith and to conform himself to the melody, although he may be utterly ignorant of music?[289]

[289] Longinus, *On the Sublime,* trans. W. Rhys Roberts (Cambridge: University Press, 1935), XXXIX, 2.

A similar reference to the impact of emotions conveyed by music is mentioned the great French writer, Michael Montaigne (1533–1592), who seemed amazed by the emotional power of the music he was hearing everywhere in society.

> No heart is so flabby that the sounds of our drums and trumpets do not set it ablaze, nor so hard that sweet music does not tickle it and enliven it; no soul is so sour that it does not feel touched by some feeling of reverence when it contemplates the somber vastness of our Churches, the great variety of their decorations and our ordered liturgy, or when it hears the enchantment of the organ and the poised religious harmony of men's voices. Even those who come to scoff are brought to distrust their opinion by a shiver in their heart and a sense of dread.[290]

[290] Michel de Montaigne, *Essays,* trans. M. A. Screech (London: Penguin, 1993), II, xii, 670.

By the end of the Renaissance, when composers of secular music had begun to write music with deeper emotional content, one finds descriptions of listeners with reactions which seem as familiar as one would notice among listeners today. For example, consider this first-hand account of a performance by the lute player, Francesco da Milano.

The tables cleared, he took up a lute and, as if merely essaying chords, he began, seated near the foot of the table, to strum a fantasy. He had plucked no more than the first three notes of the tune when all the conversation ceased among the festive throng and all were constrained to look there where he was, as he continued with such enchanting skill that little by little, through the divine art in playing that was his alone, he made the very strings to swoon beneath his fingers and transported all who listened into such gentle melancholy that one present buried his head in his hands, another let his entire body slump into an ungainly posture with members all awry, while another, his mouth sagged open and his eyes more than half shut, seemed, one would judge, as if transfixed upon the strings, and yet another, with chin sunk upon his chest, hiding the most sadly taciturn visage ever seen, remained abstracted in all his senses save his hearing, as if his soul had fled from all the seats of sensibility to take refuge in his ears where more easefully it could rejoice in such enchanting symphony.[291]

[291] Pontus de Tyard, *Solitaire second* (1555).

And yet, as obvious as it would seem that everyone understands that the purpose of music is to communicate feelings, and notwithstanding the testimony given above by famous persons, the fundamental role of the emotions in music has never been completely accepted, even to the present day.

One reason for this lies with the early Roman Christian Church and its attempt to create a new kind of Roman citizen. Regarding emotions as the first step toward sin, the Church attempted to remove emotions from the lives of the new Christians by discouraging attendance at the theater, at the circus and in the nature of their clothes and cosmetics. St. Basil went so far as to declare that a good Christian should not even laugh, for laughter is a form of emotion. It was this position which resulted, when the Church reopened the schools, in redefining music as a branch of mathematics.

When the books of Aristotle and the other ancient Greek philosophers, which the Church had banned and had attempted to burn, began to reappear in new translations from extant copies in Arabic libraries, a strong encouragement resulted in the old idea that in man Reason should rule. This, together with the medieval division of music studies into two branches, the theoretic and performance, created in academic circles an entirely new "rational" branch of music which has remained a strong influence in music education until the present day. Of course this is a misnomer of enormous consequences, for everything rational (left hemisphere of the brain) about music is not actually music.

The influence of this new "rational" perspective of music remains very strong, as for example in the music contests where only the accuracy of performance of the musical grammar is judged and not music itself. It is also this background which has resulted in two widely quoted definitions of music itself.

> Stravinsky:
> I consider that music is, by its very nature, powerless to express anything at all, whether a feeling, an attitude of mind, a psychological mood, a phenomenon of nature, etc ... If, as is nearly always the case, music appears to express something, this is only an illusion, and not a reality.[292]

> Hindemith:
> Music cannot express the composer's feelings.[293]

[292] *Chronicle of My Life* (English edition), 91ff.

[293] *A Composer's World.*

These comments at first take on an appearance of dishonesty, if not sarcasm, for the actual compositions of these two men are in every way normal subjective and emotional oriented as any other fine composer. But they did help mislead a generation of young composers, encouraging cerebral music which found no audience and of which not a single composition remains in the repertoire today.

Nonsense or not, this academic perspective, taken together with a significant twentieth century rebellion against some excesses of late nineteenth century Romanticism, has resulted in many performances today which seem to have as their only purpose of merely playing the notes on the page. And that is exactly what you get in such a performance, only the notes on the page with no expression of feeling or even of life itself. How many of us can sympathize with this lament by Bekker:

Most of us have probably experienced concerts with atmospheres that could have been described as "a chaste boredom ... raised to the highest virtue."[294]

This quotation is found in the most important new book on performance practice, *The End of Early Music*, by my friend and long time professional oboist in the Netherlands, the late Bruce Haynes. Bruce wrote,

> Emotion might be called the meaning in music ... For a musician to play or sing a piece without their perceiving its meaning would be like learning to speak a foreign language by rote, imitating sounds without understanding words.[295]

Bruce spoke of walking down the street, seeing a lovely home but on looking in the window finding no one at home. That, he said, is a metaphor for many performances, a pretty performance of the notes on the page—but no one at home. One early writer, the poet, Gottfried von Strassburg, who died in 1210 AD, in his *Tristan*, goes even further in saying that if the emotions are missing it is not even music.

> Although it is a very common thing, what one plays superficially in a heartless and soulless way cannot really claim to be music.[296]

Haynes provides many examples to make the point that musicians did not play that way in earlier times. He documents "considerable weeping, loud and open" in Paris at the premiere of an opera by Gluck in 1774.[297] He quotes Johann Quantz in his discussion of performance practice of 1752 speaking of "the inner feeling—the singing of the soul," adding,

> If musicians are not themselves moved by what they play, they cannot hope for any profit from their efforts, and they will never move others through their playing, which should be their ultimate aim.[298]

K. P. E. Bach wrote that one should play from the soul, and not like a trained bird. Like Quantz, he added,

[294] Quoted in Bruce Haynes, *The End of Early Music* (New York: Oxford University Press, 2007), 171.

[295] Ibid., 168.

[296] Gottfried von Strassburg, *Tristan*, trans. Arthus Hatto (Harmondsworth: Penguin Books, 1960), 141.

[297] Ibid., 171.

[298] This and following quotations are from Ibid., 175.

> Musicians cannot move others unless they themselves are moved; it is essential that musicians be able to put themselves in each emotion they wish to rouse in their audience, for it is by showing their own emotion that they awaken sympathy. In languishing, sad passages, they languish and grow sad. That is visible and audible.

Bach's father, the great Johann Sebastian Bach, was once the host for a visit by the English writer, Charles Burney, in the early 1700s.

> After dinner ... I prevailed upon him to sit down again to a clavichord, and he played, with little intermission, till near eleven o'clock at night. During this time, he grew so animated and *possessed*, that he not only played, but looked like one inspired. His eyes were fixed, his under lip fell, and drops of effervescence distilled from his face. He said, if he were to be set to work frequently, in this manner, he should grow young again.

Many eighteenth century writers report that in Italy, in particular, one hears the most moving performances. We have quoted above a first-hand account of Corelli playing. Another visitor found similar physical movements by even ensemble violinists. The instrumental compositions one hears there, "affect the feelings, the imagination, and the soul with so much strength that the violinists who play them cannot prevent themselves from being transported and seized with fury because of them; that they torture their violins and their bodies, that they are agitated like those possessed ... " These accounts are the antithesis of performances where "no one is at home."

Instrumental performances such as these gained much of their support from opera, the new form which began in 1600. According to Pirrotta, the whole idea of the *stile recitativo* and *stile rappresentativo* lay not "so much in the adherence to recitation of the text ... as in the vivid immediacy with which a character's inner emotional reactions were to be presented live to the audience."[299] This is very clear when one looks at the actual music of the early operas. One sees notes and rhythms set to the text, but the emotions were

[299] Nino Pirrotta, in *Music and Culture in Italy from the Middle Ages to the Baroque* (Cambridge: Harvard University Press, 1984), 280.

added by the singer through improvisation. This had to be, for those words of the left hemisphere have in themselves no emotions.

According to the great Spanish playwright, Lope de Vega, even in drama the emotions were supplied by music, which is quite remarkable.

> The instruments occupied the front part of the theater, without being seen, and to their harmony the actors sang the verses; all the effects, such as surprise, lamentation, love, anger, being expressed in the composition of the music itself.[300]

All of the above accounts of musicians communicating the emotional meaning of the music have their medieval origin in the performance tract, and not in the conceptual tract, when music education divided into two branches. The conceptual tract was taught in the schools and the performance tract by those who were actually performing music. But one must not think that the values we recognize in performance were not yet appreciated. The great mathematician, Boethius (475–524 AD), believed that perception through all the senses was something present due to nature and that this genetic information is something different from rational description. He goes even further and states that the genetic aspect makes the power of music inseparable from man himself.

> From all these accounts it appears beyond doubt that music is so naturally united with us that we cannot be free from it even if we so desired.[301]

[300] Emilio Cotarelo y Mori, *Historia de la Zarzuela* (1934), 36.

[301] Boethius, *Fundamentals of Music*, trans. Calvin Bower (New Haven: Yale University Press), I, i.

Music as the Language of Truth

> Anyone who still hasn't got past the stage of the beauty of music knows nothing about music ... Music is Truth.
> Sergiu Celibadache (1989)

THE REAL SECRET TO THE POWER of music is that it is the expression of experiential Truth dealing with feeling. It is only the left hemisphere of man's brain which is capable of lying, thus making suspect all reading, writing, speech, history, poetry, oratory and theater. But, the right hemisphere of our brain, the domain of the experiential nature of music, does not lie and has no equivalent of "No."[302] This is clear to everyone in the example of love. You can use the left brain (speech, thought) in trying to talk yourself in or out of your feelings of love, but it is always quite clear to yourself what those feelings *really* are. And so it is with music, as was accurately observed by Confucius (551–479 BC) in a treatise on music:

> Music is the one thing in which there is no use trying to deceive others or make false pretenses.

The agent that makes Truth in music so powerful to the listener is the fact that the communication is always first person present tense, it occurs live, lock-step in time with the listener. In the performance of music, the listener *experiences* the music immediately and has an *instantaneous* connection with the inner artistic idea of the composer.[303] This is an important distinction between music and painting or sculpture. The observer of a canvas first employs *exclusively* the eye. If he is going to be successful in going beyond this to see and communicate with the inner artistic idea of the artist, he must make a *shift* from vision to mental contemplation. In other words, he must get past the experience of the eye before he can get to the experience of the artist. It is this delay, this circumnavigation which robs art and sculpture of the power of music.

[302] A discussion of the clinical research can be found in Robert Ornstein, *The Right Mind* (New York: Harcourt Brace, 1997), 93.

[303] W. H. Auden observed, "A verbal art like poetry is reflective; it stops to think. Music is immediate, it goes on to become." Quoted in George Marek, *Schubert* (Viking, 1985), 5.

But there are additional important distinctions. First, the art work of the painter is "frozen" in time. In this way it is like a photograph. If you think of someone you know well, you can "see" in your mind much of his features. But if you happen to have a photograph of that person, when you look at that a much more vivid picture of the person comes to mind. But the picture *never becomes the real person*. A recording of music, by the way, is analogous with a photograph.

Another important distinction lies in the nature of the existence of the art work. A finished canvas exists as a work of art even if it is hanging in a closed museum where no one can see it. A composition, on the other hand, exists as genuine music *only* in performance, which implies the presence of a listener—as there would be no purpose in a performance if there were no one to hear it. Therefore in a musical performance the listener is not an observer at all, but a *participant* in a live aesthetic experience. And in this regard let us remember that a single wealthy individual can own a canvas of Leonardo, and keep it secret from the public if he so desires, but no one owns Beethoven. Music, as is appropriate for a special form of Truth, belongs to all mankind.

Among the early Greek philosophers Plato (427–347 BC) made three important points which most of the following philosophers would agree. First, he sets music apart from the other arts and theater as, he says, these are only "imitations" of the real thing. He seemed to understand that music was not an imitation of something, nor a symbol of something, but the *real thing* expressed from composer to musician or listener. This is why, he points out, that a singer cannot be fooled, he knows immediately if a composition is good or bad and if the composer has a "good or bad soul."[304]

[304] *Laws*, 812b and following.

Second he, as with so many early philosophers, makes the connection between music and the divine. Speaking of the poets, whom let us not forget were musicians who sang their works before the public, Plato observes,

> For poets are a divine race, and often in their strains, by the aid of the Muses and the Graces, they attain Truth.[305]

[305] *Laws*, 682.

He follows this with the suggestion that music was genetically given to man by the gods.

> And did we not say that the sense of harmony and rhythm spring from this beginning among men, and that Apollo and the Muses and Dionysus were the Gods whom we had to thank for them?

The third, and most important, point which Plato makes is the distinction between entertainment music and that aesthetic music which represents Truth. He condemned those who had allowed music to fall to the level of mere entertainment, "ignorantly affirming that music has no truth … and can only be judged by the pleasure of the public."[306] Quite the contrary, he contends that "being pleasant" is not an appropriate criterion for selecting music for performance or for judging the value of music.

> AN ATHENIAN STRANGER. When anyone says that music is to be judged by pleasure, his doctrine cannot be admitted; and if there be any music of which pleasure is the criterion, such music is not to be sought out or deemed to have any real excellence, but only that other kind of music which is an imitation of the Good, and bears a resemblance of its original.
> CLEINIAS. Very true.
> AN ATHENIAN STRANGER. And those who seek for the best kind of song and music ought not to seek for that which is pleasant, but for that which is True.[307]

Aristides Quintilianus, who lived sometime during the first four centuries AD, was not so strict as Plato, believing that music could give pleasure and still be true to its basic purpose.

> We should not avoid song altogether just because it gives pleasure. Not all delight is to be condemned, but neither is delight itself the objective of music. Amusement may come as it will, but the aim set for music is to help us toward virtue.[308]

It is interesting that he also wrote directly to the point of why music is so potent in its communication of emotions,

[306] Ibid., 656d.

[307] Ibid., 668b.

[308] Aristides, *De Musica*, Book II. All our quotations are from the translation by Andrew Barker, *Greek Musical Writings* (Cambridge: Cambridge University Press, 1989).

because the emotion expressed in the music is identical with that felt within the listener (due to the genetic similarity in all men with respect to the basic emotions).

> Music persuades most directly and effectively, since the means by which it makes its imitation [*mimesis*] are of just the same kind as those by which the actions themselves are accomplished in reality.

The ancient Romans, who in general were more interested in entertainment than the Greeks, do not speak of this topic much. The Roman philosopher, Quintilian (30–96 AD), in the course of a discussion of oratory, seemed to believe that all the arts dealt with Truth. He observed that since all art must be based on direct perception, "Art can never deal in false ideas."[309]

Cicero (106–43 BC) rarely discusses or praises music at all, but we do find one interesting passage. Many early philosophers who comment on oratory point out that the successful orator is one who gets the crowd excited, even if what he says is completely untrue. Cicero, on this subject, seems to suggest that musicians are true to themselves, without regard to the audience, while the orator is the reverse. He phrased it this way,

> Can it be that while the aulos players and those who play the lyre use their own judgment, not that of the crowd, ... the [orator], endowed with a far greater skill, searches out not what is most true, but what the crowd wants?[310]

This reminds us of a comment by Mendelssohn, "the public is more attracted by outward show than by Truth."[311]

The poets of the early Christian Era contribute some interesting comments on Truth in music. The fourth century poet, Ausonius, using the name of one of the Greek gods of music, writes "Phoebus bids us speak truth."[312] But, he points out, Truth in music is not found in the externals.

> Because with purchased books thy library is crammed, dost think thyself a learned man and scholarly, Philomusus? After this sort thou wilt lay up strings, keys, and lyres, and, having purchased all, tomorrow thou wilt be a musician.[313]

[309] Quintilian, *The Education of an Orator* (*Institutio Oratoria*), trans. H. E. Butler (London: Heinemann, 1938), II, xvii, 17.

[310] *Tusculan Disputations*, V, 104.

[311] Letter to Conrad Schleinitz, Berlin, August 1, 1838.

[312] *Ausonius*, trans. Hugh G. Evelyn White (London: Heinemann, 1921), II, 17. One fifth century poet, Julianus, City Prefect of Rome, found, on the other hand, that the public did not always want the truth.

> The flame that gives life to Art was my gift, and now from Art and fire I get the semblance of ceaseless pain. Ungrateful of a truth is the race of mankind. [*The Greek Anthology*, trans. W. R. Paton (London: Heinemann, 1918), V, 87.]

[313] "To Philomusus a Grammar Master," in Ibid., II, 161.

If the reader recalls that all early poetry was sung, and therefore usually cataloged as music, he will find interesting the suggestion by Sidonius (fifth century) that if there be Truth in music, it follows that it must reflect his own life as well.

> As for me, my anxiety absolutely forbids me to make the content of my poetry different from the content of the life I lead.[314]

[314] *Sidonius Poems and Letters*, trans. W. B. Anderson (Cambridge: Harvard University Press, 1965), II, 443.

Boethius (475–524 AD), the famous mathematician, included music with the other known sciences as being concerned with Truth, but it is interesting that he adds that only music is also concerned with morals.

> There happen to be four mathematical disciplines [arithmetic, music, geometry, and astronomy], the other three share with music the task of searching for truth; but music is associated not only with speculation but with morality as well.[315]

[315] Boethius, *Fundamentals of Music*, trans. Calvin Bower (New Haven: Yale University Press), I, i.

As the Medieval Period progressed there were still occasional references in poetry to Truth in music. Two eighth century examples from England are interesting. The poem, "The Wonders of Creation," suggests that it is the aspect of Truth in music which helps man understand life.

> It is, thinking man, an obvious example
> to every one who by wisdom
> can comprehend in his mind all the world,
> that long ago men, well-advised people,
> could often utter and say a truth
> in the art of song, by means of lays,
> so that most of mankind, by always asking
> and repeating and remembering,
> gained knowledge of the web of mysteries.[316]

[316] *The Exeter Book* (Oxford University Press, 1958), II, xiv, 8ff.

Another poet declares he can write only of Truth in his songs:

> Let none of human kind imagine,
> that I of lying words compose my lay,
> or write my verse![317]

[317] "The Phoenix," Ibid., II, iv, 546ff.

During the years of the "Pre-Renaissance," the twelfth and thirteenth centuries, one finds many references in the secular songs to the Truth being communicated by the singer/composer. In one example by Vogelweid (c. 1170–1230), he says that the Truth in his song is so obvious that only someone with no experience in love could possible misunderstand it.

> Many there are that mock my pain,
> And ever say that 'tis not truly from the heart I sing;
> These but spend their breath in vain,
> Since they can never yet have known love's joy and suffering;
> And so it is they judge me wrong:
> Whoever knows
> All that from true love flows,
> Would not misunderstand my song.[318]

With the growing movement toward a return to the importance of emotions in music, and departing from the Church's 1,000 years of pretending that music was a branch of mathematics, it is perhaps fitting that the Renaissance begins with an extraordinary insight by Johannes de Grocheo (1255–1320 AD). In his *De Musica*, he observes that not only is music used to express the feelings of the composer or musician, but that music is the means by which the "practical" part of the brain "explains and exposes its functions."[319] This is an amazing early reference to the actual fact that the right hemisphere of the brain is otherwise mute. He is saying that music is the only means that we have for understanding the nature of Truth as it exists in the right hemisphere. We are reminded of a similar remark in Sir Philip Sidney's (1554–1586) *The Countesse of Pembrokes Arcadia*, where we find,

> Then she remembered this song, which she thought took a right measure of her present mind.[320]

In the early Renaissance we find some remarkable references to Truth on our experiential or emotional side. In Boccaccio a character says "don't listen to the words of my song. Listen to what the feeling reveals when I sing it."

> Love, heed not what my voice sings, but rather how much my heart, your subject, is filled with desire.[321]

---

[318] *Selected Poems of Walter von der Vogelweide*, trans. W. Alison Phillips (London: Smith, Elder, & Co., 1896), 43.

[319] Johannes de Grocheo, *De Musica*, trans. Albert Seay (Colorado Springs: Colorado College Music Press, 1967), 9.

[320] Sir Philip Sidney, *The Countesse of Pembrokes Arcadia*, in *The Prose Works of Sir Philip Sidney*, ed. Albert Feuillerat (Cambridge: Cambridge University Press, 1962), I, Book II, xxv.

[321] *L'Ameto*, trans. Judith Serafini-Sauli (New York: Garland, 1985), 40.

A passage with the same meaning is also found in Machaut:

> And if it please you, my dear lady, to consider the last little song I sang, of which I composed both words and music, you can easily tell whether I'm lying or speaking the truth.[322]

There are two comments by Chaucer which are worthy of consideration relative to our topic. In one place, after concluding that Beauty is something which cannot be described in words, Chaucer offers a definition for Beauty that it is Truth. "Truth," he says, "is the crown of Beauty."[323] We believe he was also thinking along these lines when he wrote, "Nature does not lie."[324]

During the Baroque we find an interesting reference to our subject in a poem by Antonio Abbatini in which he provides a first-hand description of one of the early academies. He describes a period of discussion and argument after which a period of three hours is set aside during which time each man exposes his real character before all through performance.

> Then to the harpsichord the company transfers,
> and each man takes upon himself to show, with song
> and sound, his virtue, which binds the heart and soul.[325]

There are several other similar comments from this period which make the same point, that words are somehow inadequate but that music expresses the real thing. The French philosopher, Jean-Baptiste Du Bos (1670–1742), thought the key to the power of music lay in the fact that its sounds came directly from nature, whereas language can only be the *symbol* of the real thing.

> All these sounds have a wonderful power to move us because they are the signs of the passions that are the work of nature herself, from whence they have derived their energy. Spoken words, on the other hand, are only arbitrary symbols of the passions.[326]

A passage in Calderon's *Life is a Dream* (II, i) makes the same point. Here, Astolfo observes,

---

[322] Guillaume de Machaut, "Remede de Fortune," trans. James Wimsatt and William Kibler (Athens: The University of Georgia Press, 1988), 374.

[323] "A Complaint unto Pity," 75.

[324] "The Parliament of Birds," 629.

[325] Quoted in Lorenzo Bianconi, *Music in the Seventeenth Century*, trans. David Bryant (Cambridge: Cambridge University Press, 1989), 290ff.

[326] "*Reflexions critiques sur la poesie et sur la peinture*" (Paris, 1719), quoted in Peter le Huray and James Day, *Music and Aesthetics in the Eighteenth and Early Nineteenth Centuries* (Cambridge: Cambridge University Press, 1981), 18.

> Tell the eyes
> In their music to keep better
> Concert with the voice, because
> Any instrument whatever
> Would be out of tune that sought
> To combine and blend together
> The true feelings of the heart
> With the false words speech expresses.

Du Bos' reference to Nature reminds us that there were instances in early music when it was recommended that performance should literally imitate Nature. For example, Aurelian of Reome, in his early music treatise, *Musica Disciplina* (c. 843 AD), recommends forming cadences in chant like ocean waves.

> We pray the singer to begin concluding all the verses of the nocturnal responses from the fifth syllable before the end; and this is according to the musicians who have maintained that not more than five waves of the sea also remove all storms from the same.[327]

In another example, Guido, in his *Micrologus* (c. 1026–1028 AD), recommended basing the interpretation of cadences on the slowing down of horses.

> Towards the ends of phrases the notes should always be more widely spaced as they approach the breathing place, like a galloping horse, so that they arrive at the pause, as it were, weary and heavily.[328]

The famous vocal teacher, Tosi, reminds his students that if they sing from the heart the listener will understand it is true.

> Oh! how great a master is the heart! Confess it, my beloved singers, and gratefully admit, that you would not have arrived at the highest rank of the profession if you had not been its scholars... Admit, when the heart sings you cannot dissemble, nor has truth a greater power of persuading.[329]

During the nineteenth century the association between Art and Truth remained strong, as we can see in these two statements:

---

[327] Aurelian of Reome, *The Discipline of Music*, trans. Joseph Ponte (Colorado Springs: Colorado College Music Press, 1968), XIX.

[328] *Hucbald, Guido, and John on Music*, trans. Warren Babb (New Haven: Yale University Press, 1978), 175.

[329] P. F. Tosi, *Observations on the Florid Song* (London: Wilcox, 1743), IX, xliv.

> The first universal characteristic of all great art is tenderness, as the second is truth.
> *John Ruskin, 1859*

.....

> It is the glory and good of art
> That art remains the one way possible
> Of speaking the truth.
> *Robert Browning, "The Ring and the Book," 1868*

Jacques Barzun, in his wonderful study of culture in society, *From Dawn to Decadence*, makes an interesting observation.

> Art has been defined over and over as Man's highest spiritual expression, and in one respect superior to religion in that it is the only activity that does not lead to killing.[330]

And with the dawn of the Romantic Era, Art becomes itself almost a religion. The famous critic, E. T. A. Hoffmann, speaks of himself as belonging,

> to that invisible church whose members are transfused by the celestial fire of art and desire nothing but the purest integrity and Truth.[331]

As we have pointed out, the real person is found only in the right hemisphere and that is the only hemisphere which cannot lie. By the nineteenth century this realization had become a subject of much interest, leading people to give more thought to who they really are, as we see in these expressions, "who are we," and "the inmost Essence of ourselves."

> Music whispers to us dim secrets that startle our wonder as to who we are.
> *Emerson*

.....

> [Music] shuts us off from the outer world, as it were, to let us gaze into the inmost Essence of ourselves.
> *Wagner*[332]

[330] Jacques Barzun, *From Dawn to Decadence* (New York: Harpers Collins, 2000), 713.

[331] *E. T. A. Hoffmann's Musical Writings* (Cambridge: Cambridge University Press, 2003), 445.

[332] Quoted in *Richard Wagner's Prose Works*, trans. William Ashton Ellis (New York: Broude), V, 77.

.....

You use a glass mirror to see your face; you use works of art to see your soul.
    George Bernard Shaw[333]

[333] *Back to Methuselah*, 1921.

E. T. A. Hoffmann writes in several places of music drawing us to meditate on a deeper spiritual level. In one place he writes,

> Our kingdom is not of this world, say musicians, for where in nature do we find the prototypes for our art, as painters and sculptors do ... But music is a universal language of nature; it speaks to us in magical and mysterious resonances; we strive in vain to conjure these into symbols, and any artificial arrangement of hieroglyphs [notation] provides us with only a vague approximation of what we have distantly heard.[334]

[334] Hoffmann, *E. T. A. Hoffman's Musical Writings,* 163ff. See also pp. 88 and 196.

One can find many nineteenth century references to this association of music and the inner life of man.

Chopin:

A long time ago I decided that my universe will be the soul and heart of man.[335]

[335] Letter to Delphine Potocka. Chopin's last words were reported to be, "Play Mozart in memory of me."

Clara Schumann, on Brahms:

It is really moving to see him sitting at the piano, with his interesting young face which becomes transfigured when he plays.[336]

[336] Clara Schumann, *Diary* (September, 1853).

Arthur Rubinstein:

When I play, I make love—it is the same thing.[337]

[337] *Arthur Rubinstein—Love of Life* (film, 1975).

Tchaikovsky:

Here are things which can bring tears to our eyes. I will only mention the adagio of the D minor string quintet. No one else has ever known as well how to interpret so exquisitely in music the sense of resigned and inconsolable sorrow. Every time Laub played the adagio I had to hide in the farthest corner of the concert-room, so that others might not see how deeply this music affected me.[338]

[338] Letter to von Meck, March 16, 1878.

Kierkegaard:

I am in love with Mozart like a young girl. Immortal Mozart! I owe you everything; it is thanks to you that I lost my reason, that my soul was awestruck in the very depths of my being … I have you to thank that I did not die without having loved.[339]

[339] *Either/Or* (1843).

Bruno Walter:

At no time and in no place has music been merely playing with sounds. The vibrations themselves which we perceive as musical sounds are not exclusively material in nature—emotional elements are active in them, lending inner meaning and coherence to the sound phenomenon: only thus can the successive and simultaneous arrangement of notes become a musical language whose eloquence speaks to the human soul.[340]

[340] Bruno Walter, *Of Music and Music-Making* (New York: Norton, 1957), 65.

And this is the great opportunity for music education, the opportunity to be the only teachers in the school building who have the tools to reach the *real* student. But, music educators are not taught to understand this and they continue down the road no student is interested in, devoting themselves to the grammar of music, talking *about* music. They aspire to make music like the rest of the curriculum, like English, Geography, Math and History.

But these kinds of subjects have nothing to do with the real student. These kinds of subjects only bombard the student with external facts, outside the experience of the student as a unique, individual person.

But music is different. Music deals with Truth at the individual level, the *real* student. Since music is not taught this way in school, and thus is of little value in helping the student discover who he is, his only hope is to figure it out by himself. Some have been fortunate enough to do this, as was the case with Wagner, when one day walking "aimlessly in the country side of Italy,"

I suddenly realized my own nature; the stream of life was not to flow to me from without, but from within.[341]

[341] Richard Wagner, *My Life* (New York: Tudor, 1936), 603.

2
In the Beginning

What was the Earliest Music Like?

IN 1966 I HAD THE OPPORTUNITY, in cooperation with the US State Department, to give French horn recitals in all the major cities of South America and Mexico. When in La Paz, Bolivia, I was strongly urged to go hear native musicians playing in a local coffee house. The owner of this establishment would fly out in a helicopter a few miles into the alto plano where people lived virtually as if still in the Stone Age, completely unconnected with modern civilization. He would then capture some musicians, bring them back to La Paz to perform, appearing in chains for dramatic effect, for his coffee house. After a few days in La Paz these musicians would make a culture leap of several thousand years into the present time, so the owner would let them go and fly out and capture some more natives to replace them in his coffee house.

    The ensemble I was privileged to hear was extraordinary. They played with great emotion and with surprising tonal and dynamic variety. Their instruments were simple instruments made by themselves. The flautist, for example, performed on a piece of bamboo, perhaps eight inches long, with five holes punched in it to make possible diatonic music. His technique was truly incredible; he could play as many notes per second as any flute graduate from the Paris Conservatory.

This performance made a profound impression on me for two reasons. First, I realized that I was having the rarest of opportunities, to hear musicians who had never been exposed to written music. If I would have held up before them a score from my recital program, they would have not recognized that what they were seeing was "music" or that it had any relationship to what they were doing. No doubt they would have thought that they were simply looking at some foreign symbolic language, as indeed they would have been. It was for me a step back to a very distant time when all music was understood to be for the ear. That may seem a peculiar comment to the reader, but the fact is that I find myself in the twenty-first century continually reminding musicians who work with me that music is for the ear and not the eye. The following chapter will be devoted to the historic revolution which occurred when music first began to be notated. It resulted in a fundamental change in how musicians think about music and I have always believed the musicians lost more than they gained by the introduction of music symbols written on paper.

The second strong impression which hearing this native performance made on me was that there is no reason to conclude that those musicians were doing anything more advanced than similar musicians I might have heard a thousand years before. As men, those of a thousand years before were no less developed physically and emotionally than we. Indeed, I once had an anthropologist tell me that if one could go back in time, through some sort of time-machine, and capture an infant from 15,000 years before and returned him to be reared by a modern family, that child would experience no necessary adjustment of any kind. He would be developmentally just like a child born of our time. Probably one would have to go back 200,000 years or more in order to find fundamental physical differences. All this means that music did not begin with Gregorian chant,[1] as we are informed in undergraduate music history. Rather we have a very rich

[1] We are also not informed that "Gregorian chant" was not from the time of Gregory at all, but that is a different story.

background in the nature and purpose of music which is passed on to us genetically.

As music of the remote past existed before notation, meaning would have depended on a much greater diversity of subtle articulations, rhythmic and dynamic variety. Because all their senses would have been more highly developed than ours, it would seem likely that they would have had a richer palate of emotions and may have even had the kind of extrasensory perception that dogs sometime seem to have. Perhaps, then, it is we who are more limited in our ability to communicate our emotions in music, or perhaps it is just that we have been schooled to express less than we feel.

We may also be sure that if there was a flute player 200,000 years ago, he had a teacher. We know for sure that the teaching of music is the oldest profession and the names we know of actual music teachers were musicians who worked for pharaohs whose names have been forgotten. We know they did not teach from manuals, but rather by demonstration, "it should sound like this." Models for some elements of music, such as melody and rhythm, may have been found in nature. No doubt some idioms followed vocal sounds, even before there was language. Anyone who has ever had a dog knows how much can be communicated by simple vowel sounds. A complex sound like "Mama," even if it was not yet thought of as language would nevertheless consist of noticeable components of pitch, dynamics and rhythm, as a matter of expression and not as a matter of notation.

Simple elements such as these not only suggest a tradition, communicated by the teacher, but also the presence of a listener capable of understanding the "performance." This must have been an important goal far back in time for the need to communicate through music seems to us inseparable from the desire to perform. The reader may be surprised to know that Plato gave much thought to the requirements of a musician and he makes it clear in *Ion* that the fundamental role is to communicate emotions to the listener. Imagine the reaction today if you suggested to the faculty that this become a primary expectation of the semester jury!

If we focus on musicians who lived 12,500 years ago, the period when Plato maintained that organized music education existed, can we speculate on their repertoire? We may assume their emotional and physical needs were identical with ours and we may assume that, as in our time, musicians played to communicate feelings. Of course they would not have had common repertoire as we use the term, but it is possible that there were recognizable melodic patterns which they had come to associate with specific kinds of feelings. This may be the basis of some modern clinical research which has indicated the brain has a preference for certain kinds of melodic patterns and not others.[2]

Of course, what we call improvisation would have been very common. This is so much a part of us that musicians have rebelled against notation every step of the way. We can see an illustration of this in the treatise by Gafurius, *Practica musicae* (1496), where he confirms not all notes were capable of notation.

> Sounds which cannot be written down are committed to memory by usage and practice so that they will not be lost, for their delivery flows imperceptibly into the past.[3]

This is no where better illustrated than on the German tour made by Berlioz to introduce his music there. He was conducting his *Symphonie fantastique* with the court orchestra in Frankfurt and in rehearsal, in the second movement which begins with a dialog between the English horn and oboe, the old gentleman playing oboe began at once to improvise. Berlioz stopped and explained to the old gentleman that he, Berlioz, was the composer of this music and he would appreciate it very much if he would just play what he had written on paper. The old gentleman meant no harm, was embarrassed and promised to just play his part as written. And so he did for the remaining rehearsals, but on the concert he could not help himself and began to improvise. It was what he had done his entire career; it was his job.

Certainly it is understood that in the Baroque and Classical Periods composers left the scores "unfinished" and the

[2] Clinical research has indicated that the brain does not recognize retrograde melodic patterns. So much for 12-Tone theory!

[3] *The Practica musicae of Franchinus Gafurius,* trans. Irwin Young (Madison: University of Wisconsin Press, 1969),18.

players were expected to finish them. Mozart never intended musicians to play all those arpeggio passages, whose only point is to indicate the chord,[4] nor in the Baroque did Vivaldi ever imagine that anyone would play those *Alberti bass* parts as written. During our time the expectations for improvisation have been greatly reduced, but, on the other hand, no artist today would ever think of playing exactly what he saw on paper.

[4] I once gave a lecture in Hungary on the four circumstances where Mozart expected improvisation. Afterwards someone told me that if I had given that lecture in Vienna I would have been hanged from a lamp post!

What was Early Music Education Like?

WE HAVE SPECULATED above on what "repertoire" meant 12,500 years ago and now we must ask the same question regarding "music education." Education has evolved to the point that today it has become associated with preparing someone to earn a living. This, of course, would have been a very minor consideration during the 10,000 years of established educational principles in Egypt which Plato speaks of. What then was the purpose of early music education?

I think a good place to consider this question is with a definition provided by Baldassare Castiglione (1478–1529), who, as a diplomat for the Duke of Urbino and Popes Leo X and Clement VII, had the opportunity to observe Italian culture at its highest level. From this experience came one of the most famous books of the Renaissance, *Il Cortigiano* (The Courtier), which attempts to describe the attributes of the perfect gentleman.[5] Here Castiglione says the central purpose of the teacher must be to instill moral values.

> It is necessary to have a master who by his teaching and precepts stirs and awakens the moral virtues whose seed is enclosed and buried in our souls and who, like a good farmer, cultivates and clears the way for them by removing the thorns and tares of our appetites which often so darken and choke our minds as not to let them flower or produce those splendid fruits which alone we should wish to see born in the human heart.[6]

In turn, this morality-based education fosters ideal learning attitudes in the student. He follows this thought with an interesting observation on France.

> Socrates was perfectly right in affirming that in his opinion his teaching bore good fruit when it encouraged someone to strive to know and understand virtue; for those who have reached the stage where they desire nothing more eagerly than to be good have no trouble in learning all that is necessary.

This idea that the teaching of music has as an important part of its purpose the teaching of morals has a very long

[5] *The Courtier*, II, 145ff., trans., George Bull (New York: Penguin Books, 1967).

[6] Ibid., III, 291.

history. This, in turn, must have had an ancient connection with the association of music and religion. Roger Ascham, the personal tutor of Elizabeth I of England, for example, in his *Toxophilus*, quotes the medieval medical writer, Galen, as observing that the lower crafts man learned by observing animals, such as learning weaving by watching spiders. However, the higher arts man learned from the gods, such as shooting and music from Apollo.[7]

[7] *Toxophilus*, in *The Whole Works of Roger Ascham*, ed. Rev. Giles (London: John Russell Smith, 1864), II, 19.

Other early writers, such as St. Augustine (354–430 AD), in his book *The Teacher*, found the earliest instruction in music in nature, in particular from birds.

> What good singer, even though he be unskilled in the art of music, would not, by the same natural sense, keep in his singing both the rhythm and the melody known by memory? And what can become more subject to measure than this? The uninstructed man has no knowledge of it. Nevertheless, he does it by nature's doing.[8]

[8] *The Teacher*, trans. Robert Russell (Washington, D.C.: The Catholic University of America Press).

The goal of these early educational associations with morals and nature must have had as their goal the most ancient of Greek advice: Know Thyself. We can see this goal in a poem by a writer known as Angelus Silesius (1624–1677):

> All proofs and arguments
> Cannot distort the sight
> Of him who is awakened
> To his own inner light.[9]

Nikaure and Rewer were both music teachers in ancient Egypt during the Fifth Dynasty (2,563 to 2,433 BC). Why has history preserved their names from a period when even the names of the kings and the dates of their reigns are not fully understood? Why, in the tomb paintings of ancient Egypt, do you find scenes of actual music education in progress? Was music education really that important? The reader may be quite surprised to find that the values and principles of good music education were discussed and set in place far before any form of written language. Plato (428–348 BC) suggested that once the values of good music education were understood and established no changes were

[9] *The Book of Angelus Silesius*, trans. Frederick Franck (New York: Knopf, 1976), 110. Scheffler studied at the Elizabeth Gymnasium and as a medical student at the University of Strasbourg and at the University of Padua. In 1653 he became a Catholic and took the name Angelus Silesius ("God's Silesian Messenger").

allowed for the next 10,000 years! What were these values and what constituted good music education among the ancient Egyptians, the most ancient culture we know much about?

First, the primary value of music education, they felt, was in the development of character and this depended on the use of only the best repertoire and no other. Second, they found no need for notation because they had discovered that music must be taught by personal, present tense experience. And third, they believed good music education must be accompanied by strict discipline. This included the discipline of the teachers and when the ancient music education system seemed to break down by the first century BC, Plutarch blames the teachers. The reader will find in the following pages centuries of experience during which these values are reconsidered and redefined.

The early views on music education in ancient Greece, as well as the traditions of the Hebrews, all came from Egypt, where both Plato and Pythagoras studied.[10] Although accounts of live performance have been lost in history, it would appear that music education extended throughout much of society. According to Athenaeus, late second century to early third century AD, in the city of Alexandria, at least, he found a remarkable knowledge in music which extended to everyone.

> I would have you know that there is no record in history of other people more musical than the Alexandrians, and I am not speaking merely of singing to the harp, for even the humblest layman among us, even one who has never learned his ABC's, is so familiar with that, that he can immediately detect the mistakes which occur in striking the notes; no, even when it comes to pipes, they are most musical.

In addition to the earliest emphasis of Greek music education on character formation, we should point out that this objective was clearly associated with only music of the highest quality. Indeed, in the play, *The Thesmophoriazusae*, by Aristophanes, it would seem that the character of the music and the musician were one and the same.

[10] The reader will find 400 pages of discussion of early writers on music education in David Whitwell, *Foundations of Music Education*, ed. Craig Dabelstein (Austin: Whitwell Books, 2011).

Answer me. But you keep silent. Oh! just as you choose; your songs display your character quite sufficiently.

The reason and purpose for using only the highest quality of music is often mentioned by the early writers. Athenaeus, in reviewing this subject, observes, "It is plain to me also that music should be the subject of philosophic reflection."[11] In another place he quotes a remark by Eupolis, "Music is a matter deep and intricate," adding his own observation that music is always supplying something new for those who can perceive.[12] And, he adds, music was in the beginning performed at banquets, but not for entertainment purposes.

> For, since the songs are sung in concert, if discourse on the gods has been added it dignifies the mood of every one ... It is plain, therefore, in the light of what we have said, that music did not, at the beginning, make its way into feasts merely for the sake of shallow and ordinary pleasure, as some persons think.[13]

For Plutarch, this educational purpose in listening to good music was the point at which one could call music "useful" to mankind.

> Therefore, if it be the aim of any person to practice music with skill and judgment, let him imitate the ancient manner; let him also adorn it with those other sciences, and make philosophy his tutor, which is sufficient to judge what is in music decent and useful.[14]

It appears, on the basis of many references, that all forms of early education was accompanied by severe discipline. Even in this remote age we find it mentioned by Cicero:

> The laws of the Cretans, in accordance with Jupiter's wishes, as the poets tell, and those of Lycurgus too, train the young men by making them toil, hunting and running, going hungry and thirsty, feeling cold and heat. At Sparta, in fact, boys are received at the altar with such blows that,
> *much blood flows from the flesh,*
> sometimes even, as I heard when I was there, to the death. Not only did none of them ever cry out, none even groaned.[15]

[11] Athenaeus, *Deipnosophists*, XIV, 632.

[12] Ibid., XIV, 623.

[13] XIV, 627ff.

[14] *Concerning Music*.

[15] Cicero, *Tusculan Disputations*, II, 34.

Plato on Music Education

PLATO (427–347 BC) was born in comfort, was an experienced soldier, and had won prizes for physical feats in the Isthmian games. His coming into contact with Socrates changed his life and he would later observe, "Thank God I was born Greek and not barbarian, freeman and not slave, man and not woman; but above all, that I was born in the age of Socrates."[16]

After the death of Socrates, Plato, a young man of twenty-eight, began a period of travel, first to Egypt for a period of study at Heliopolis, then to Sicily, Italy and finally returning to Greece where he visited the members of the school founded by Pythagoras. He returned to Athens in 387 BC, a man of forty years of age and fully prepared to begin his historic writing. As everyone knows most, and perhaps all, of the writings of Plato are composed as if the author were Socrates, as if they were notes taken from the classes of Socrates. We will use the name of Plato, who, after all wrote the works. In the end, whether the reference is to Socrates or Plato is perhaps not so important to the reader, as both represent a common philosophical perspective of a particular time and place twenty-four centuries in the past.

One of the most startling passages about music in the works of Plato, and certainly a passage intended to inform us regarding the age before his, tells us that the "Golden Age" of Greek music had already passed and that during his time a decay had set in caused by a change in values in the direction of entertainment music. He begins by a brief reference to earlier, noble music such as hymns to the gods and lamentations.

> And they used the actual word "laws" for another kind of song; and to this they added the term "citharoedic." All these and others were duly distinguished, nor were the performers allowed to confuse one style of music with another. And the authority which determined and give judgment, and punished the disobedient, was not expressed in a hiss, nor in the most unmusical shouts of the multitude, as in our days, nor in

[16] Quoted in Will Durant, *The Story of Philosophy* (New York: Simon & Schuster, 1926), 13.

applause and clapping of hands. But the directors of public instruction insisted that the spectators should listen in silence to the end; and boys and their tutors, and the multitude in general, were kept quiet by a hint from a stick. Such was the good order which the multitude were willing to observe; they would never have dared to give judgment by noisy cries.

And then, as time went on, the poets themselves introduced the reign of vulgar and lawless innovation. They were men of genius, but they had no perception of what is just and lawful in music; raging like bacchanals and possessed with inordinate delights—mingling lamentations with hymns, and paeans with dithyrambs; imitating the sounds of the aulos on the lyre, and making one general confusion; ignorantly affirming that music has no truth, and, whether good or bad, can only be judged of rightly by the pleasure of the hearer. And by composing such licentious works, and adding to them words as licentious, they have inspired the multitude with lawlessness and boldness, and made them imagine that they can judge for themselves about melody and song.[17]

[17] *Laws*, 700ff.

Plato, after getting to know an uneducated slave boy, concluded that all men must enter the world with some genetic knowledge.[18] This perhaps was confirmed also by his brilliant analogy of a magnet representing the process of divinity speaking to the poet, who then communicates with the performer and through him to the audience.[19]

[18] *Meno*, 85e.

[19] *Ion*, 533d, 535e.

For Plato, the important values in music education had to do with the development of character, a value as the reader has seen above continued well into the Renaissance. We see this association of philosophy and music in a tale he tells about Socrates. At the end of his life, waiting in prison, Socrates is described as taking up the topic of pleasure and pain. At this time he confides having a reoccurring dream that he should "Set to work and make music." But while he apparently did compose at least one hymn in prison, he curiously interpreted his dream as meaning he should concentrate on philosophy.

> I had imagined that this was only intended to exhort and encourage me in the study of philosophy, which has been the pursuit of my life, and is the noblest and best of music.[20]

[20] *Phaedo*, 60e. It would have been interesting to hear him argue this with Beethoven, who said "Music is a more lofty revelation than all wisdom and philosophy!"

It was the absence of this kind of philosophical association with music which prevented Plato from holding a high regard for the amateur performer of music. Plato describes them as people so busy running around hearing concerts, and presumably performing concerts, that they never stop to contemplate on the higher meaning of the music they are playing. In fact, he says, very few artists are capable of both attaining beauty *and* contemplating on it.

> Musical amateurs, too, are a folk strangely out of place among philosophers, for they are the last persons in the world who would come to anything like a philosophical discussion if they could help it; while they run about at the Dionysiac festivals as if they had let out their ears for the season to hear every chorus, and miss no performance either in town or country. Now are we to maintain that all these and any who have similar tastes, as well as the professors of quite minor arts, are philosophers?
>
> Certainly not, I replied; they are only an imitation.
>
> ...
>
> And this is the distinction which I draw between the sight-loving, art-loving, practical class which you have mentioned, and those of whom I am speaking, and who are alone worthy of the name of philosophers.
>
> How do you distinguish them? he said.
>
> The lovers of sounds and sights, I replied, are, as I conceive it, fond of fine tones and colors and forms and all the artificial products that are made out of them, but their mind is incapable of seeing or loving absolute beauty.
>
> The fact is plain, he replied.
>
> Few are they who are able to attain to this ideal beauty and contemplate it.
>
> Very true.[21]

[21] *Republic*, 476c.

When Plato speaks of "Truth" in music he is, of course, thinking of experiential Truth and specifically that regarding emotion. He makes this clear in his discussion, *Symposium*, where he defines music as "a science of the phenomena of love in [its] application to harmony and rhythm."[22]

This is perhaps the appropriate place to reflect on Plato's definition of a good composition, for this was at the time inseparable from performance. We begin with several isolated observations. First, Plato declares "Musically" is the

[22] *Symposium* 187b. Pliny the Younger, at the end of the first century AD. He writes of the daughter of Calpurnia Hispulla,
> She has even set my verses to music and sings them, to the accompaniment of her lyre, with no musician to teach her but the best of masters, love.

very "name for correctness in the art of music."[23] Second, we know Plato was assuming a contemplative listener when he writes of "musical instruments used to charm the souls of men."[24] Third, Plato seemed perfectly aware of the importance that compositions be composed with "wonderful care."

> AN ATHENIAN STRANGER. Because all discourses and vocal exercises have preludes and overtures, which are a sort of artistic beginnings intended to help the music which is to be performed; lyric measures and music of every other kind have preludes framed with wonderful care.[25]

Plato believed that composers should write not from rules but from inspiration. He mentions this in the *Apology*:

> I learnt that not by wisdom do poets write poetry, but by a sort of genius and inspiration.[26]

Another characteristic of good music must be the contemplation of the beautiful.

> For what should be the end of music if not the love of beauty?[27]

It is clear that Plato had given considerable thought to the values and goals of music education. In one place he refers to music education as the true education of the inner being. Who could phrase a better definition of music education? Indeed, in another place, Socrates, in a dialog with Glaucon, a brother to Plato, suggests that music is "a more potent instrument than any other" in the education of the soul.[28]

Music education creates a man who is graceful, who perceives the omissions or faults in art and nature and develops a soul characterized by the noble and good.

Rhythm and harmony find their way into the inward places of the soul, on which they mightily fasten, imparting grace, and making the soul of him who is rightly educated graceful, or of him who is ill-educated ungraceful; and also because he who has received this true education of the inner being will most shrewdly perceive omissions or faults

[23] *Alcibiades I*, 108d.

[24] *Symposium*, 215c.

[25] *Laws*, 722d.

[26] *Apology*, 22c.

[27] *Republic*, III, 403c.

[28] *Republic*, 401d.

in art and nature, and with a true taste, while he praises and rejoices over and receives into his soul the good, and becomes noble and good, he will justly blame and hate the bad, now in the days of his youth, even before he is able to know the reason why; and when reason comes he will recognize and salute the friend with whom his education has made him long familiar.

> Yes, he said, I quite agree with you in thinking that it is for such reasons that they should be trained in music.[29]

[29] *Republic*, 401d.

Aside from those formidable accomplishments, Plato continues with additional side-effects of music education and they are that a man becomes characterized by self-discipline, courage, liberality and magnanimity.

> Even so, as I maintain, neither we nor the guardians, whom we say that we have to educate, can ever become musical until we and they know the essential forms of temperance [self-discipline], courage, liberality, magnanimity, and their kindred, as well as the contrary forms, in all their combinations, and can recognize them and their images wherever they are found, not slighting them either in small things or great, but believing them all to be within the sphere of one art and study.

Plato identifies as one goal of music education as being that it, through a kind of catharsis, creates calm minds in children who are otherwise fearful and producing a "sound mind in place of their frenzy."[30]

[30] *Laws*, 791.

A very important goal of music education, in Plato's view, was training the child for a lifetime appreciation of good music.

> Now the irregular strain of music is always made ten thousand times better by attaining to law and order, and rejecting the honeyed Muse—not however that we mean wholly to exclude pleasure, which is characteristic of all music. And if a man be brought up from childhood to the age of discretion and maturity in the use of the orderly and severe music, when he hears the opposite he detests it, and calls it illiberal; but if trained in the sweet and vulgar music, he deems the severer kind cold and displeasing. So that while he who hears them

gains no more pleasure from the one than from the other, the one has the advantage of making those who are trained in it better men, whereas the other makes them worse.³¹

[31] Ibid., 802.

Closely related to this, Plato make a very important aesthetic statement when he contends that we cannot call a composition good if its purpose is merely to offer pleasure. "Pleasure," he says is a "doctrine which cannot be admitted." Instead, the goal is the "good," and most important, "Truth."

> AN ATHENIAN STRANGER. When anyone says that music is to be judged by pleasure, his doctrine cannot be admitted; and if there be any music of which pleasure is the criterion, such music is not to be sought out or deemed to have any real excellence, but only that other kind of music which is an imitation of the good, and bears a resemblance to its original.
> CLEINIAS. Very true.
> AN ATHENIAN STRANGER. And those who seek for the best kind of song and music ought not to seek for that which is pleasant, but for that which is true.³²

[32] *Laws*, 668b.

One of the most interesting and unusual discussions to be found in Plato is his view on the requirements of a serious music student. First he must have a good ear and understand theory (systems compounded out of pitches). But he hastens to qualify this by observing that this is not what we mean by being a musician.

> SOCRATES. But you would not be a real musician if this was all that you knew; though if you did not know this you would know almost nothing of music.³³

[33] *Philebus*, 17c.

Second, he must understand how emotions appear and "come to be in the movements of bodies," meaning how they affect the listener.

Third, in another place Plato adds the basic requirement of knowing how to tune. Here he also mentions that the musician speaks "in a gentle and harmonious tone of voice."³⁴

[34] *Phaedrus*, 268e.

Fourth, the music student loves his teacher.

> And as to the artists, do we not know that he only who has love for his instructor emerges into the light of fame?—he whom Love touches not walks in darkness.³⁵

[35] *Symposium*, 197.

The second of these expectations, regarding emotions and the subsequent "movements of bodies," uses a now archaic expression to mean the communication of emotions, "to move the emotions of" the listener. One finds the use of "movement" in seventeenth century France to mean moving the emotions and not a term related to form, as in first movement. However, while living in Europe I have heard people refer to a symphony's first movement and second movement meaning one emotion and then a second and different emotion in the second movement. I heard my landlord there once after attending a concert refer to the first and second movements in the initial movement, meaning the first tonal section and the second tonal section, which vary in feeling as well.

The point then is that the good music student must learn how, in his performance, to move the emotions of the listener. Plato illustrates this by presenting his conversation with Ion, a professional performer who, in a form of singing unknown to us, presented to the public memorized works such as the poems of Homer.

> I wish you would frankly tell me, Ion, what I am going to ask you: When you produce the greatest effect upon the audience in the recitation of some striking passage, such as the apparition of Odysseus leaping forth on the floor, recognized by the suitors and shaking out his arrows at his feet, or the description of Achilles springing upon Hector, or the sorrows of Andromache, Hecuba, or Priam,—are you in your right mind? Are you not carried out of yourself, and does not your soul in an ecstasy seem to be among the persons or places of which you are speaking ... ?
>
> ION. That proof strikes home to me, Socrates. For I must frankly confes s that at the tale of pity my eyes are filled with tears, and when I speak of horrors, my hair stands on end and my heart throbs.
>
> SOCRATES. Well, Ion, and what are we to say of a man who at a sacrifice or festival, when he is dressed in an embroidered robe, and has golden crowns upon his head, of which nobody has robbed him, appears weeping and panic-stricken in the presence of more than twenty thousand friendly

faces, when there is no one despoiling or wronging him;—
is he in his right mind or is he not?

ION. No indeed, Socrates, I must say that, strictly speaking, he is not in his right mind.

SOCRATES. And are you aware that you produce similar effects on most of the spectators?

ION. Only too well; for I look down upon them from the stage, and behold the various emotions of pity, wonder, sternness, stamped upon their faces when I am performing.[36]

[36] *Ion*, 534, c - 535e.

Finally, Plato, as does Aristotle, presents a lengthy discussion on the pedagogy of music education. This has little value for the modern teacher as it deals with instruments no longer in use and in particular with the character of the Greek modes, such as Dorian, Lydian, etc. We know these terms referred to the styles and character of the music of individual tribes of people, but no one today knows what the musical distinctions were.

Aristotle on Music Education

WILL DURANT CALLED ARISTOTLE a one-man "Encyclopedia Britannica of Greece."[37] That is not a bad description for the subjects of Aristotle's *extant* writings include politics, every branch of science known at the time, the arts, government, the art of public speaking, philosophy and ethics. And we must not fail to mention that he invented the philosophical branch of study we call Aesthetics.

Fortunately, Aristotle was born in 384 BC into circumstances which made possible the fulfillment of his genius. His father was a physician to the King of Macedonia, the grandfather to Alexander the Great, whom Aristotle would tutor. At age fifty-three, Aristotle founded in Athens his own school, known as the Lyceum. It is assumed that the many students who were drawn to this school shared in the burden of his work, collecting data, carrying out observations and experiments, and perhaps even in the actual writing. This must have been the case if some ancient writers were correct in attributing to him between 400 and 1,000 books.

In subjects such as logic or rhetoric, where Aristotle needed only his native intelligence and his love for step by step rational analysis, his writings must still impress every modern reader. In the field of science, however, we are startled at some of the "Weird Science" we find in his pages. How, for example, could he have concluded that the brain is cold, bloodless, and *fluid* in nature, or that the delay in the closure of the cranial bone in infants has to do with the need for "evaporation?"[38] And how could he have not guessed that it is in the brain that we experience the senses, concluding instead that it is in the heart?

> For the passages of all the sense-organs ... run to the heart.[39]
>
> .....
>
> Because the source of the sensations is in the heart, therefore this is the part first formed in the whole animal.[40]

[37] Will Durant, *The Story of Philosophy* (New York: Simon & Schuster, 1961 edition), 46.

[38] *De Partibus Animalium*, II.6. Unless otherwise noted, all translations are from *The Works of Aristotle* (Oxford: Clarendon Press).

[39] *De Generatione Animalium*, V.2.

[40] Ibid., II.6.

His understanding of the physical nature of musical sounds seems to have been the result of casual observation and consequentially results in some curious conclusions:

> In the case of oboes and other instruments of the same class, the sounds produced are clear when the breath emitted from them is concentrated and intense. For the impacts on the external air must be of that kind, and it is in this way that they will best travel to the ear in a solid mass.
>
> .....
>
> The reeds of oboes must be solid and smooth and even, so that the breath may pass through smoothly and evenly, without being dispersed. Therefore mouthpieces which have been well steeped and soaked in grease give a pleasant sound, while those which are dry produce less agreeable notes.[41]

But, Aristotle was also an interested observer of music and musicians. He recognized the difference between the musical and the unmusical performance[42] and he noticed that quality of birth or wealth was not the factor that resulted in a good player.[43] In various places, Aristotle mentions the institution of the chorus, how it is supported,[44] that the conductors should be elected,[45] and the modes in which their music was composed.[46] The breadth of observations which he lists in his *Problemata*, in a chapter devoted to music, is very impressive. Among them are:

- A sound made by a chorus travels farther than that of a solo singer.

- Most people prefer hearing music they already know.

- Most people prefer to hear an accompanied singer, rather than a solo singer.

- Low notes which are out of tune are more noticeable than high notes which are out of tune.

- A large chorus keeps better time than a smaller one.

The interesting thing is, while we have numerous observations of, and references to, music throughout his writings, and while he once specifically mentions the concert hall in

[41] *De Audibilibus*, 802a.9, and 802b.19.

[42] *Coming-to-be and Passing-away*, II.6.

[43] *Politica*, 1283a.

[44] *Atheniensium Respublica*, 56.2.

[45] *Politica*, 1299a.17.

[46] *Problemata*, 922b.10. He says they do not use Hypodorian or Hypophrygian, but like everyone else in ancient Greece, he assumes the reader knows what these terms mean. He only reminds us that the first was "magnificent and steadfast," and that the second had "the character of action."

Athens,[47] he never once mentions a specific musical performance nor does he ever speak of music in personal terms. But, on the other hand, one finds some hints that he was, in fact, a contemplative listener. For example, there is his observation that we get the most pleasure in hearing music which is "expressive of meaning."[48] In another place we find his judgment that "a woeful and quiet character and type of music" is "more human."[49]

Due to Aristotle's great use of logic, he arrives at some very important generalizations which are an important background for the philosophy of music. For example, he finds that while speech is not universal, emotions are the same for the whole of mankind.[50] And with respect to universality,

> The many are better judges than a single man of music and poetry.[51]

One of his most quoted definitions is,

> Words spoken are symbols or signs of emotions or impressions of the soul; written words are the symbols of words spoken.[52]

This is his foundation for his careful explanation that the knowledge of music is not the same thing as music itself.[53]

As he understood emotions to be universal, it is no surprise that he found music to also be universal. "Why," he asks, "do all men love music?"

> Is it because we naturally rejoice in natural movements? This is shown by the fact that children rejoice in [rhythm and melody] as soon as they are born. Now we delight in the various types of melody for their moral character, but we delight in rhythm because it contains a familiar and ordered number and moves in a regular manner; for ordered movement is naturally more akin to us than disordered, and is therefore more in accordance with nature ... We delight in concord because it is the mingling of contraries which stand in proportion to one another. Proportion, then, is order, which, as we have said, is naturally pleasant.[54]

We find pleasure when we concentrate on the things we love most. He provides the example of an aulos player

---

[47] *Metaphysica*, 1010b.12.

[48] Ibid., 918a.33.

[49] Ibid., 922b.20.

[50] *On Interpretation*, I, trans. Harold P. Cook (Cambridge: Harvard University Press, 1962).
[51] *Politica*, III, 1281b.8.

[52] *On Interpretation*.

[53] *Categories*, VIII.

[54] *Problemata*, 920b.28.

when playing his instrument is oblivious of conversation around him.[55] The best pleasures, he finds, are those which contribute to a virtuous life.

> The happy life is thought to be virtuous; now a virtuous life requires exertion, and does not consist in amusement. And we say that serious things are better than laughable things and those connected with amusement, and that the activity of the better of any two things ... is the more serious.[56]

As a final example of his general definitions we point out that Aristotle used the word "Art" to refer to the creative process, and not to the art object itself nor to the man creating the art work. It is interesting in this discussion that Aristotle makes a point of saying that chance plays a role in all art works.[57] "Good" art is that in which "it is not possible either to take away or to add anything."[58]

In Aristotle we find a surprisingly long discussion of Music Education. Unlike his treatment of most other subjects, where he usually has a very clear idea to present, here we find him struggling with the idea itself.[59] It is as if we are observing him in the act of talking to himself, trying out arguments and testing his deductions. Or, to say it a different way, he goes to great lengths to frame the question and since the expression, "our discussion," appears, perhaps this entire discussion may even be formed from notes taken by one of his students. One must read the original very carefully, for after these long "pros and cons" Aristotle will then sometimes slip in his answer in the briefest of comments.

Aristotle first makes three very important prerequisite conclusions.

1. It is evident that there is a sort of education in which parents should train their sons, not as being useful or necessary, but because it is liberal or noble.[60]
2. This much we are now in a position to say, that the ancients witness to us; for their opinion may be gathered from the fact that music is one of the received and traditional branches of education.[61]

---

[55] Ibid., 1175b. Aristotle, rather unwittingly, here hits upon the fundamental problem of music for the voice: the listener simply cannot concentrate on the "music" (right hemisphere) and the words (left hemisphere) at the same time equally with both hemispheres. The whole era of the recitative and aria was one solution, or perhaps we should say avoidance, for the "solution" was to merely take turns.

[56] Ibid., 1177a.

[57] Ibid., 1140a.

[58] Ibid., 1106b.8.

[59] The discussion is found in the *Politica*, beginning with line 1337.

[60] Ibid., 1338a.30.

[61] Ibid., 1338a, 35.

3. It is clear that in education practice must be used before theory.[62]

[62] Ibid., 1338b.5.

But, Aristotle now wonders, what exactly does music contribute to society? "It is not easy," he says, "to determine the nature of music, or why anyone should have a knowledge of it."

a) Is it for the sake of amusement and relaxation, like sleep and drinking, which are not good in themselves, but are pleasant, and at the same time "make care to cease," as Euripides says?[63] And for this end men also appoint music, and make use of all three alike, sleep, drinking, music, to which some add dancing.

[63] *Bacchae*, 381.

b) Or shall we argue that music conduces to virtue, on the ground that it can form our minds and habituate us to true pleasures?

c) Or does it contribute to the enjoyment of leisure and mental cultivation? Now obviously youths are not to be instructed with a view to their amusement, for learning is no amusement, but is accompanied with pain. Neither is intellectual enjoyment suitable to boys of that age, for it is the end, and that which is imperfect cannot attain the perfect end. But perhaps it may be said that boys learn music for the sake of the amusement which they will have when they are grown up.

Accepting for now this definition, Aristotle next raises an important question, Do you have to actually learn to *perform* music in order to *learn* music?[64] Is it not possible to obtain the values of music without actually being a musician? Certainly, he says, it is absurd to say that we must learn cooking, just because we need to eat! Aristotle seems to be pondering the dimensions of this question relative to music education, when he asks the following questions:[65]

[64] Beginning, *Politica*, 1339a.

[65] Beginning Ibid., 1339a.34.

a) Why, like kings, can they not just listen to other musicians and not learn to play themselves?

b) Even granting that music may form the character, the objection still holds: "why should we learn ourselves?"

c) Why cannot we attain true pleasure and form a correct judgment from hearing others? Why should we learn ourselves instead of enjoying the performances of others?

d) Zeus does not himself sing or play on the lyre. Nay, we call professional performers vulgar; no freeman would play or sing unless he were intoxicated or in jest.

"We leave these unanswered for the present," says Aristotle. Now Aristotle returns to the original question: Should Music be part of education?

> The first question is whether music is or is not to be a part of education. Of the three things mentioned in our discussion, which does it produce?—education or amusement or intellectual enjoyment, for it may be reckoned under all three, and seems to share in the nature of all of them.[66]

[66] Ibid., 1339b.10.

The intellectual enjoyment of music, Aristotle observes, is universally acknowledged to contain not only an element of the noble, but is also pleasant and results in happiness.

Aristotle next turns to the belief held so strongly by the ancient Greeks, that music forms the character of youth. His primary discussion has to do with reviewing what he knows of the old Greek modes, but as we have explained above this information is not of use to us today. Now, after this discussion, Aristotle presents his conclusion:

> Enough has been said to show that music has a power of forming the character, and should therefore be introduced into the education of the young.[67]

[67] Ibid., 1340b.10.

In another place, Aristotle attributes one factor in this conclusion to hearing itself. He makes the interesting observation that of everything perceived by all our senses, only that perceived by hearing, specifically music, influences character.

> Why is it that of all things which are perceived by the senses that which is heard alone possesses moral character? For

music, even if it is unaccompanied by words, yet has character; whereas a color and an odor and a savor have not.[68]

[68] *Problemata*, 919b.26.

Now Aristotle returns to the question, is it necessary for the student to actually learn to play an instrument or can he be taught in a sort of music appreciation class? Yes, he concludes the students must be taught to be performers,[69] but it should not continue into the adult years when more important things (business) must occupy them.[70] And they need not reach the technical level of the professionals.

[69] Ibid., 1340b.31

[70] Ibid., 1341a.5.

> The right measure will be attained if students of music stop short of the arts which are practiced in professional contests, and do not seek to acquire those fantastic marvels of execution which are now the fashion in such contests, and from these have passed into education.[71]

[71] Ibid., 1341a.10.

And again,

> Thus then we reject the professional instruments and also the professional mode of education in music (and by professional we mean that which is adopted in contests), for in this the performer practices the art, not for the sake of his own improvement, but in order to give pleasure, and that of a vulgar sort, to his hearers ... The result is that the performers are vulgarized, for the end at which they aim is bad. The vulgarity of the spectator tends to lower the character of the music and therefore of the performers.[72]

[72] Ibid., 1341b.9.

The final topic of importance with regard to the purposes of education is the goal of the catharsis, the famous end which he proposed in his book on Tragedy and where, in his discussion there, he established the branch of philosophy known as aesthetics.

> In education the most ethical modes are to be preferred, but in listening to the performances of others we may admit the modes of action and passions also. For feelings such as pity and fear, or, again, enthusiasm, exist very strongly in some souls, and have more or less influence over all. Some persons fall into a religious frenzy, whom we see as a result of the sacred melodies—when they have used the melodies that excite the soul to mystic frenzy—restored as though they had

found healing and purgation. Those who are influenced by pity and fear, and every emotional nature, must have a like experience, and others in so far as each is susceptible to such emotions, and all are in a manner purged and their souls lightened and delighted. The purgative melodies likewise give an innocent pleasure to mankind.[73]

After Aristotle we have some fragments of two books by his student, Aristoxenus (b. c. 379 BC), a writer frequently quoted due to the scarcity of other literature from this period. Unfortunately there are extant only one chapter of his book, *Elements of Rhythm*, and three chapters of his *Elements of Harmony*. As he was apparently the author of a great many books, I personally think it is risky to assume he was primarily a musician, but nevertheless, in the lost book on Harmony, we find in one of the surviving chapters a passage which would seem to reflect some doubt on the old assumption that music affects character.

> Some consider Harmonie a sublime science, and expect a course of it to make them musicians; nay some even conceive it will exalt their moral nature. This mistake is due to their having run away with such phrases in our preamble as ... "one class of musical art is hurtful to the moral character, another improves it"; while they missed completely our qualification of this statement, "in so far as musical art can improve the moral character."[74]

On the other hand, Plutarch quotes the following which he knew from one of the lost books of Aristoxenus:

> Now that the right molding or ruin of ingenuous manners and civil conduct lies in a well-grounded musical education.[75]

In the following century we find a philosopher, Eratosthenes (276–194 BC), who takes the position that the role of music is to entertain, not instruct. The philosopher, Strabo (63 BC – 24 AD), attacked him for this viewpoint, which suggests that Eratosthenes was an exception.

> Why, even the musicians, when they give instruction in singing, in lyre playing, or in aulos playing ... maintain that these studies tend to discipline and correct the character.[76]

[73] Ibid, 1342a. Some of these modes were apparently so associated with particular forms, that Aristotle cites [1342b.] an instance of a performer who attempted to perform a dithyramb, "acknowledged to be Phrygian," in the Dorian and could not do it.

[74] Aristoxenus, *The Elements of Harmony*, 16, trans. Henry S. Macran (Hildesheim: Georg Olms Verlag, 1974), 31.

[75] Quoted by Plutarch in *Concerning Music*.

[76] *The Geography of Strabo*, trans. Horace L. Jones (Cambridge: Harvard University Press, 1960), I.2.3.

In this period after Aristotle we also begin to have a few surviving anecdotes which reflect actual teaching techniques in music.[77] There is an interesting comment on these teaching techniques by Epictetus (53–135 AD), who seems surprised that such a severe learning environment could produce such pleasant results.

[77] See "Greek Views on Music Education after Aristotle," in David Whitwell, *Foundations of Music Education*, ed. Craig Dabelstein (Austin: Whitwell Books, 2011), 70ff.

> Every art, when it is being taught, is tiresome to one who is unskilled and untried in it ... This you will see still more in the case of music, for if you are by when a man is being taught you will think the process of all things the most unpleasant, yet the effects of music are pleasant and delightful for unmusical persons to hear.[78]

[78] *The Discourses of Epictetus*, trans. P. E. Matheson (New York: Random House, 1957), 308.

No early writer addresses the topic of the influence music plays on character development with more heartfelt passion than the historian Polybius (203–120 BC). He departs from his description of the internal wars of the period 220–216 BC to give a fervent testimonial to the role music plays in shaping the character of entire peoples. He offers the illustration of the Cynaetheans and what happened to them when they neglected music education, together with a plea that they return to this use of music to save themselves. In addition to some detail not found elsewhere in ancient Greek literature, he gives us one of the most extraordinary pictures of the educational use of music ("I mean *real* music," he says) in ancient Greece.

> It is worth while to give a moment's consideration to the question of the savagery of the Cynaetheans, and ask ourselves why, though unquestionably of Arcadian stock, they so far surpassed all other Greeks at this period in cruelty and wickedness. I think the reason was they were the first and indeed the only people in Arcadia to abandon an admirable institution, introduced by their forefathers with a nice regard for the natural conditions under which all the inhabitants of that country live. For the practice of music, I mean real music, is beneficial to all men, but to Arcadians it is a necessity ... The early Arcadians had good reason for incorporating music in their whole public life to such an extent that not only boys, but young men up to the age of thirty were compelled to study it constantly, although in other matters their lives were most austere.

.....
The primitive Arcadians, therefore, with the view of softening and tempering the stubbornness and harshness of nature, introduced all the practices I mentioned, and in addition accustomed the people, both men and women, to frequent festivals and general sacrifices, and dances of young men and maidens, and in fact resorted to every contrivance to render more gentle and mild, by the influence of the customs they instituted, the extreme hardness of the national character.

The Cynaetheans, by entirely neglecting these institutions, though in special need of such influences, as their country is the most rugged and their climate the most inclement in Arcadia, and by devoting themselves exclusively to their local affairs and political rivalries, finally became so savage that in no city of Greece were greater and more constant crimes committed . . .

If Heaven ever grant them better fortune, they may humanize themselves by turning their attention to education and especially to music; for by no other means can they hope to free themselves from that savagery which overtook them at this time.[79]

[79] Polybius, *The Histories*, IV.20.5ff, trans. W. R. Paton (Cambridge: Harvard University Press, 1954).

From the writer Aristides Quintilianus (third century AD), the last of the ancient Greek philosophers, we have an extensive discussion of music education. This discussion, which is a portion of his larger treatise, *De Musica*,[80] clearly follows the thinking of Plato, but is much more detailed. It is, therefore, valuable not only for filling in philosophical details, but because of its very existence it seems to suggest that these ideas may have been continuously held by Greek philosophers for six or seven centuries. He begins with the following promise:

[80] Aristides discussion begins Book II. All our quotations are from the translation by Andrew Barker, *Greek Musical Writings* (Cambridge: Cambridge University Press, 1989), II, 457ff.

> We ought to investigate whether it is possible to educate by means of music or not; whether such education is useful or not; whether it can be given to all or only to some; and whether it can be given through just one kind of composition or through several. We must inquire whether the kinds thought unsuitable for education have no use at all, or whether even these can sometimes be found beneficial.

First we should like to point out that Aristides (he is known by this name) was one of the earliest philosophers who seemed to understand that we consist of two separate sides of our personality, that which we associate today with our bicameral brain with its rational side and its experiential side. Furthermore, he very correctly understood that in the experiential side, which he called the irrational side, music was the most dominant characteristic. One branch, he maintains, deals with the rational part, it keeps this part pure by "gifts of wisdom." The other branch deals with the irrational part, "as though it were some savage beast that is moved without order," taming it, allowing it neither "excesses nor to be wholly subdued." The "leader and high priest" of the first branch of learning is philosophy, the "ruler" of the second is music.

This second branch of education is especially important for children, for they would reject mere words, as they contain no pleasure, and it permits education "which does not stir up the rational part before its time." Everyone understands that children are by nature attracted to music.

> Song always comes readily to all children, as we can see, and so do patterns of joyful movement: nor would anyone in his senses forbid them the pleasure they get from such things.

We are also impressed that Aristides was one of the earliest to understand very clearly that music differs from the other arts in the fact that the communication between composer and listener is immediate and direct.

> Music persuades most directly and effectively, since the means by which it makes its imitation [*mimesis*] are of just the same kind as those by which the actions themselves are accomplished in reality.

Aristides next turns to music education which he says was so clearly understood by the ancients.

> Why then are we surprised to find that it was mostly through music that people in ancient times produced moral correction?—for they saw how powerful a thing it is, and how effective its nature makes it. Just as they applied their intelligence to such other human attributes as health and bodily well-being, seeking to preserve one thing, working to increase another,

limiting to what is beneficial anything that tended towards excess, so also with the songs and dances to which all children are naturally attracted. It was impossible to prohibit them without destroying the children's own nature: instead, by cultivating them, little by little and imperceptibly, they devised an [educational] activity both decorous and delightful, and out of something useless made something useful.

After mentioning that music is especially valuable in dealing with the emotions, which the rational part of us is noticeably unsuccessful, he makes the comment that the only people who have doubts about the use of music are either poor musicians or popular musicians.

> Those who neglected music, melody and unaccompanied poetry alike, were utterly crude and foolish; [and second] those who had involved themselves in it in the wrong way fell into serious errors, and through their passion for worthless melodies and poetry stamped upon themselves ugly idiosyncrasies of character.

Aristides brings up this topic because other writers from this last period of ancient Greece speak of a decline in the practice of music, an apparent reference to increasing interest in entertainment music. Aristides points out that the important thing is to "separate out the best from the worst" music and to keep in mind that the true purpose of music is the moral education of the student.

> We should not avoid song altogether just because it gives pleasure. Not all delight is to be condemned, but neither is delight itself the objective of music. Amusement may come as it will, but the aim set for music is to help us toward virtue.

By "the aim of music to help us toward virtue," Aristides specifically means the use of music to form the character. "Music," he says, "is the most powerful agent of education, rivaled by no other, [and it can be shown] that our characters commonly deteriorate if they are left undisciplined, lapsing into base or brutal passions."

> Of those among whom music has been perverted against its nature into depravity and cultural corruption, the peoples

that cultivate the appetites have souls that are too slack, and improper bodily affectations, like those who live in Phoenicia and their descendants in Africa; while those that are ruled by the spirited part lack all mental discipline—they are drunkards, addicted to weapon-dances no matter whether the occasion is right, excessive in anger and manic in war, like the Thracian peoples and the entire Celtic race. But the races that have embraced the learning of music and dexterity in its use, by which I mean the Greeks and any there may be who have emulated them, are blessed with virtue and knowledge of every kind, and their humanity is outstanding. If music can delight and mold whole cities and races, can it be incapable of educating individuals? I think not.

"Now," Aristides says, "it is time to explain what kinds of melody and rhythm will discipline the natural emotions." Here he promises to not only set forth the principles written down by the great philosophers, but to reveal to us some of the things they did not write about—those "esoteric secrets" they reserved "for their discussions with one another." The subject he is thinking of here is the way music is the key to the education of the emotions and hence the key to music education. He must do this, he says, because now,

> indifference to music (to put it politely) is so widespread, we cannot expect people with only a mild interest in the subject to tolerate being faced with a book in which not everything is explicitly spelled out.

To demonstrate how character is found in melody, Aristides provides a lengthy discussion of the male and female qualities of vowels, diphthongs, consonants, etc., all of which makes little sense to the modern reader. Although he says these same principles which apply to melody are valid with respect to instruments, he does not explain this.

It is the identification of these emotional characteristics in a melody which is the first step in affecting character through music education. Unfortunately he does not explain this process beyond indicating that one selects a melody of a desired character in order to introduce this character into children, "and older people too," in which this character is missing.

If it is obscure and hard to diagnose, you should begin by applying whatever melody comes to hand. If this is effective in influencing the soul, you should persist with it, but if the patient remains unaltered you should introduce a modulation [meaning introducing another style of music]; for it is likely that someone who is resistant to one sort of melody will be attracted by its opposite.

Aristides next turns to rhythm, which he also considers in terms of emotion and character. Rhythms composed of short syllables are faster and "more passionate," those composed only of long syllables are slower and calm and mixtures have the qualities of both. Compound rhythms are more emotional and tempestuous. Running rhythms inspire us to action, other are supine and flabby. In fact, observes Aristides, rhythm is so closely associated with character, it follows that one can judge a person by his manner of walking.

> We find that people whose steps are of good length and equal, in the manner of the spondee, are stable and manly in character: those whose steps are long but unequal, in the manner of trochees or paions, are excessively passionate: those whose steps are equal but too short, in the manner of the pyrrhic, are spineless and lack nobility: while those whose steps are short and unequal, and approach rhythmical irrationality, are utterly dissipated. As to those who employ all the gaits in no particular order, you will realize that their minds are unstable and erratic.

Following a discussion of associations between character and various instruments, Aristides concludes with a rather vague notion that all these things are somehow connected with the bodies of the universe.

Music Education in Ancient Rome

WRITERS OF THE EARLIEST PERIOD of ancient Rome were all agreed that their cultural arts were indebted to ancient Greece. One Roman feature, something one finds little trace of in ancient Greece, was a strong interest in the solo singer, a practice which extended to the members of the highest level of society. For example, Sulla, though a harsh ruler, was a good singer. The consul Lucius Flaccus (fl. c. 19 AD) was a diligent trumpet player, practicing daily it would appear.[81] And while we know nothing specific of Julius Caesar's interest in music, perhaps his sympathy for it is reflected in the fact that upon his death and ritual cremation, the musicians of Rome threw their professional clothes onto the fire as an expression of grief.[82] And, in one place, Cicero mentions a conversation in which he heard of a knight who had studied music as a boy and was still practicing his singing.[83]

This dilettante activity included the female members of society, although the philosopher, Sallust, grumbles that a lady should not have too much skill.

> Among their number was Sempronia, a woman who had committed many crimes that showed her to have the reckless daring of a man. Fortune had favored her abundantly, not only with birth and beauty, but with a good husband and children. Well educated in Greek and Latin literature, she had greater skill in lyre playing and dancing than there is any need for a respectable woman to acquire.[84]

On the other hand the status of music in society at large was quite different in Rome. Although information is sparse, it would seem that the decay in the quality of music reported in the most recent and final periods of ancient Greece was accompanied by a new practice of having music supplied by slaves. It was for this reason that the historian Nepos (100–22 BC) wrote that the practice of music and singing were not appropriate to a man of distinction.[85] And Cicero once criticized a member of the aristocracy, Chrysogonos, whom he felt supported too much slave music.

[81] Alfred Sendrey, *Music in the Social and Religious Life of Antiquity* (Rutherford: Fairleigh Dickinson University Press, 1974), 391.

[82] Suetonius, *Lives of the Caesars*, Book I, lxxxiv.

[83] Cicero, *De oratore*, III, xxiii, 87.

[84] *The Conspiracy of Catiline*, 25, 5.

[85] Sendrey, *Music in the Social and Religious Life of Antiquity*, 407.

But what am I to say about his vast household of slaves and the variety of their technical skill? I say nothing about such common trades, such as those of cooks, bakers, litter-bearers: to charm his mind and ears, he has so many artists, that the whole neighborhood rings daily with the sound of vocal music, stringed instruments, and auloi, and with the noise of banquets by night. When a man leads such a life ... can you imagine his daily expenses, his lavish displays, his banquets? Quite respectable, I suppose, in such a house, if that can be called a house rather than a manufactory of wickedness and a lodging house of every sort of crime.[86]

On the other hand, the vast number of these slaves made possible some very large performing forces. A procession in the time of Ptolemaeus Philadelphus (283–246 BC), for example, included no fewer than 600 singers and 300 kithara players.[87] A similar report by Horace reports numerous aulos and lyres accompanying songs in the temple of Venus.[88] Many of these musicians were Greeks who fled to Rome after the conquest of Macedonia in 167 BC and the destruction of Corinth in 144 BC.[89]

Music education seems to have been available, but not required, in the schools of Rome from a very early period. We know that in the late third century BC, for example, the music teachers were more highly paid than those of reading or gymnastics. This education consisted of instruction in music theory and performance on the kithara, with examinations at the end of the school term.

Music education on a private basis was also highly organized, as we know from a papyrus dating from 206 BC. This document is a contract between a music teacher and a young slave named Narcissus and details specific amount of repertoire to be learned, as well as specifying study on two kinds of aulos, panpipes and kithara.[90]

During the final period of ancient Rome, the Empire (14–476 AD), in what one normally thinks of as the period of decline, one is surprised by the significant numbers of the aristocracy who still had a serious interest in music. Among the members of the Senate, for example, we know of Caius Calpurnius Piso, one of the conspirators against

[86] Cicero, *Pro Sexto Roscio Amerino*, XLVI, 134.

[87] Ibid., 411.

[88] *Carmina*, IV, 1, 22.

[89] Their instruments went with them, but changed names. Marcus Varro, in *On the Latin Language*, VI, 75 and VIII, 61, gives *tuba* for trumpet and *tubicines* for the players (*liticines* and *bucinator* for the other types of trumpet); *cornicines* for "horn blowers"; *tibiae* for auloi and *tibicines* for the players; and *cithara* for lute.

[90] Ibid., 404.

Nero in 65 AD, who was an accomplished lyre player.[91] The musical accomplishments of many of the emperors is also surprising.[92] Caligula (12–41 AD) received an education which included both vocal and instrumental music and used to perform in private concerts before the aristocracy. Caligula once asked a famous singer, Apelles, whether he considered he or Jupiter the greater. When the singer unfortunately hesitated in his answer, Caligula had him scourged, but complimented his voice as being attractive even in his cries of pain! We are also told that "if anyone made even the slightest sound while his favorite was dancing, he had the person dragged from his seat and scourged him with his own hand."[93]

Nero (37–68 AD), the most debauched and cruel of the emperors (he murdered his mother when age twenty-two!) considered himself a serious singer and studied the lyre, with which he accompanied his singing, with the foremost teacher of his time, Terpnos. We will mention here only some of the specific educational theories under which he practiced, as is described by Suetonius.

> … he little by little began to practice himself, neglecting none of the exercises which artists of that kind are in the habit of following, to preserve or strengthen their voices. For he used to lie upon his back and hold a leaden plate on his chest,[94] purge himself by the syringe and by vomiting, and deny himself fruits and all foods injurious to the voice … So far from neglecting or relaxing his practice of the art, he never addressed the soldiers except by letter or in a speech delivered by another, to save his voice; and he never did anything for amusement or in earnest without an elocutionist by his side, to warn him to spare his vocal organs and hold a handkerchief to his mouth.[95]

[91] Sendrey, *Music in the Social and Religious Life of Antiquity*, 391.

[92] Ibid., 392ff.

[93] Suetonius, *Lives of the Caesars*, Book IV, lv.

[94] This information comes from Pliny the Elder, *Natural History*, XXXIV, xliv, 167, who says,

> Nero, whom heaven was pleased to make emperor, used to have a plate of lead on his chest when singing songs *fortissimo*, thus showing a method for preserving the voice.

[95] Suetonius, *Lives of the Caesers*, Book VI, xxff.

Quintilian on Music Education

IT IS FROM THIS FINAL PERIOD that we have the only extant significant discussion on music education in ancient Rome. The author, Quintilian (30–96 AD) was born in Spain and was sent to Rome to study by his well-educated father. There he studied law and rhetoric and eventually opened his own school of rhetoric and among his students were Pliny the Younger and perhaps Tacitus. His discussion of music education is only a part of a larger work and one notes that he begins with an acknowledgement of the Greek's emphasis on music education.[96]

[96] Quintilian, *The Education of an Orator* (*Institutio Oratoria*), trans. H. E. Butler (London: Heinemann, 1938), I, x, 9ff.

> For myself I should be ready to accept the verdict of antiquity. Who is ignorant of the fact that music was in ancient times the object not merely of intense study but of veneration: in fact Orpheus and Linus, to mention no others, were regarded as uniting the roles of musician, poet and philosopher.
>
> .....
>
> It was not therefore without reason that Plato regarded the knowledge of music as necessary to his ideal statesman or politician, as he calls him; while the leaders even of that school, which in other respects is the strictest and most severe of all schools of philosophy, held that the wise man might well devote some of his attention to such studies. Lycurgus himself, the founder of the stern laws of Sparta, approved of the training supplied by music.

He concludes his introduction by suggesting that the importance of music education is so universally understood that he is fearful that in saying too much he risks the impression that the idea needs defense. These comments are particularly interesting in their suggestion that music education was much more the norm in Roman education than extant literature suggests.

> If there were anything novel in my insistence on the study of music, I should have to treat the matter at greater length. But in the view of the fact that the study of music has, from those remote times when Chiron taught Achilles down to our own day, continued to be studied by all except those who

have a hatred for any regular course of study, it would be a mistake to seem to cast any doubt upon its value by showing an excessive zeal in its defense.

Finally, Quintilian gives several vivid examples of the power of music over behavior, including the case of,

> an aulos player accused of manslaughter because he had played a tune in the Phrygian mode as an accompaniment to a sacrifice, with the result that the person officiating went mad and flung himself over a precipice.

3
The Arrival of Notation

Sounds which cannot be written down are committed to memory ... so that they will not be lost.[1]
 Franchino Gaffurio (1451–1518)

The fact is we write a thing differently from the way in which we execute it.[2]
 François Couperin (1668–1733)

The important things are not found in the notes.
 Gustav Mahler

[1] *The Practica musicae of Franchinus Gafurius*, trans. Irwin Young (Madison: University of Wisconsin Press, 1969), 18.

[2] Couperin, *L'Art de toucher.*

A LAYMAN reading comments such as the above might well conclude that while we have a notational system for writing music on paper, musicians ignore it. And that is exactly right; that is what we do. The reason why we ignore what is on paper, to put it into modern terms, has to do with our bicameral brain. The notation is a symbolic language and is thus stored in the left hemisphere, but the experience of music is in the right hemisphere. The human result is exactly like trying to write a love letter, where we expect the left hemisphere to write about something it knows nothing about.

The first problem for musicians today is that to be considered musical they must not play what is on paper. The analogy with the love letter is very close, for our modern notational system was created by late medieval Church musicians who were trained as mathematicians and understood they were not to account for emotions, something the early Church was trying to remove from the lives of the new Christians. And so we are left today with a notational system which still to this very day includes not a single symbol for feelings or emotions, even though the principal purpose of music is to communicate feeling and emotions. It follows that if one performs what is on paper, the important things will be missing. Johann Mattheson, a great Baroque German musician and critic, observed in 1739 that if a musician does that, plays what is on paper and the composer is in the audience he may well not even recognize his own composition![3]

The second problem for the performer is that those notes on paper are in the wrong time zone. They are past tense, while the performer is in the present tense. Charles Burney, during his travels in Europe in the eighteenth century, reports a conversation he had with the great Henry Purcell. Purcell, he tells us, complained that writing everything out robs music of its special quality of being performed in the present tense. When one plays written music, it is automatically music of the past ("obsolete and old fashioned").[4] This is why the listeners who were in the audience of the earliest European public concerts found they preferred musicians playing in the present tense rather than from printed music. The philosopher John Donne, in a letter of c. 1600, points this out.

> For both listeners and players are more delighted with voluntary than with sett musicke.[5]

The great English philosopher Thomas Hobbes makes the same point in creating the analogy that the written music is like the bones and the performance the flesh.[6]

Very closely related to this problem is the fact that notation introduced the eye into the realm of music, which obviously is of the domain of the ear.[7] Moreover the written form of music turns music *ipso facto* into a noun, whereas the very definition of music is a verb, "to make music," something which happens live before a listener. This, in turn, changed a long tradition of judging music in performance

[3] Johnann Mattheson, *Der Volkommene Capellmeister* (1739). Denise Restout, in *Landowska on Music* (Stein and Day, 1964), 356, reports that Wanda Landowska told the story of Chopin having heard one of his Nocturnes performed by Liszt, asked in all seriousness, "Whose piece is this?"

[4] Charles Burney, *A General History of Music* [1776] (London, 1935), II, 443.

[5] John Donne, quoted in *Selected Prose*, ed. Helen Gardner (Oxford: Clarendon Press, 1967), 5. John Donne (1573–1631) studied at both Oxford and Cambridge, but as a born Catholic was not permitted to receive a degree. After various attempts at professions brought him to poverty, he converted to the official Church, became famous for his sermons and eventually became dean of St. Paul's.

[6] *The English Works of Thomas Hobbes*, ed. William Molesworth (London: Bohn, 1839), IV, 455.

[7] To make this point, Ricardo Muti sometimes tells his conducting students that they are to meet at an art gallery to smell some paintings!

into the judging of something on paper, which ironically is not even music to begin with. Everything on paper is only the grammar of music, but not the music. This is why the great oboist, Bruce Haynes, wrote that no one should ever hold up a piece of paper and say "this is music!" And this is why, in the quotation at the top, Mahler was reminding us that the important things are not found on paper. Consider the ramifications of this: music schools emphasize the wrong thing and music contests adjudicate the wrong thing.

The implications for performance are just as critical. Take the case of the conductor. He has before him the printed score, a version of the music which may even have printed errors. Second, in rehearsal he is hearing a live version of the music, which may well include sounds not written on paper. Finally in his head he maintains his own idealized version of the score, which he recreated from studying the notes left behind by the composer. Which of these three scores does he conduct? Or consider the pianist performing a Beethoven sonata. There are no feelings written on the page, and Beethoven is of no help since he is dead. Who shall represent the composer? Mozart answered this question:

> The performer should play so that one believes that the music was composed by the person who is playing it.[8]

[8] Mozart in a letter of 1778.

In the final analysis, one must acknowledge that we have a music notational system which does not support good musicianship. How did we get into this ambiguous situation?

A Brief History of Western Notation

A CLAY DOCUMENT from 3,000 BC Sumeria, which describes the music of the temple, identifies several musicians by title, one of whom was responsible for the rehearsal of the choir. A document from Akkad from the same period mentions some temple musicians who "know the melodies" and are "masters of the musical movements." These may well be the earliest descriptions of a conductor.

We first *see* a conductor among the tomb paintings of the Old Kingdom of ancient Egypt (2686–2181 BC). Although little is known of the actual music of ancient Egypt we must presume the possibility of art music for many of the tomb paintings seem to show people listening to the music. In one remarkable painting a female musician plays the trumpet for the god Osiris, who is pictured shedding tears.[9] Frequently there is pictured among these persons who seem to be listening one who is always positioned directly facing one or more musicians and appears to be making some kind of hand gestures or signals. He is called by scholars a *chironomist*, "one who gestures with his hands," a definition first given by the rhetorician, Marcus Fabius Quintilinus (35–100 AD).

Of course there was no known music notation at this early time, but one thing the players would need, then as now, is someone to make a decision on tempo and it is a good guess that this chironomist–conductor was filling this role. It is interesting that in all forms of Western notation from this time forward the issue of tempo was never addressed as part of the actual notation. Even the familiar metronome of the nineteenth century is an addition above the score. Clearly the reason no consensus would make possible the notation of tempo, is that tempo is closely tied to the emotions, which are by definition an individual thing. This was addressed by Johann Mattheson, the great composer and critic of the German Baroque.

> Movement is a "spiritual thing," not a physical thing, and depends not on "precepts and prohibitions," but "feeling and

[9] Lise Manniche, *Music and Musicians in Ancient Egypt* (London: British Museum Press, 1991), 58.

emotion." To find the correct movement, the performer must "probe and feel his own soul" as well as "feel the various impulses which the piece is supposed to express."[10]

[10] Johann Mattheson, *Der vollkommene Capellmeister* (1739), trans. Ernest Harriss (Ann Arbor: UMI Research Press, 1981), II, vii, 18ff.

The earliest symbols of Western music notation are the neumes of the ninth century, curious squiggles written above the music and whose meaning is unknown. Traditional musicology has always taken these to be indications for a conductor to follow with his hands and that the probable purpose was to aid memory. I have always thought they were more related to performance itself and that their origin was whatever that chironomist–conductor in the Egyptian tomb paintings was doing.[11] Guido of Arezzo in his *Mirologus* (c. 1026–1028 AD), goes further and associates them with the emotions.

[11] One scholar has attempted to create a musical scale corresponding to the hand positions in the paintings. See Heinrich Besseller and Max Schneider, *Musik des Altertums, Lieferung* 1 (Leipzig: Beutscher Verlag für Musik, 1961), 86.

> Let the effect of the song express what is going on in the text, so that for sad things the neumes are grave, for serene ones they are cheerful, and for auspicious texts exultant, and so forth.

In the following chapter I will discuss the early medieval Roman Church history which resulted in the closing of the schools and the eventual reopening of them. Since the Church had taken a very strong stand against emotions, and since for the ordinary person that is the point of music, the Church could only be convinced to allow music into the new curriculum if it were made a branch of mathematics. Thus the initial attempts at notation which leads to that which we use today were invented by Church men who were trained in mathematics. It retains to the present day very much of this arithmetic character, "two of these equals one of those," etc.

What prompted the Church to begin to create a new notational system was the necessity to find a way to train the boy sopranos faster, for the old rote teaching system was not producing enough singers.[12] We can see this intent clearly in an early effort by Odo of Cluny (878–942 AD), in his *Enchiridion musices* of c. 935 AD, the first system in which letters were used as symbols for pitch in the modern sense. In his preface remarks, Odo says he has taught boys in a

[12] Women singers were not yet allowed in the Church.

few days to read "without fault anything written in music," something which he states that until now ordinary singers could not do even after fifty years experience.[13]

Of course to be functional for teaching purposes, copies were required. Thus there were many full-time monks whose job it was to copy manuscripts, persons whose names we do not know but who played a vital role in the music of the Middle Ages. One wrote on the manuscript he was working on,

> Careful with your fingers! Don't touch writing! You don't know what it is to write. It's a crushing task; it bends your spine, blurs your eyesight, creases your stomach and cracks your ribs.[14]

By the Renaissance it is clear that many musicians had lost interest in the old mathematics Church traditions, including the polyphony we still hear so much about in school. The first educational treatise which began to move away from the old school was the *Compendium Musices* (1552) by Adrian Coclico, a Flemish theorist who taught at the university in Wittenberg in 1545. Coclico repeatedly renews his criticism of mathematics-based learning. No sooner has he begun writing about scales, for example, than he stops and observes that this can only be understood in performance.

> I have wished to train this boyish industry in music through but few words and precepts on that account, so that no youth running to the books of musician-mathematicians will waste his life in reading them and never arrive at the goal of singing well.[15]

He is quick to point out that his own study was with that "most noble musician, Josquin," from whom he learned "incidentally, from no book." Coclico's goal was to teach the boys to be musical and he begins by stating his purpose as teaching "correct, smooth and elegant singing."

> I see today German youth not only ignorant of the traditions of music, of which many praises will be expounded elsewhere, but also ruined and kept back from the true force and reason of singing. As long as they pass over the memorizing of

[13] Odo, *Enchiridion musices*, in Oliver Strunk, *Source Readings in Music History* (New York: Norton, 1950), 104.

[14] Late Medieval manuscript, quoted in Jacques Barzun, *From Dawn to Decadence* (New York: HarperCollins, 2000), 235.

[15] Adrian Coclico, *Musical Compendium*, trans. Albert Seay (Colorado Springs: Colorado College Music Press, 1973), 10.

precepts, for them to learn to sing rapidly and correctly cannot be done.[16]

[16] Coclico, Ibid., 5.

He quickly adds a significant qualification to the last sentence, noting,

> I would say that whoever keeps his students too long on precepts and theory lacks judgment and evidently is ignorant of the goal of music.

The whole treatise reflects his personal struggle with trying to make music out of the mathematics-based notation and accompanying rules. Good musicians were soon not satisfied to perform from copies written in the old notational system and to make music they found it necessary to express themselves by adding various ornaments and improvisation. Therefore Vincenzo Galilei warns the student,

> And let it not come into your mind to try to defend yourself with the silly excuse of some who say they did not feel called upon to do more than that which they found written or printed ...[17]

[17] Vincenzo Galilei, *Fronimo* (1584), trans. Carol MacClintock (Neuhasen-Stuttgart: Hänssler-Verlag, 1985), 83. In the case of opera there was, of course, a great deal of improvisation.

Beginning with the late fifteenth century there are a number of first-hand reports of performances in which it is evident the performers were not just reproducing the notes on the page. Angelo Poliziano attended such a concert and recalled,

> No sooner were we seated at the table than Fabio was ordered to sing, together with some other experts, certain of those songs which are put into writing with those little signs of music, and immediately he filled our ears, or rather our hearts, with a voice so sweet that (I do not know about the others) as for myself, I was almost transported out of my senses, and was touched beyond doubt by the unspoken feeling of an altogether divine pleasure ... Now it was varied, now sustained, now exalted and now restrained, now calm and now vehement, now slowing down and now quickening its pace, but always it was precise, always clear and always pleasant.[18]

[18] Quoted in Nino Pirrotta and Elena Povoledo, *Music and Theatre from Poliziano to Monteverdi* (Cambridge: Cambridge University Press, 1982), 36.

By the time of the Baroque Period the freedom which performers took from what the eye saw on paper resulted in a wide variety of dynamics and tempi. This is quite clear from the remarks that Georg Muffat made in the Foreword to his collection of concerti, *Auserlesene Instrumental-Music* (1701).

> At the direction *piano* or *p* all are ordinarily to play at once so softly and tenderly that one barely hears them, at the direction *forte* or *f* with so full a tone, from the first note so marked, that the listeners are left, as it were, astounded at such vehemence.[19]

"Astounded" seems a strong expectation of the listener, but Muffat mentions a similar astonishment again with respect to tempo.

> In conducting the measure or beat, one should for the most part follow the Italians, who are accustomed to proceed much more slowly than we do at the directions *Adagio, Grave, Largo*, etc., so slowly sometime that one can scarcely wait for them, but, at the directions *Allegro, Vivace, Presto, Piu presto*, and *Prestissimo* much more rapidly and in a more lively manner. For by exactly observing this opposition or rivalry of the slow and the fast, the loud and the soft, the fullness of the [ripieno] and the delicacy of the [concertino], the ear is ravished by a singular astonishment, as is the eye by the opposition of light and shade.

Even in the case of something so common as the military signals played on the natural trumpet in the eighteenth century, the author of a contemporary treatise observes that the trumpet signals had become less artistic, a fact which he attributed to the introduction of notation.[20]

During the era of the court composer, where often new compositions were demanded on short notice, these contributions by the performers were considered as "finishing the composition." Most composers expected this. Heinrich Schütz, for example, in the preface to his *Resurrection History* (1623), recommends that the long sustained chords in the organ part should be performed with "decorative and appropriate runs or passages."[21] Again, in his *Cantiones sacrae*, Op. 4, of 1625, he writes,

[19] Quoted in Oliver Strunk, *Source Readings in Music History* (New York: Norton, 1950), 451.

[20] Ernst Altenburg, *Versuch einer Anleitung zur heroischmusikalischen Trompeter- und Pauker-Kunst* ... (Halle, 1795), trans. Edward Tarr, 54.

[21] Hans Moser, *Heinrich Schütz* (St. Louis: Concordia, 1936), 367.

> You organists, however, who wish to satisfy more sensitive ears I request not to spare the pains to fill in all the voices. If in customary manner you accompany only according to the *basso continuo*, I would consider this wrong and unmusical [*vanum et inconcinnum*].[22]

[22] Ibid., 402.

This freedom in performance, the understanding that the performer was not expected to just play what is on paper continued throughout the nineteenth century. It would be only in the twentieth century that, for the first time in more than 1,000 years, performers were expected to play only what the eye saw on the page. This period, beginning in the 1930s was a reaction to Romanticism and is now known as the "Modern Style." The European oboist, Bruce Haynes, characterizes as,

> Accuracy, good intonation, literalism in reading scores, automatic tempos and limited personal expression. Music reduced to audible mathematics functioning like an automaton.[23]

[23] Bruce Haynes, *The End of Early Music* (London: Oxford University Press, 2007), 50.

Leon Botstein, writing under the subject "Modernism," in the *Grove Dictionary of Music* (1980), describes the new style as,

> An austere, explicitly anti-sentimental ... approach to performance evolved at mid-century and came to dominate; examples include the conducting of Arturo Toscanini, Georg Szell, Hermann Scherchen and Fritz Reiner, ... the pianism of Artur Schnabel, Rudolf Serkin and Glenn Gould and the refined approach to the violin displayed by Joseph Szigeti and Jascha Heifetz.

It is for every reader to accept or reject this approach to performance as he sees fit. Let me rephrase that: it is quite appropriate for the reader to reject this approach to music if it doesn't reflect his own feelings. In my experience in the field of education this approach has had the effect of making students afraid to express themselves in their recital performances. It may be their recital, but the performance belongs to the teacher. A young Korean pianist said to me, after her recital, "Now I can finally play like I want to!" She only wanted her performance to communicate her feelings to the listener. That is what music is all about.

4
The Great Divide

Musica speculativa vs *Musica practica*

As everyone today knows we have a bicameral brain, a left side which specializes in rational information and a right side which specializes in experiential information. If we could pose a rhetorical question, and if both sides could answer, we might get quite different answers. If, as an illustration, we were to ask "What is Love?," the right side would answer,

> Love is something one comes to understand as a result of his personal experience with various kinds of love throughout the course of his life;

but the left side would answer,

> Love is a concept one learns about from reading books.

Both answers are correct, given their perspective, but since the real person as an individual exists only on the right side, it is safe to say that most persons would identify with only one of these answers.

The perception of Music is very similar. The right side would answer,

> Music is something one comes to understand as a result of his personal experience in hearing (and playing) music throughout the course of his life;

but the left side would have a different perspective,

Music is something you learn about from reading books and hearing lectures.

But in the case of Music, there is a vital difference. What is known of Music on the left side is not music at all, it is only language and grammar. Music notation is on the left side, but that is not music. "Music" is a verb, "to make music," and this experience is found only in the right hemisphere of the brain. This distinction was very clear even in the most ancient of times. This is precisely what Plato meant in the following dialog:

> SOCRATES. And yet not by knowing either that sound is one or that sound is infinite are we perfect in the art of speech, but knowledge of the number and nature of sounds is what makes a man a grammarian.
> PROTARCHUS. Very true.
> SOCRATES. And the knowledge which makes a man a musician is of the same kind.
> PROTARCHUS. How so?
> SOCRATES. Sound is one in music as well as in grammar?
> PROTARCHUS. Certainly.
> SOCRATES. And there is a higher note and a lower note, and a note of equal pitch—may we affirm so much?
> PROTARCHUS. Yes.
> SOCRATES. But you would not be a real musician if this was all that you knew.[1]

[1] Philebus, 17c.

Although ancient persons did not have the advantage we have of the results of clinical research on the brain, one can suppose that most persons on the basis of their own observations understood that there were those who performed music and others who knew conceptual ideas about music, much as people today. This view of man and his music came to a dramatic crises with the dawn of the new Roman Christian Church. As part of its desire to create a new Roman citizen the Church developed a very narrow perspective in which only Reason was to be the ruler of all thoughts and actions.

The Church closed the old philosophical schools, such as the one in Athens which had been founded by Aristotle.

When it began to formulate a new philosophy of education it could find a place for music only as a branch of mathematics, due to the very strong prejudices the Church had against any form of activities which involved the emotions.[2] We can see their resulting curriculum as it was expressed by the Venerable Bede (672–735 AD):

> We are to be initiated in *grammatica*, then in *dialectia*, afterward in *rhetorica*. Equipped with these arms, we should approach the study of philosophy. Here the order is first the quadrivium, and in this first *arithmetica*, second *musica*, third *geometria*, fourth *astronomia* ...[3]

But the appearance here of Music referred to the "science" of music and not the performance of music. In fact, for a long time during the early years of the Christian Era there was a strong prejudice against those who only performed music and did not know the "science" of music. We can see this reflected in an anonymous treatise, *On Music,* written c. 1100 AD where we find that the musician who performs without "knowing" what he is doing is nothing but a beast!

> From the musician to the singer how immense the distance is;
> The latter's voice, the former's mind will show what music's nature is;
> But he who does, he knows not what, a beast by definition is.[4]

Some three hundred years later we find this paraphrased by the great theorist, Tinctoris (1435–1511):

> There is a big difference between musicians and singers.
> These know, those talk about, what music is.
> And he who doesn't know what he talks about is considered an animal.[5]

Perhaps the origin of this remarkable prejudice was St. Augustine (fourth century), who declared that even the audience members who listen to music without understanding the "science" of music are also beasts!

> AUGUSTINE. And what's more, aren't those who like to listen to [performers] without this science to be compared to beasts?[6]

---

[2] St. Basil wrote that a good Christian should not even laugh, for that too is a form of emotion!

[3] *De elementis philosophiae*, quoted in Nan Cooke Carpenter, *Music in the Medieval and Renaissance Universities* (Norman: University of Oklahoma Press, 1958), 20, fn. 12.

[4] John gives the source as the "Micrologus," but it actually comes from the beginning of Guido's "Regulae rhythmicae."

[5] *Dictionary of Musical Terms*, trans. Carl Parrish (New York: Free Press of Glencoe, 1963), 45.

[6] *On Music*, trans. Robert Taliaferro in *Writings of Saint Augustine* (New York: Fathers of the Church), I, iv.

We are sorry to report that this attitude continues to the present day. We have heard a University of California professor say in public that "a clarinet player is to music, as a typewriter is to literature."

Eventually a more thoughtful discussion emerged and in a treatise by Al-Farabi, *Ihsa al-ulum* (c. 900 AD), we find the first extant description of what we have called in the name of this chapter, "the Great Divide," or the separation of the study of music into two branches, the conceptual and performance.

> As for the Science of Music, it comprises, in short, the investigation into the various kinds of melodies, and what they are composed of, and for what they are composed, and how they are composed, and in what forms it is necessary that they should be in order that the performance of them be made more impressive and effective. And that which is known by this name [music] comprises two sciences. One of them is the science of practical music, and the second is the science of theoretical music.[7]

[7] Quoted in Henry George Farmer, *Al-Farabi's Writings on Music* (New York: Hinrichsen, 1934), 13ff.

These two branches took on the names, *musica speculativa* and *musica practica*. Education authorities said, in effect, "We will teach the first, and leave to you, the performers on the street, the second." Thus, the prejudice we have seen in the medieval music treatises concerning "science" versus "practice" now, with the appearance of the new, modern universities, becomes institutionalized and proposition becomes dogma. Thus, for example, at the university in Oxford, one finds in the fourteenth century new treatises by Walter Odington and Simon Tunstede which are organized on the basis of *musica speculativa* and *musica practica*.[8] Of the six books which constitute Odington's treatise, by the way, the first three are purely mathematical.

[8] Nan Cooke Carpenter, *Music in the Medieval and Renaissance Universities* (Norman: University of Oklahoma Press, 1958), 86.

One can understand, therefore, how important an harbinger it was when the first treatises on *musica practica* began to appear, one of the first of which was the *Practica musicae* by Franchino Gaffurio (1451–1518). In his dedication, he begins by stressing how important music is for its role in moral education.

It is readily apparent, illustrious Prince, how much influence the profession of the art of music had and with what veneration it was held among the ancients. We know this both from the example of the greatest philosophers, who, when they were very old, devoted themselves to this discipline as if in it they put the finishing touch to their studies, and from the practice of the strictest governments, which with the utmost diligence saw to it that whatever was harmful to public morals should be eliminated. Not only did these states not banish the art of music; they cultivated it with the utmost zeal as the mother and nurse of morals.[9]

[9] *The Practica musicae of Franchinus Gafurius*, trans. Irwin Young (Madison: University of Wisconsin Press, 1969), 3.

He adds that music plays an active role in affecting morals and makes the interesting observation that it was thought that Music was the first of the Liberal Arts.

Now music is not, like the other learned disciplines, merely a speculative pursuit: it reaches out into practice, and as was said previously, is connected with morality ... Thus this field of music theory is valuable not only because of the knowledge it gives music itself, but also because its roots extend very far; it aids other disciplines. This has been verified by the testimony of very influential men who have acknowledged that they learned literature from music above all else. Fabius Quintilian declares, on the authority of Timagenes, that this art "is the most ancient of all studies in liberal education."[10]

[10] Ibid., 5ff.

Gaffurio mentions that he is astonished that some musicians can understand things like harmony without having studied theory. But we know today that it is perfectly reasonable that one can know music without knowing *about* music, as is most perfectly demonstrated in the child prodigy[11] and many popular artists who "know nothing" about music and, in some extraordinary cases, do not even read music. Gaffurio's explanation for this "incredible" fact is the correct one: musicians learn the fundamentals of music experientially.

[11] Music is the only field of man's endeavors in which it is possible to have a child prodigy.

Next Gaffurio makes the observation that the theoretical musician cannot really understand the principles of theory unless he hears them in actual music.

There are also those who hold things valueless if they are not put to use. These people feel that the practice of vocal music has contributed most to the development of harmony, not because of the multitude of possibilities inherent in practice, but because it exhibits perfection itself.

> The mechanics of music are found in the movement of sounds producing consonances and melody. It is true that these sounds are assembled in vain by theory and science unless they are expressed in practice. Hence one must become thoroughly conversant with the highness, lowness, and the combinations of these sounds not only through one's mind and reason but also through the habit of listening to and articulating them.[12]

[12] Ibid., 12.

Gaffurio concludes his treatise, "Practica musicae," by once again observing that after having written two treatises on *musica speculativa*, the kind of books he knows the readers are weary of, he felt compelled to add a volume on *musica practica*.

> Now, most gracious reader, I have presented my thoughts on musical practice with perhaps no less talent and industry than you wished for, though your wish was unspoken. For of course, since you must have grown weary reading my books on theory, you needed this just as some sharp foods are needed to revive and refresh the taste. Nor did I think I could escape blame if, when I taught the art of music and unveiled its innermost secrets (if I may use the phrase), I held back in silence from this part as well, which is called *practica* and consists of and is perfected by the actual practice of music itself.[13]

[13] Ibid., 266.

As the Renaissance progressed, with growing sophistication in both composers and performers, there appears to have been some debate relative to the respective importance of theory and performance and one finds more and more comments such as one by Leonardo da Vinci, who said, "Words are of less account than performances."[14]

[14] *The Literary Works of Leonardo da Vinci*, ed. Jean Paul Richter (London: Phaidon, 1970), I, 78.

During the sixteenth century the debate over the relative importance of theory and performance continued. The Italian theorist, Zarlino, almost seems to be pleading for more respect for theory, employing a nice analogy of going to the doctor.

> Accordingly, just as it would be insane to rely on a physician who does not have the knowledge of both practice and theory,

so it would be really foolish and imprudent to rely on the judgment of [a musician] who was solely practical or had done work only in theory.[15]

Hercole Bottrigari also took the view that practice cannot be respected without theory, but his argument looks back to the medieval dogma that the person who "knows" is to be respected more than the person who "does," or, the mind must be judged higher than the hand.

> But I will add also that it does not seem to me to be a great honor to accomplish things and not to be able to give the reasons for them.[16]

During the sixteenth century there were some of the Church theorists who strongly advocated the old prejudices against performance. One, Andreas Ornithoparchus' *Musice active micrologus*, of 1517, gives an almost hostile view of performers and makes the ridiculous claim that speculative understanding of music judges not by the ears, but by "wit and reason," and he is quick to point out that this is hard work "and should not be lightly esteemed."[17]

Next he argues for three categories of musician: performers, poets and critics (those who judge music only by "speculation and reason"). It is the first category which he discusses at length, following the old Church prejudices against musicians who are "merely" performers, craftsmen who engage in performance while understanding nothing they do.

> The first category deals with instruments, such as harpists, organists and all others who prove their skill by instruments. They are removed from the intellectual part of music, being as servants, and using no Reason, void of all speculation and following their sense only. Now though they may seem to do things with learning and skill, yet it is plain that they have no knowledge, because they do not comprehend what they profess.[18]

It is clear that he was aware of the Humanist movement and its broad attack against the old mathematic-based polyphony of the Church. That, no doubt, is why he also sensed that his treatise would not receive universal praise.

[15] Gioseffo Zarlino, *On the Modes*, trans. Vered Cohen (New Haven: Yale University Press, 1983), 106.

[16] Hercole Bottrigari, *Il Desiderio*, trans. Carol MacClintock (American Institute of Musicology, 1962), 36.

[17] Ornithoparchus, *Musicae active mirologus* and Dowland, *Introduction: Containing the Art of Singing* (New York: Dover, 1973), 123.

[18] Ibid., 123.

> I doubt not that there will be some who will snarl at it and backbite it, condemning it before they read it and disgracing it before the understand it. Some would rather seem, than be, musicians, not obeying authors, or precepts or reasons, but whatsoever comes into their hair-brain Cockscomb ... To whom I beg you (gentle Readers) to lend no ear ... for it is in vain to harp before an ass.[19]

The first German writer who completely rejected the old views of the Church was Adrian Coclico, who wrote a treatise, *Compendium Musices* in 1552, another treatise intended as an aid in the training of boy singers. He almost completely rejects the old speculative tradition and his book is filled with comments such as the following which begins his discussion of scales.

> I have wished to train boys in music through but few words and precepts on that account, so that no youth running to the books of musician-mathematicians will waste his life in reading them and never arrive at the goal of singing well.[20]

This is really the first book which advocates the values of performance with almost no importance given to theory. We can understand his perspective when he mentions his own experience, giving us a particularly valuable and interesting account of his own teacher, the great French-Flemish composer, Josquin des Prez (d. 1521):

> In Belgian cities, where prizes are given to singers and, because of the prizes to be gained, no procedure or labor is undertaken unless it pertains to the goal of singing well, no music is written down or prescribed by precept.
> My teacher, Josquin des Prez, never rehearsed or wrote out any musical procedures, yet in a short time made perfect musicians, since he did not hold his students back in long and frivolous precepts, but taught precepts in a few words at the same time as singing through exercise and practice.[21]

Rather than theoretical background, Coclico looked for enthusiasm, zeal and love of music in a prospective student.

> First, adolescents or better, boys ... should bring to their teacher a great zeal and desire for learning music, together

---

[19] Ibid., 211.

[20] Adrian Coclico, *Musical Compendium*, trans. Albert Seay (Colorado Springs: Colorado College Music Press, 1973), 10. Seay adds, "Music by 1550 was less and less of a liberal art and more and more a fine art, while theory had begun to lose most of its speculative character in favor of the purely practical."

[21] Ibid., 16.

with their natural enthusiasm, so that they may listen as eagerly and attentively as possible to whoever teaches and guides … He, however, who is possessed by a certain single-minded zeal for learning …, this person I hold myself committed that he will be an excellent musician. In a Greek proverb it is beautifully stated: Love teaches music.[22]

[22] Ibid., 5ff.

This natural enthusiasm he felt was particularly necessary in the case of the student who desired to compose.

> The student should be led to composing by a great desire, and by a certain natural impulse he will be driven to composition, so that he will not taste food nor drink until his piece is finished, for, since this natural impulse so drives him, he accomplishes more in one hour than others in a whole month. Composers to whom these unusual motivations are absent are useless.[23]

[23] Ibid.

The late sixteenth century was a remarkable highpoint in early music. The rich, emotionally expressive music of Monteverdi, de Rore, Gesualdo and Gabrieli was widely recognized due to the new publishing houses in Venice. Michael Praetorius thought this music was so special that he concluded in 1619 that he believed no further progress in the field of composition was possible.[24] The compositions of these composers played a fundamental role as harbingers of a strong fascination with the expression of emotions in music. And that, contrary to many older music history texts, is the proper definition of music of the Baroque, 1600–1750.

[24] *Syntagma musicum*, III. The fact that he was twenty years into the Baroque Period and had noticed no changes says something for the chalk line we draw on blackboards to indicate the beginning of the Baroque.

The quality of the late sixteenth century compositions clearly influenced composers to raise their work to higher levels of art and it would appear that performance itself was being taken more seriously. We can see this in a letter of 1607, Monteverdi explains that he is sending the music to a singer in advance,

> so that he can rehearse it and get a firm grasp of the melody together with the other gentlemen singers, because it is very difficult for a singer to perform a part which he has not first practiced, and greatly damaging to the composition itself, as it is not completely understood on being sung for the first time.[25]

[25] Letter to Annibale Iberti (July 28, 1607), quoted in *The Letters of Claudio Monteverdi*, trans. Denis Stevens (Cambridge: Cambridge University Press, 1980), 51.

A letter of 1620 gives some indication of what he meant by sufficient rehearsal.

> Now consider, Your Lordship: what do you think can be done when more than four hundred lines, which have to be set to music are still lacking? I can envisage no other result than bad singing of the poetry, bad playing of the instruments, and bad musical ensemble. These are not things to be done hastily, as it were; and you know from *Arianna* that after it was finished and learned by heart, [then!] five months of strenuous rehearsal took place.[26]

For the celebrations of the wedding of Austria's Ferdinand III (1637–1657) and Maria Anna, daughter to Philip III of Spain, in January 1667, even a horse ballet was given for which rehearsals began six months earlier!

These new higher standards in performance developed into a standard which is still true today. We see this in John Playford's observation "Art admitteth no Mediocrity."[27] Nicolas Boileau, in his *L'Art Poëtique* of 1674, addresses a number of ethical concerns regarding the art of poetry. First he contends that in art, unlike science or the trades, there is no second place, no "mean betwixt the best and worst," because no reader is indifferent. If the young poet cannot bear this burden, Boileau advises he be a stone mason, "tis a useful art."[28] And so it is today in music performance, be it student or professional; there is no middle ground, it is either good or it is bad. No audience member was ever heard to say, "It was almost a good concert!"

At the same time a new version of "The Great Divide" appeared, due in large part to the intellectual freedom initiated by the "Enlightenment Period." The "rationalistic" philosophy led by Descartes promised the concept of the "Laws of Nature," which explain and define rules for everything, even the arts.[29] It was this spirit which led in Paris to the founding of the *Académie Françasie*, the Royal Academy of Painting and Sculpture, the Academy of Dance, the Academy of Science, the Academy of Music, the Academy of Architecture, and more. And it was from this rationalistic perspective that Immanuel Kant ranked music in a low position among the arts

[26] Letter to Alessandro Striggio (January 9, 1620), quoted in Ibid., 160.

[27] John Playford, *An Introduction to the Skill of Music* [1674] (Ridgewood: Gregg Press, 1966), 41. Playford (1623–1686) was a publisher and amateur composer and theorist.

[28] Boileau, *The Art of Poetry*, quoted in Albert Cook, *The Art of Poetry* (Boston: Ginn, 1892), 210. The English translation is by Dryden, based on an earlier effort made in 1680 by William Soame.

[29] A good summary can be found in Walter Jackson Bate, *Prefaces to Criticism* (Garden City: Doubleday, 1959), pp. 14ff. Much material on the French philosophers can be found in David Whitwell, *Aesthetics of Baroque Music in France*, ed. Craig Dabelstein (Austin: Whitwell Books, 2012).

because of its overwhelming sensuous appeal. In his view, music merely "plays with sensations."[30]

In trying to force everything into their world of Reason, the philosophers of the Rationalistic school created much nonsense, as for example when Descartes claimed that a drum covered with sheep skin will not emit a sound if a drum covered with wolf skin is played at the same time.[31] These kinds of statements, and many more, resulted in Voltaire finally saying, "few people still read Descartes, whose works have in fact become totally useless."[32] We believe Barzun goes right to the heart:

> Faith in this type of reason is a creed, often passionate, called Rationalism. It differs from the workaday use of our wits by its claim that analytical reasoning is the sole avenue to truth ... That is the great difficulty. The more science proves its worth, the harder it is for "nature" or "the heart" to feel free. Reason should guide—all moralists agree—but, as others point out, mind is not separate from heart. The astute Chinese have a character for heart-and-mind. They perceived that the urge to reason is itself a drive from the heart, which explains why rationalists are often fanatics.[33]

And the Frenchman, Blaise Pascal (1623–1662) adds,

> The heart has its reason, which reason does not know. We feel it in a thousand things.[34]

Needless to say, the newly founded universities at Oxford, Paris and Bologna were quick to grasp the Rationalistic philosophies of music. The philosopher, Jean Bodin, who studied in Paris, found formal education more interested in grammar than ideas.

> Clearly this grammatical pest begins to infest the approaches to all disciplines, so that instead of philosophers, orators, mathematicians, and theologians, we are forced to endure petty grammarians from the schools.[35]

The one who argued the most strongly against the idea that grammar or mathematical concepts could describe music was the German composer and critic, Johann Mattheson.

---

[30] Ernst Behler, *Immanuel Kant Philosophical Writings: The Critique of the Faculty of Judgment*, trans. J. D. Meredith (New York: The Continuum Publishing Company, 1986), Section 46. Fine Arts as the Art of Genius.

[31] Stuart Isacoff, *Temperament* (New York: Random House, 2001), 174.

[32] Ibid., 176.

[33] Jacques Barzun, *From Dawn to Decadence* (New York: HarperCollins, 2000), 202.

[34] Blaise Pascal, *Pensees* (New York: Modern Library, 1941), III, 277.

[35] Jean Bodin, *Method for the Easy Comprehension of History*, trans. Beatrice Reynolds (New York: Columbia University Press, 1945), 8. Boden (1530–1596) was educated in Paris and served as a counselor of Henry IV.

Mathematics, he writes, can measure the elements of music, but not how these elements are used. It is the latter, not the former, which concern feelings in music.

> A perfect understanding of the human emotions, which certainly are not to be measured by the mathematical yardstick, is of much greater importance to melody and its composition than the understanding of tones ... This is certain: it is not so much good *proportion*, but rather the apt *usage* of the intervals and keys, which establishes the beautiful, moving and natural quality in melody and harmony. Sounds, in themselves, are neither good nor bad; but they become good and bad according to the way in which they are used. No measuring or calculating art teaches this.[36]

[36] Johann Mattheson, *Der vollkommene Capellmeister* (1739), trans. Ernest Harriss (Ann Arbor: UMI Research Press, 1981), Foreword, VI.

How then does one describe the role mathematics plays in music, together with its other elements? Mattheson offers following metaphor:

> The human mind is the paper. Mathematics is the pen. Sounds are the ink; but Nature must be the writer. Why have a silver trumpet if a competent trumpeter is not available?

Mattheson points out that sculptors know and can measure the proportions of the human body, but "heart and soul ... and beauty is not on this account to be found in such mathematical measuring; but only in that force which God put in Nature." Similarly, in painting, when "mathematics ceases entirely, true beauty really first begins." And so with music,

> A composer can succeed quite well without special mathematical skills. Many who virtually climbed to the pinnacle of music can hardly name or interpret all parts of mathematics; not to mention anything more.... However, the best mathematician, as such, if he were to want to compose something, could not possibly achieve this with mere logic. Let it be said once in fact for all: Good mathematical proportions cannot constitute everything: this is an old, stubborn misconception.

The point, he says, is this: "music draws its water from the spring of Nature; and not from the puddles of arithmetic." The composer expresses something understood from Nature.

Only then can this be mathematically expressed, but not the other way around. When Mattheson speaks here of Nature, he is also thinking of God.

> Mathematics is a human skill; nature, however, is a divine force ... Now the goal of music is to praise God in the highest, with word and deed, through singing and playing. All other arts besides theology and its daughter, music, are only mute priests. They do not move hearts and minds nearly so strongly, nor in so many ways ... Music is *above*, not in *opposition* to mathematics.

In another place Mattheson becomes rather critical of the theoretical aspect of music because of the impression it renders to the ordinary person. His argument is that emphasis of the theory side of music gives the impression to the layman that they know nothing about music if they have not had this training. Mattheson knew by observation what we have learned today through clinical brain research. The fact is *all* men are born with enough genetic knowledge to understand this language of music. Of the conceptual music teacher Mattheson concludes,

> For they are persuaded that this beautiful and perfect creation, which a beneficent God has given us men for our pleasure, and likewise as a model of the eternal, harmonious Splendor, depends solely upon deep learning and laborious knowledge. To prove this, they dispense their philosophical rules and scholarly vagaries, not only with great authority, but likewise with such obscurity that one has a rightful aversion for the stuff, and would rather remain in permanent ignorance than to go through such *horrenda*.[37]

Mattheson, having been a performer, knew that rational concepts cannot well describe the experience of music. Thus he advises the pursuit of performance, after the necessary foundation, as a means of finding a "healthy idea of music, purified of all unnecessary school-dust."

We know we are in a new era with the regard to the recognition of performance when François Couperin contended,

> Just as there is a difference between grammar and Eloquence, so there is an infinitely greater one between notated music and the art of fine playing.[38]

[37] Johann Mattheson, *Das Neu-Eröffnete Orchestre* (Hamburg, 1713), 2ff. Mattheson also writes at length in opposition to the old dogma that mathematics is the basis of music in his book, *Das Forschende Orchestre* of 1721.

[38] François Couperin, *L'Art de toucher* (Paris, 1717, reprinted Wiesbaden: Breitkopf & Härtel, 1933), Preface.

Roger North (1651–1734) of England, at this time also refers to the "grammar" of music and suggests that he found a distinction between theoretical studies and what he calls the "real knowledge" necessary to being a performer.

> The teaching of music and languages are very different, although the masters of the former [follow] the methods used by them of the other; that is, a sort of grammar to be [learned] by heart, whether it be or be not understood. The difference lies in this, that languages are mere memory, and come from the arbitrary use of nations, and may be as well one way or another; and this use grammarians endeavor to reduce to rule, which must be learnt and remembered. But music is taken from nature itself, and depends on body in a physical sense, even as the mathematical sciences do, and takes place finally in our imagination and fancy; and therefore should be taught by explaining it to the understanding as well as by giving the rules to which the practice of it is reduced. And for this reason it is that in the musical science the rules are very few, and those but introductory as it were to show what the subject matter is, that the learner might not have the trouble of being an original inventor of the whole science ... And yet the real knowledge that belongs to music is dilated enough, and it is through that, that a man must learn the skill of a musician, whether he be showed it, or gathers it of himself by observation, as generally is done ... As for children, I think easier ways might be found than the soured and mysterious Gamut, which they must rehearse *antrorsum & retrorsum*, without the least proffer to them of an explanation of it.[39]

[39] Quoted in John Wilson, *Roger North on Music* (London: Novello, 1959), 59.

Descartes observed that the performer, since his art is practiced live before an audience, automatically has a kind of check and balance in his decisions which the theorist escapes.

> For the consequences of the [practical study] will soon punish the man if he judges wrongly, whereas the [speculative study] has no practical consequences and no importance for the scholar except that perhaps the further they are from common sense the more pride he will take in them, since he will have had to use so much more skill and ingenuity in trying to render them plausible.[40]

[40] *Discourse on the Method* (1637), I, 9ff.

Voltaire ridicules the old scholastic emphasis on "conceptual music" in his fictional debate among the inmates of the hospital *Quinze Vingt*.

A deaf man reading this short history, acknowledged that these blind people were quite wrong in pretending to judge of colors; but he continued firmly of the opinion that deaf people were the only proper judges of music.[41]

Most of the Baroque musicians clearly understood how different their music was from the old mathematics-based Renaissance Church polyphony. In one of Johann Heinichen's (1683–1729) most valuable passages, one which demonstrates brilliant deductions regarding the physiology of music aesthetics, he addresses the fundamental distinction between Baroque music and earlier music. The old music, he says, was for the eye (Reason and conceptual understanding), but modern music is for the ear.

> The old musicians side more with Reason, but the new with the Ear; and since both parties do not agree on the first fundamental, it is evident that the conclusions and consequences made from two contrary fundamental principles should breed just as many controversies of inferior rank and thousands of diametrically opposed hypotheses. Musicians of the past, we know, chose two judges in music: Reason and the Ear. The choice would be correct since both are indispensable to music; yet, because of the use of these two concomitants, the present cannot reconcile itself with the past, and in this the past is blamed for two errors. First, it wrongly classed the two judges and placed the Ear, the sovereign of music, below the rank of Reason or would divide its commanding authority with the latter. Whereupon the blameless Ear must immediately cede half of its monarchical domain. In addition, unfortunately, the composers of the past poorly explained the word ratio. In those innocent times (in which one knew nothing of present day good taste and brilliance in music, and every simple harmony seemed beautiful), they thought Reason could be put to no better use than the creation of supposedly learned and speculative artificialities of note writing. Therefore, they began on the one hand to measure out theoretically innocent notes according to mathematical scales and with the help of the proportioned yardstick, and on the other hand, to place these notes in musical practice on the staves (almost as if they were on a rack) and to pull and stretch them (or in the language of counterpoint, to augment them), to turn them upside down, to repeat and to change their positions, until finally from the latter resulted a practice with an overwhelming

[41] "The Ignorant Philosopher," in *The Works of Voltaire* (New York: St. Hubert Guild, 1901), XXXV, 293.

number of unnecessary instances of contrapuntal eye-music and from the former resulted a theory with amassed metaphysical contemplations of emotion and reason. Thus, one no longer had cause to ask if music sounded well or pleased the listener, but rather if it looked good on paper. In this way, the Visual perceptibly gained the most in music and used the authority of the imprudent Reason only to cover its own lust for power. Consequently, the suppressed Ear was tyrannized so long that finally it hid behind table and chairs to await from the distance the condescending, merciful glance of its *usurpatores regni* (*ratio & visus*). This grave injustice to the musical sovereign, the Ear, has been reprehended more by present-day musicians than by those of the past. They have begun vigorously to understand the many absurd and preposterous principles of the past and to form completely new ideas about the noble art of music unlike those of the learned ignoramuses. Above all, they return to the oppressed Ear the sovereignty of its realm; they displace Reason from its judicial duties and give it [Reason] to the Ear, not as Domino or co-regent, but as an intelligent minister and counselor with the absolute mandate to warn its master (the occasionally deceived Ear, if indeed "deceived" can be spoken of) of every false step; but otherwise, Reason differs in opinion, it must serve the Ear with the complete obedience and employ all of its skill, not for the visual appearance on paper, but to give the Ear the satisfaction of an absolute ruler.[42]

Voltaire would agree with all of this for, as he observes,

Is it not an amusing thing, that our eyes always deceive us, even when we see very well, and that on the contrary our ears do not?[43]

We must add one more comment by Heinichen relative to our discussion:

It is impossible to find the tenderness of the soul of music with mere numeric changes of dead notes.[44]

With the second half of the eighteenth century, the Classical Period, we encounter yet another Great Divide. We might call this new philosophy, Formalism, and it refers to a series of standard expectations with regard to form. The Sonata Form, for example, is rather rigidly expected to have three

[42] Johann David Heinichen, *General-Bass Treatise* [1711], quoted in George Buelow, *Thorough-Bass Accompaniment according to Johann David Heinichen* (Ann Arbor: UMI Research Press, 1986), 278.

[43] *Philosophical Dictionary*, "Prejudice".

[44] Johann David Heinichen, *General Bass Treatise*, 330.

large sections: the Exposition, Development and Recapitulation sections. The Exposition section must have four sections: the First Theme, an Episode which modulates, the Second Theme at the dominant harmony and a Closing Section. This is traditionally taught in a "Form and Analysis" course in which this form is spread across a blackboard. This is a perfect example of useless information, useless because the student will never again use this information, be he player, composer or conductor. And this is because in performance one never stands at the side of a Sonata Form, as if it were the side of a barn. The information with respect to form would only be of use if it were instead a system which taught one to, in effect, stand at the beginning of the form and from that perspective see it through to the end. As it is, the student will only use this information again if he should be assigned to teach a "Form and Analysis" course.

How did the composers of the Classical Period deal with such strict Formalism? Most composers, having no desire to confuse the listener, probably followed the fashion and consequently forced their ideas into the form. But Josef Haydn once said,

> Art is free ... and I consider myself as competent as anyone to make up rules. Artificial standards have no value.[45]

And Mozart, in his Vienna Period, often seemed so carried away with the emotions of the music he was writing that he would write as he felt with the result of often bending the barriers of the form out of balance. The famous early nineteenth century critic, E. T. A. Hoffmann, in thinking of Mozart's early and late operas makes an appropriate observation:

> Instinct matures into awareness of Truths, and from this awareness emerge distinctive ideas, the personal expression of these Truths which no longer looks back to received notions or to defined forms that find their justification merely in what temporary artistic convention seems to demand.[46]

Perhaps the most useful advice is found in a comment by Samuel Johnson, the English writer (1709–1784):

[45] Quoted in *Allgemeine musikalische Zeitung* (Leipzig, 1798–1848), xo. 23 August 1809, col. 740.

[46] "Further Observations on Spontini's Opera *Olimpia*," in *E. T. A. Hoffmann's Musical Writings* (Cambridge University Press, 1989), 443.

> It ought to be the first Endeavour of a writer to distinguish Nature from custom; or that which is established because it is right, from that which is right because it is established.[47]

[47] Walter Jackson Bate, *Prefaces to Criticism* (Garden City: Doubleday, 1959), 19.

I make a point of this because I have found many musicians today who perform music of the Classical Period in a very cold and rigid manner, as if their job is to reproduce exactly what is on paper and nothing more. This is nothing more than poor musicianship and the reader may be surprised to find there were poor musicians in the Classical Period as well. We find this very complaint in the famous book on the art of flute playing by Johann Quantz published in 1752.

> The Delivery is poor when everything is sung without warmth or played at the same level without alternation of Piano and Forte ... one contradicts the Passions that should be expressed, or executes everything in general without sensitivity, without Passion, without being moved one's self, so the impression is given that the musician is singing or playing as an agent for someone else.[48]

[48] Johann Quantz, *Versuch einer Anweisung die Flöte traversiere zu Spielen.* [1752], 11: 21.

Unfortunately, that is the kind of performance one gets if the goal is to play only what the eye sees on the page. Our goal, many would say, is to rehearse what we see on the page until it is perfect, then we can present it to the public. But Bruce Haynes in discussing this very problem points out,

> The problem is that if you spend hours working on playing in tune and together, you can't expect an inspired concert—you can expect a concert that is in tune and together.[49]

[49] Bruce Haynes, *The End of Early Music* (New York: The Oxford University Press, 2007), 62

Part II

The Reformation of American Music Education

THE PREVIOUS TWO HUNDRED PAGES have presented the reader with the core thinking of great thinkers, educators and musicians of the past two millennia about music education. The fundamental values for the individual child have been stated and reaffirmed consistently during that long period of time. During the middle of the twentieth century American music educators elected to abandon these long proven values in order to create a new philosophy of music education which centered on talking about music instead of making music. How would those musicians and teachers of the past view the present results? Here are my views.

1. Music education, like every other kind of education, should pass on to the next generation the highest of civilization's accomplishments. Students in American music education are being exposed to the lowest quality of music.

2. The goal of music education should be to educate the child, not entertain him. The real child, in so far as he is a unique individual, is found in the right hemisphere of his brain. Everything relevant to the left hemisphere is passed on information from other people, and is past tense as well. In American music education specific techniques and goals for educating the right hemisphere of the child are virtually non-existent.

3. Because of the enormous potential which music has for the education of the right hemisphere, the real child, it follows that all children deserve to experience making music. There is no effort in the United States to do this.

4. Music education which does not have at its core actual performance is a contradiction in terms. American music education is a contradiction in terms.

We urgently need a reformation in American music education, a return to the values affirmed by two millennia of civilization's greatest thinkers and musicians on the subject of music education. The following pages are organized in two broad parts. Part One is a detailed discussion of the fundamental curricular obligations necessary for a reformation in music education. Part Two offers a discussion of specific benefits to the individual child if there were such a reformation in music education following the curricular obligations given in the first part. Almost all of these specific benefits to the individual child are missing today. That alone is perhaps the strongest argument for the needed reformation.

Professional Prerequisites for the Reformation of American Music Education

The Musical Excellence of the Teacher

THE WORD "MUSIC" IS A VERB, meaning "to make music." It is a word referring to a live present tense activity. A record, therefore, is not music, it is *recorded* music. Not being a noun, "music" should not be used to identify music notation, etude books and solo materials, teaching methods and for the individual parts of a composition or the composition itself. It follows that if the subject is teaching *music*, then the pedagogy must be found in live performance. The first prerequisite for a music education teacher, therefore, is his experience and ability as a performer of music. This definition is necessarily narrow because the subject of music education is located in the right hemisphere of teacher and student, not in the various forms of data mentioned above, all of which are intended for the wrong hemisphere of the brain. Those materials are also past tense, whereas the teacher and student are in the present tense. This is only one reason why conductors, for example, should memorize their scores. How can the conductor expect to function with one foot in the present tense and one foot in the past tense?

Let me give a personal example. In my first university teaching position, I had the kind of schedule one often finds in small colleges. I was assigned to perform with the faculty quintet and the university orchestra, teach all low brass lessons, all percussion lessons, teach a course in music education, a course in sight-singing—and be the sole person expected to produce the shows, arrange the music and rehearse a marching band. Now with regard to the private lessons in percussion, I had had music education courses in college devoted to teaching percussion, I had done some part-time teaching of young percussion students in a nearby town when I was in college and I had performed more than a thousand concerts with the USAF Band and Orchestra in Washington, D.C., where I daily observed and heard fine percussionists. But all that background really meant very little in view of the fact that I was not a percussionist myself; I lacked the personal experiential background for teaching these instruments. I felt like an imposter and the students could not be fooled. I could have taught them endless background information on historical percussion instruments and percussion technique and I could have selected interesting materials to teach from, but again all that is left hemisphere and has no relevance to what the students needed—someone who could teach in the present tense from the experiential perspective found only in the right hemisphere.

There is a spiritual aspect of music and of music teaching. Recertification should address this in order to keep the music teacher centered. Therefore, perhaps a music teacher should be expected to perform in a public recital once a year. The issue is a matter of insuring that the teacher himself remains musically in the present tense. This kind of recertification cannot be substituted by attending workshops and carrying home the latest hand-outs of the commercial publishing business.

> Method, school mannerisms, advance improvement indeed, but narrowly, one-sidedly. Ah, teachers! how ye sin against yourselves!
> Robert Schumann[50]

[50] *Neue Zeitschrift für Musik*, 1834, "Criticisms of the Davidbündler."

The second of concern is the quality of person we are accepting into the music education program. One very significant problem is that we have a vicious circle by which activity driven students become activity driven teachers. I ran into this in my first semester of teaching in Los Angeles. In a beginning conducting class I was stressing some basic concern with a student and I said, "You are going to have to be able to do this when you get out and become the conductor of a high school band." The young man answered, "I don't want to be a conductor, I want to be a band director!" By this he meant the world of marching (which is often year long in California), contests and trophies. True music education will never cross his mind. He will model what he has experienced and reproduce that model. In this regard I recall I used to receive lists of seniors, together with their intended majors, from some of the large high school band programs in Southern California. Often I would find on the entire list not a single student who intended to major in music. On the other hand in the case of my high school band, in a small town in Oklahoma, where we performed works like an arrangement of the entire Brahms *Academic Festival Overture* and original works commissioned by our conductor, we devoted as little time and effort to marching as possible. Fifteen seniors in that band became music majors. The conductor plays a significant role in determining the model, and the model has a strong influence in determining the quality of the next generation of music teachers. If the band teacher presents as his model the marching band, then he presents a model which has nothing to do with music education. It is the model of an activity which employs music for entertainment purposes.

In this regard I have found over the years that some university music education departments do not care what kind of job their graduates get and they certainly feel no moral or ethical responsibilities to develop attitudes which would raise the profession. They do not tell the would-be teachers that they will be working in an environment where they will be considered teachers of a second class activity. They do not tell them about the increasing mountain of paperwork demanded by government. They do not explain that the administrator will demand participation in some activity which has no penalty for poor performance nor any incentive for excellence. We must find a way to break this vicious circle of poor students becoming poor teachers.

The third area of real concern has to do with the musical preparation of the new teachers. We have a problem here and I think the time has come when we need to be honest and face it for the sake of future children. The fact is that the most gifted performers among our music majors do not aspire to be music educators. Our music major has invested many hours, even years, in working to improve his performance on his instrument. As he nears graduation from college, however, he sees few performance jobs and the possibility that he is unlikely to have a career in performance. He is aware that he could be a public school music teacher and earn a living, but why is it so difficult to make up his mind to follow this alternative?

All children are much aware of self. The music major has found a way to express himself, through his performance. This, together with all the investment in study, is why performance is such a personal thing to him. I believe the basic obstacle for the music major is that electing to be a teacher means giving up his identity as a performer, something which has been a very meaningful part of his life. But it need not be so. I can recall a time when the musical reputation of a music educator was based solely on the demonstrated musicality of the students of his or her choirs and ensembles in the performance of the highest aesthetic quality. When music teaching is centered in performance, the music educator also feels centered in performance. And it is in the lessons of performance the he fulfills his most effective role as a music educator. As the Baroque singing teacher, Tosi, remarked,

> Let the student hear as much as he can ... because, from the attention in hearing [concerts], one reaps more advantage than from any instruction whatsoever.[51]

[51] P. F. Tosi, *Observations on the Florid Song* (London: Wilcox, 1743), VI, xiiiff.

Unfortunately, in the United States this is no longer true. A major turning point in the middle of the twentieth century resulted in the change of the nature of music education from *playing* music to talking *about* music. They call it "conceptual" teaching. All children love music, but they are not fooled by this distinction. And so they go home and teach themselves to play, sing and compose; literally hundreds of thousands of students at this very moment studying music with absolutely no supervision by professional music educators.

In my opinion, there are two more fundamental problems in American music education. First, anyone who has had the opportunity to be around children after the age of five or so knows that children think they are older than they are. We, on the other hand, tend to treat them as if they were younger than they are. Perhaps, given appropriate repertoire, they are capable of much higher understanding, musicianship and level of performance than we imagine. My view is perhaps influenced by the fact that I have heard, in person, a grade school orchestra perform in public the final movement of the Tchaikovsky *Fourth Symphony*—from memory. The conductor of such a performance could not help but feel himself to be a performer as well.

The second fundamental problem with public school music, in my opinion, is the extremely low quality of the repertoire. Can our music major imagine himself as participating in authentic performance when conducting music of so little value? It is a great mistake to blame the publishers, for they are in the business of making money by selling music. If all the schools in the United States decided to use only music for bass recorders, that is what the music publisher would turn out and everything else would disappear overnight.[52]

Europe is quite a different story. The traditions of Orff, Kodaly and Dalacroze are based on quality music, often arrangements of works by great composers. It follows that performance is the point and every one of these teachers I have met in Europe introduce themselves as musicians, not music educators. It is the repertoire which makes all the difference whether one's self identity is *performing* with a group of students or merely as a teacher supervising a student activity.

Apart from my belief that a music educator should feel he is also a performer, regardless of the level, I would like to

[52] As an antidote we recommend the site for distinguished original band repertoire, Maxime's Music (http://maximesmusic.com).

recommend that the selection of school repertoire be judged not on its potential for entertaining the students, but on its value in educating the right hemisphere of the child. The hope that the student has fun draws one into the world of pop music which has no important educational value at all. One of the most ancient truths of performance is that you cannot make a bad piece of music sound good.

I am sorry to say I do not believe you can find among the United States music publishers the kind of music I would recommend for young children. I am thinking, as an illustration, of perhaps creating a piece of music which consists of the first theme of the first movement of Schubert's 9th Symphony. You could simplify it, but not re-harmonize it. I would give it a name something like "Noble Feeling." The inherent quality of Schubert's melody would not be lost. The great spiritual quality of this music would be felt by the music educator as well; he, too, would be filled with the spiritual rewards of performance.[53] It is the music which matters and that is why Schubert matters.

> In every child there lies a wondrous depth.
>
> .....
>
> No children can be brought to healthy manhood on candy and pastry. Spiritual like bodily nourishment must be simple and solid. The masters have provided it; cleave to them.
>
> *Robert Schumann, Maxims for Young Musicians*

---

[53] Shortly after this paragraph was written I received the following note from an old friend, Willis Traphagan, an emeritus professor from the University of Massachusetts/Lowell.

> We started our five year old grandson with piano lessons a few months ago—his teacher, who certainly understands what you are talking about, uses a series of materials which address this issue to some degree, to wit: Our grandson is now working on two very much simplified excerpts from Beethoven. One is a theme from the 6th Symphony and the other a very simple version of the "Ode to Joy" from the 9th Symphony. Both preserve the feeling of the music and I am delighted to see the boy absorbing those feelings and attempting to express them in his playing. He is not an unusual child, nor is he any sort of a prodigy. I think this anecdote illustrates your point rather strongly.

Music Learning must be through Performance

> One learns music by playing.[54]
> *Erasmus*

> Practice make men better informed than mere knowledge.[55]
> *Martin Luther*

THESE TWO ABOVE QUOTATIONS are very much in line with the real definition of music, that it is a verb meaning to make music. But owing to the "Enlightenment" music theorists during the Baroque became more active and began to formulate more rules. With his usual very pointed style, Voltaire said, No, "the man who judges by rule, judges wrong."[56] The German composer, Johann Heinichen, agreed with Voltaire and others in insisting that music is for the ear, not for the eyes to read treatises on mathematics or grammar.

What has the visual to do with music? Could anything more absurd be stated? The art of painting is for the eye, music, however, for the ear. Similarly, food is for the sense of taste and flowers for the sense of smell. Would it not be ridiculous to say the dinner was especially good because it smelled good, even though it was disagreeable to the taste and stomach? It is just as absurd if one should say along with pedants: this is outstanding music because it looks so fine (I mean pedantic) on paper, even though it does not please the ear, for which music is solely made ... As we must now admit unanimously that our *Finis musices* is to stir the affections and to delight the ear, the true *Objectum musices*, it follows that we must establish all our musical rules according to the Ear.[57]

The most famous early critic of the nineteenth century, E. T. A. Hoffmann, agrees and makes the point that the layman is certainly not going to be confused about music being for his ear [and here Hoffmann provides a little satire on what listening to the musical grammar would be like] and in performance even the highly trained musician will also be caught up in the music and will forget about all those rules he studied. The subject is Mozart's greatest opera.

[54] "Adages," in *The Collected Works of Erasmus* (Toronto: University of Toronto Press, 1992), XXXII, 25.

[55] In a conversation of 1538 reported by Anthony Lauterbach, in *Luther's Works* (St. Louis: Concordia, 1961), LIV, 274.

[56] *The Works of Voltaire* (New York: St. Hubert Guild, 1901), XXI, 250, 256.

[57] Johann David Heinichen, *General-Bass Treatise* [1711], quoted in George Buelow, *Thorough-Bass Accompaniment according to Johann David Heinichen* (Ann Arbor: UMI Research Press, 1986), 278. Heinichen (1683–1729) was a prolific composer in Dresden, but is known today only because of this important treatise which deals on many aspects of performance practice.

The layman does not recognize the technical structure, which is not what matters anyway, but is powerfully swept along by the dramatic momentum. In *Don Giovanni* the statue of the Commendatore intones its terrible "Yes!" on the tonic E, but the composer then takes this E as the third above C and thus modulates into C major, the key taken up by Leporello. Now no musical layman will understand the technical structure of this transition, but he will tremble inwardly with Leporello; and the musician who has attained the highest level of knowledge is equally unlikely, at the moment of greatest tension, to think of the structure, since for him the scaffolding disappeared long ago, and so his response coincides with that of the layman.[58]

[58] *E. T. A. Hoffmann's Musical Writings* (Cambridge: Cambridge University Press, 1989), 153.

The juxtaposition of the layman and the highly trained musician here reminds us of one of the most powerful aspects of music. The performance on the stage is sent out to the audience in the form of an epitome of an emotion, or what Wagner called the *melos*. This basic form of the emotion, let us say "sadness," is then sifted individually through each listener's personal experience with sadness in his right hemisphere memory, resulting in a personal understanding of this emotion in the music, which will be different from the person sitting next to him. Thus music is understood at once on both a general and an individual level. And it is here that the individual artist, or the conductor, has such power over the emotions of the audience. The French Baroque philosopher, Pontus de Tyard, demonstrates this power nicely in an account of a performance he heard after a banquet in Milan, when,

> a lute player ravished the guests utterly out of themselves by his divinely languorous playing; and then, by a more vigorous tune, restored to them the souls which he had before stolen.[59]

[59] Quoted in Frances Yates, *The French Academies of the Sixteenth Century* (London: University of London, 1947; Nendeln: Kraus Reprint, 1968), 41.

Concepts cannot describe Music

The idea of beauty is given in our feeling, and cannot be construed for conceptualization.[60]
Jean Paul Richter

[60] Eduard Berend, *Jean Pauls Sämtliche Werke* (Weimar, 1927–1944), I: 16, 411.

> While composing music is not the time to recall the rules which might hold our genius in bondage.[61]
> *Jean-Philippe Rameau*

> Art comes from a *natural* vivacity of the pen and is not obtained from the study of books.[62]
> *Pietro Aretino*

As ARISTOTLE FIRST POINTED OUT, words are only representatives of the real thing and it is for this reason that he made a careful explanation demonstrating that knowledge of music is not the same thing as music itself.[63]

Pedro Calder, one of the great poets of the Spanish Baroque, points out this is true even in an art work based on words.

> That the poet's words but shadow
> What the poet had intended.[64]

The same is true, of course, in music; what we see in the notation on paper is only a representative of something else. And as Calder, in his *Life is a Dream* (III, i), reminds us, only the left hemisphere of the brain can lie.

> Tell the eyes
> In their music to keep better
> Concert with the voice, because
> Any instrument whatever
> Would be out of tune that sought
> To combine and blend together
> The true feelings of the heart.
> With the false words speech expresses.

And in painting as well, verbal or written concepts are very inadequate in revealing the form of Truth represented by the artist's canvas. There is a famous story told by Wilhelm Wackenroder of a young Italian painter who was dissatisfied with his attempts to copy the paintings of Raphael. The young artist wrote to Raphael begging to reveal his secrets. Raphael answered that the young artist should find someone else's works to copy, as he could not explain his own technique.[65]

---

[61] Rameau, *Le Nouveau Systeme de musique theorique* [1726], quoted in Morgenstern, *Composers on Music* (New York: Pantheon, 1956), 41.

[62] Aretino, Letter to Doni, in Claude V. Palisca, *Humanism in Italian Renaissance Musical Thought* (New Haven: Yale University Press, 1985), 297ff.

[63] *Categories*, VIII.

[64] *Belshazzar's Feast*, at the ending.

[65] *Wilhelm Heinrich Wackenroder's "Confessions" and "Fantasies,"* ed. Mary Hurst Schubert (University Park, PA and London, 1971), 90ff.

We will discuss the failure of conceptual language to represent music further below in the discussion of the grammar of music. First, however, we should like to repeat the comments by Matheson, a great seventeenth century German critic, on the impossibility for concepts or abstract mathematics to reflect much about music.

He first quotes Andreas Papius:

> The mere *cognition of the ratio* of a step, a half step, a comma, the consonances, etc., will bring the name virtuoso or artistic prince to no one, but rather the minute examination *according to the laws of nature* of the various works which are produced by great artists: from this we can understand the composer's *soul*, in regard to how and to what extent, in his particular work, one thing more than another masters the *human mind and emotions*, which is the *highest pinnacle of the discipline of music*.

Then Matheson points out that mathematics can measure the elements of music, but not how these elements are used. It is the latter, not the former, which concern feelings in music.

> A perfect understanding of the human emotions, which certainly are not to be measured by the mathematical yardstick, is of much greater importance to melody and its composition than the understanding of tones ... This is certain: it is not so much good *proportion*, but rather the apt *usage* of the intervals and keys, which establishes the beautiful, moving and natural quality in melody and harmony. Sounds, in themselves, are neither good nor bad; but they become good and bad according to the way in which they are used. No measuring or calculating art teaches this.[66]

By the end of the Baroque, we see in Avison a complete break with Scholastic dogma. It must have been much more dramatic in his time, than it seems to us, for him to state that musical communication is *not* of the realm of Reason.

> After all that has been, or can be said, the energy and grace of musical expression is of too delicate a nature to be fixed by words: it is a matter of taste, rather than of reasoning, and is, therefore, much better understood by example than by precept.[67]

[66] Johann Matheson, *Der vollkommene Capellmeister* (1739), trans. Ernest Harriss (Ann Arbor: UMI Research Press, 1981).

[67] Charles Avison, *An Essay on Musical Expression* [London, 1753] (New York: Broude Reprint, 1967), 81. Avison (1709–1770) was an organist and composer.

After the Baroque it seems quite clear in retrospect that for most persons "music" meant performance, and not theory. After all, the first modern school of music, the Paris Conservatoire, established in 1792, was a school of performance. The only study not related to one's instrument was a weekly solfeggio course and apparently one harmony course taught by Catel.

In 1865 Wagner was asked by King Ludwig II of Bavaria for advice in the establishment of a "German Music School to be founded in Munich." Wagner responded with an essay of some length and he concluded that it must be performance which is the "invisible bond" of the curriculum. He goes further and maintains that the only true way to teach aesthetics and music history is through performance.

> The invisible bond, uniting the various branches of study, will always have to be [in] performance ... In keeping with the whole plan of our Music school, this cannot be pursued upon an abstract scientific path, mayhap through academic lectures and the like; but here, too, we must strike the purely practical path of direct artistic exercise, under higher guidance for the performance ...
>
> The true aesthetics and the sole intelligible history of music ... we must teach in no other way but by beautiful and correct performances of works of classical music.[68]

[68] Ellis, *The Prose Works of Wagner*, IV, 197ff.

It is also probably fair to suggest that all the great nineteenth century composers believed that music only really existed in performance, not in the score. Perhaps the reason for this was best expressed in the often quoted observation by Mahler, "The best things in music are not found in the notes." So much for any conceptual philosophy of music! Liszt once wrote,

> Unfortunately it is not with music as it is with painting and poetry: body and soul alone are not enough to make it comprehensible; it has to be performed, and very well performed too, to be understood and felt.[69]

[69] Letter to Abbe de Lemennais, Marseille, April 28, 1845.

He expresses the same thought in a letter thirteen years later:

What is the good of anything that is written on paper, if it is not comprehended by the soul and imparted in a living manner?[70]

[70] Letter to Rosa von Milde, Weimar, August 25, 1858.

Wagner had once written to Liszt expressing this same thought:

Only the *performer* is the real, true artist. All that we create as poets and composers expresses a *wish* but not an *ability*: only the performance itself reveals that ability or *art*.[71]

[71] Letter to Franz Liszt, Zürich, July 20, 1850.

After the testimony of 1500 years by some of the greatest composers and greatest minds who ever lived, in the mid-twentieth century American music educators took it upon themselves to turn the clock again back to a medieval emphasis on teaching the "science" of music, today called the conceptual aspects of music. Any objective observer would conclude that this approach has once again failed. Just compare the small numbers of students per capita in music classes, compare the relative level of spending by the school on music, compare the content of writing in educational journals, compare the sophistication of performance—compare anything you want to compare.

The fundamental reason why conceptual teaching in music has been a failure has been because fundamentally it is not music. Aristotle reminds us that the written word, "cat," is not the real thing, it is only a *symbol* of the spoken word. And the spoken word, "cat," is not the real thing either. Thus, when we write, "cat," we are two generations away from the real thing. It is the same in music but with an additional factor of fundamental importance. Anything, be it a painting or a performance of music, which an individual judges to be beautiful is an individual judgment existing in his right hemisphere. And it is there that all persons have differing views, exactly as the old saying goes, "Art is in the eye of the beholder." It follows, therefore, that it is impossible to develop any left hemisphere language, rules, principles or curricula which applies to everyone; such judgments belong to only the person making them. This was one important principle in the philosophy of George Santayana.

> A first approach to a definition of beauty [must] therefore be made by the exclusion of all intellectual judgments, all judgments of matter of fact or of relation. To substitute judgments of fact for judgments of value, is a sign of a pedantic and borrowed criticism. If we approach a work of art or nature scientifically, for the sake of its historical connections or proper classification, we do not approach it aesthetically.[72]

[72] George Santayana, *The Sense of Beauty* (New York: Collier Books, 1961), 26.

He means it is impossible to create a rational philosophy which represents the individual experiential understanding of the right hemisphere. This is one of the flaws that makes nonsense of the entire pedagogy of conceptual teaching in music. Further it is necessary for conceptual teaching in music to stand on the premise that what is on paper is music. Any child can tell you it is not.

Subsequently, for the most part this kind of teaching in music begins and ends with teaching only the *grammar* of music. This does not happen in any other field of education. In English Literature, for example, the study of Shakespeare's grammar is noted but it is not the core of the studies; the great moral truths are. Conceptual music teachers very rarely go beyond the grammar to discuss Truth in music. It is what makes the Mahler quote so illuminating, "The most important things in music are not found in the notes!" We are simply not teaching "the important things." And we wonder why more students are not in our classes; we wonder why the financial support has disappeared and we wonder why the school board makes calculus a core subject when hardly anyone will ever use it in their lifetime.

Let us be clear. Music theory is very important. But music theory is not music. If we say we are going to teach music, then don't teach music theory. Teach music.

Let us repeat this using the terms of the early universities. We have inherited two forms of music, a *speculativa* form, which includes notation and all of theory and much of modern music education, those things which we can talk and write about, and which we learn by eye, and a *practica* form which is mostly learned by ear (the private studio teacher says, "No, it goes like this").

But in truth, the *speculativa* form does not exist as music. It is *only* the conceptual symbolic language which represents the *practica* form, which is the *real* music! Thus, when music schools teach the conceptual form, while they *call* it music, they are not really teaching music. Harmony as it is usually taught, for example, is not music and might better be identified as the grammar of music, or perhaps even as another symbolic language.

In terms of pure education there are further very significant reasons for the poverty of the current conceptual philosophy of teaching. Two come to mind immediately. First, conceptual theory joins most of the rest of education in presenting the child with rational information which is past tense. But rational information is by nature secondary and makes the child like every other child on the planet. Music, if taught experientially, has the potential to reach and teach the *real* child, the unique, individual being and in the present tense where he is.

Second, conceptual music teaching, by its very nature, will always present to the class the *teacher's* experience in music, which is past tense, and not the individual student's experience, which must be present tense. Because music is experiential, it must be based in the child. It is the *child's* experience which is the location for learning.

The Grammar of Music is not Music

> Anyone who has ever tried to convey a musical idea by means of notation knows how approximate it is. No matter how clever one is at accurately writing the idea, no matter how much detail is included, it always seems a small miracle if someone else can seize the meaning by eye without having first heard it.[73]
> Bruce Haynes

[73] Bruce Haynes, *The End of Early Music* (Oxford University Press, 2007), 105.

WE HAVE EXPLAINED in the section above the fact that no left hemisphere description of music can have a universal meaning to all readers or listeners. In addition to this there is the fact that not all the music exists in print or symbols upon the page. To illustrate an example of this common problem, an old friend of mine, Keith Wilson, of Yale University, once recalled studying the score of the band arrangement of the Hindemith *Symphonic Metamorphosis* with the composer.

> I thought that the recording that was available at the time was great. He said that some of it was, and some of it wasn't. When I was going over it with him, at one point he said, "Now see, [the conductor] completely ignores this ritard ... see how he completely ignores this ritard!" Well I couldn't find a ritard anywhere in the score and told him so. He replied, "Any fool should *feel* that ritard."[74]

So how, under Conceptual Music Education Theory, do we analyze something that is not there? And this problem has been part of music for a very long time. Franchino Gaffurio, in his late fifteenth century treatise, mentions in passing,

[74] Edwin C. Powell, "An Interview with Keith Wilson on Hindemith's *Symphonic Metamorphosis*," *Journal of Band Research* (Fall, 2002), 40. While it is only a related problem, I was once asked by a major publisher to actually compose an overture to be published under the name of a very famous composer. I refused; someone else accepted.

> Further, sounds which cannot be written down are committed to memory by usage and practice so that they will not be lost.[75]

The early nineteenth century philosopher, Jean Paul Richter, presented the point of view that in an art work individual elements cannot be judged in isolation.[76] Jacques Barzun believed that our current predilection to break things down in analysis had its origin in the philosophy of Descartes, who used the metaphor of the kitchen clock

[75] *The Practica musicae of Franchinus Gafurius,* trans. Irwin Young (Madison: University of Wisconsin Press, 1969), 18.

[76] *Jean Paul's Sämtliche Werke,* I: 2, 5.

which one breaks down into individual pieces, studies and then puts them together again.⁷⁷ Barzun has doubts over the value of this kind of breaking down of an art work, not to mention that when finished, "we also see that the pretty picture was spoiled when it was cut up."

⁷⁷ Jacques Barzun, *From Dawn to Decadence* (New York: Harper Collins, 2000), 201, 214.

E. T. A. Hoffmann thought the kind of musical analysis we are taught to do today fell into the category of autopsy.

> Yet another new anatomical slab on which our compositions will be clamped down with their limbs forcibly stretched out and dissected with ruthless cruelty. Ha! I can already see the false relations and hidden consecutive fifths severed from the flesh of their harmonic context and quivering under the glinting knife of the anatomist!⁷⁸

⁷⁸ Richter, *Jean Paul's Sämtliche Werke*, 425.

Jean Paul Richter was thinking along the same lines when he wrote,

> I recognize that reviewers must scale goldfish clean or pluck jeweled hummingbirds neat to lay bare their anatomy. And since they must deal in their refutation so closely with petty details, they have the right to refer merely in general terms to what is important.⁷⁹

⁷⁹ Richter, *Jean Paul's Sämtliche Werke*, 7.

Deryck Cooke, in his brilliant book on musical analysis, *The Language of Music*, points out that in no other art does the critic engage in the study of its grammar in the hope of understanding the whole.

> If man is ever to fulfill the mission he undertook at the very start—when he first began to philosophize, as a Greek, and evolved the slogan "Know thyself"—he will have to understand his unconscious self; and the most articulate language of the unconscious is music. But, we musicians, instead of trying to understand this language, preach the virtues of refusing to consider it a language at all; when we should be attempting, as literary critics do, to expound and interpret the great masterpieces of our art for the benefit of humanity at large, we concern ourselves more and more with parochial affairs—technical analyses and musicological minutiae—and pride ourselves on our detached, de-humanized approach.⁸⁰

⁸⁰ Deryck Cooke, *The Language of Music* (New York: Oxford University Press, 1959), x.

"Detached, de-humanized," indeed is what we see in this example from the early nineteenth century critic E. T. A. Hoffmann's analysis of the *Coriolan Overture* of Beethoven.

After the main theme has been briefly touched upon by the second violins and cellos the first period of the overture closes on the first inversion of the dominant of the relative major key of Eb.

"First inversion of the dominant of the relative major key of Eb." What would this mean to anyone reading this discussion of Beethoven's music in the newspaper, *Allgemeine musikalische Zeitung*, for 5 August 1812? Can this kind of grammar by any definition be considered music? This kind of writing means nothing to any of us because music does not communicate itself in thinking, but rather in feeling. Rameau's advice to the listener was exactly this.

> We must not think but let ourselves be carried away by the feeling which the music inspires; without our thinking at all, this feeling will become the basis of our judgment.[81]
>
> .....
>
> To enjoy the effects of music fully, we must completely lose ourselves in it; to judge it, we must relate it to the source through which we are affected by it. This source is nature. Nature endows us with the feeling that moves us in all our musical experiences; we might call her gift instinct. Let us allow instinct to inform our judgments, let us see what mysteries it unfolds to us before we pronounce our verdicts.[82]

The problem here is that we don't learn anything important about music from grammar or any other kind conceptual study. If music's primary purpose is the communication of emotions, then it is the study of emotions which must form our understanding of a score. The Spanish writer, Juan Ruiz, writing in the year 1330, gives us the path to begin:

> Examine, then, your inner self, inspect your feelings well,
> And by your heart you'll judge how others' passions surely go.[83]

This should be the true purpose of score study. The conductor, for example, draws his physical technique from the emotions of the score, not from the grammar on the page of the score, as the French philosopher, Charles Batteux (1713–1780) explains:

[81] Jean Philippe Rameau, *Observations sur notre instinct pour la musique et sur son principe*, in Sam Morgenstern, *Composers on Music* (New York: Pantheon, 1956), 44.

[82] Jean Philippe Rameau, *Le Nouveau Systeme de musique theorique*, 43.

[83] Juan Ruiz, *The Book of True Love*, trans. Saralyn Daly (University Park: Pennsylvania State University Press, 1978), 565.

Actions and passions are nearly always united and mixed together in everything men do. They are produced and announced reciprocally. They should therefore nearly always be together in the arts. When artists present an action, it should be animated by some passion; similarly when they present passions, they should be sustained by an action. That does not need to be verified by examples.[84]

[84] Charles Batteux, *Les beaux-arts*, [Paris, 1746], quoted in Peter le Huray and James Day, *Music and Aesthetics in the Eighteenth and Early-Nineteenth Centuries* (Cambridge: Cambridge University Press, 1981), 262.

Music Repertoire must be of High Aesthetic Level

> Never play bad compositions and never listen to them when not absolutely obliged to do so.
>
> .....
>
> You ought not help to spread bad compositions, but, on the contrary, help to suppress them with all your force.
> Robert Schumann, *Maxims for Young Musicians*

> Only let the pupil practice pure and good music.
> Juan Vives (1493–1540), *On Education*

> I count it but time lost to hear such a foolish song.[85]
> Shakespeare

[85] *As You Like It*, V, iii, 34ff.

THE IMPORTANCE OF DISTINGUISHING between "good" music and "bad" music is documented in the earliest literature. Athenaeus, in reviewing this subject, said in definition of good music, "It is plain to me also that music should be the subject of philosophic reflection."[86] In another place he quotes a remark by Eupolis, "Music is a matter deep and intricate," adding his own observation that music is always supplying something new for those who can perceive.[87] And, he adds, even music performed at banquets was not for entertainment purposes.

[86] Athenaeus, *Deipnosophists*, XIV, 632.

[87] Ibid., XIV, 623.

> For, since the songs are sung in concert, if discourse on the gods has been added it dignifies the mood of every one ... It is plain, therefore, in the light of what we have said, that music did not, at the beginning, make its way into feasts merely for the sake of shallow and ordinary pleasure, as some persons think.[88]

[88] Ibid., XIV, 627ff.

For Plutarch, this educational purpose in listening to good music was the point at which one could call music "useful" to mankind.

> Therefore, if it be the aim of any person to practice music with skill and judgment, let him imitate the ancient manner; let him also adorn it with those other sciences, and make philosophy his tutor, which is sufficient to judge what is in music decent and useful.[89]

[89] *Concerning Music*.

In a discussion of "good or bad" repertoire, Plato left a lengthy passage which discusses the influence on the listeners and on the danger of allowing the listeners to make repertoire decisions purely on the basis of pleasure.[90] We have quoted above, in the discussion of Plato and Music Education, his extensive comments on what characterizes good music. He concludes that good music produces "better men, whereas the other kind makes them worse."[91]

Aristotle also commented on the dangers which entertainment music has for the listeners.

> For in this the performer practices the art, not for the sake of his own improvement, but in order to give pleasure, and that of a vulgar sort, to his hearers ... The result is that the performers are vulgarized, for the end at which they aim is bad. The vulgarity of the spectator tends to lower the character of the music and therefore of the performers.[92]

It was Aristotle who first made the distinction between aesthetic music and entertainment music, a topic which we will discuss below together with catharsis.

Plutarch wrote of the ancient Greeks that they believed, "the music was ever accounted among them the best, which was most grave, simple and natural."[93] He adds that they were particularly concerned with the quality of music and poetry together.

> [The public officials] adjudged it necessary for the preservation of that gravity and seriousness of manners which was required of their youth for the attainments of wisdom and virtue, never to admit of any light and wanton, any ludicrous or effeminate poetry, which made them allow of no poets among them but such only who for their grave and virtuous compositions were approved by the public magistrate; that being hereby under some restraint, they might neither act nor write anything to the prejudice of good manners, or to the dishonor of their laws and government.[94]

Polybius, the second century BC historian, in speaking of the special attention given music by the early Greeks, was careful to clarify, " ... and by this I mean true music ... "[95]

[90] See *Laws*, 700ff.

[91] Ibid., 802.

[92] *Politica*, 1341b.9.

[93] Plutarch, *Customs of the Lacedaemonians*.

[94] Plutarch notes that when it was necessary to punish one, the guilty one had to parade around the city singing a satire of his own composition which reflected on the folly of his crime.

[95] Polybius, *The Rise of the Roman Empire*, IV, 20

During the Christian Era one continues to find concern over the impact of bad music. Martin Luther warns of young people, that we must "wean them away from love ballads and carnal songs."[96] Francesco Guicciardini (1483–1549), politician in Florence, wrote in concern for the general denigration of entertainment,

> I believe there is nothing worse in this world than levity. For lighthearted men are the ready instruments of any party, no matter how bad, dangerous, or pernicious. Therefore, flee from them as you would from fire.[97]

Can we define what good music is? A good place to begin is a treatise on the sublime by Nicolas Boileau (1636–1711), which was a study of a very important treatise, "On the Sublime" by Cassius Longinus (third century AD). Boileau writes of literature, but his thoughts apply as well to music.

> The Sublime is a certain power in literature that is able to raise and ravish the soul, and whose source is either greatness of thought and nobility of feeling, or magnificence of phrasing, or a harmonious, intense, and spirited turn of expression.[98]

Certainly one basic characteristic often mentioned by the best composers is that the music come "from the heart," an expression which means a genuine heart-felt communication of their feelings. Mendelssohn, for example, in a letter of July 13, 1831, wrote,

> I look upon it as my duty to compose just how and what is written in my heart, and to leave the effect it will make to Him who takes heed of greater and better things ... When I have produced a piece that has flowed from my heart—whether it is afterwards to bring me fame, honors, orders, or snuff-boxes, does not concern me.[99]

In a letter of advice to a young composer, Schumann wrote,

> The question is solely what is felt and experienced within a man's own breast ... In your work, go deeper into your inmost being, and let them bear a distinct stamp; let criticism and intellect rule as much as you please in all outward questions and forms, but in all inner and original thought, the heart alone, and genuine feeling.[100]

[96] Martin Luther, *Geistliches Gesangbechlein* of 1524, Preface.

[97] Francesco Guicciardini, *Maxims and Reflections*, trans. Mario Domandi (New York: Harper Torchbooks, 1965), C, 167.

[98] Nicolas Boileau, *Reflections on Longinus*, quoted in *Selected Criticism*, trans. Ernest Dilworth (New York: Bobbs-Merrill, 1965), 70.

[99] Letter to Eduard Devrient.

[100] Letter to Carl Eckert, January 26, 1842.

Schumann, in writing of his compositions of 1836–1838 adds, "There is heart's blood in them, too!"[101] Schumann also left some important advice on the subject of quality in compositions.

[101] Letter to Clara Wieck, May 10, 1838.

> When you grow older, avoid playing what is merely fashionable. Time is precious. It would require a hundred lives merely to get acquainted with all the good music that exists.
>
> .....
>
> To play overmuch in society is more injurious than advantageous. Study your audience; yet never play anything of which in your own heart you feel ashamed.[102]

[102] *Maxims for Young Musicians*. In his article, "Short Studies for Pianforte," in *Neue Zeitschrift für Musik*, 1841, Schumann adds, "Between our own four walls we may occasionally give way to frivolity, but before the world it is injurious."

With respect for maintaining the highest standards, Martin Luther warns, "Don't you know that the more wholesome something is, the less it is popular and the less it gains ground?"[103] This reminds us of a comment by Schumann, "Few strikingly original works of genius have become popular."[104]

[103] Letter to George Spalatin [1516].

[104] Schumann's *Diary*, c. 1833.

Erasmus, in an interesting passage in his "The Education of a Christian Prince," uses the analogy of music to demonstrate the importance of learning in early childhood. The additional point here is that *quality* music should be used with children.

> Pains will therefore have to be taken to accustom them from the outset to what is best, for any music sounds sweet to those who have become used to it. And nothing is harder than to withdraw someone from behavior which has already taken root in his character from habitual usage.[105]

[105] "The Education of a Christian Prince," [1516] in *The Collected Works of Erasmus* (Toronto: University of Toronto Press, 1992), XXVII, 259.

The characteristics of "bad music," for lack of a better word, have also long been recognized. Stuart Isacoff provides some examples from the late Middle Ages. A 1132 statute of the Cistercian Order complained that men should stop singing "in a womanish manner with tinkling ... as if imitating the wantonness of minstrels."[106] In 1324 Pope John XXII issued a bull on church music, complaining of faster moving notes and the use of depraved and wanton secular melodies.

Lodowick Bryskett (1546–1612), in an English treatise criticizing current manners, gives some characteristics of bad

[106] Stuart Isacoff, *Temperament* (New York: Vintage Books, 2001), 50ff.

music when he advises the young men that they must be very selective of what they listen to.

> Let it suffice that young men are to take great account of that part of music which bears with it grave melodies, fit to compose the mind to good order by virtue of the rhythms and sound ... But those which by variety in tunes, and warbling variations, confounds the words and melodies, and yields only a delight to the exterior sense, and no fruit for the mind, I wish them to neglect and not to esteem.[107]

Erasmus makes the interesting observation that in entertainment music it doesn't matter whether the singer is one of the best or one of the worst, for they are equally entertaining.[108]

Voltaire makes a point which is familiar to all musicians today: "None of the works styled academic, of any kind, have been works of genius."[109] While we should not go quite so far, there is a reason for this. One of the important parts of the definition of aesthetic music is that it have no purpose, other than the direct communication of the music from the composer's heart to the listener. Composers of music written for academic reasons, or for commissions, often become distracted from this law.

Examples of this circumstance can be found throughout the nineteenth century and in a far broader repertoire than just works written for academic purposes. No one in the nineteenth century wrote a masterpiece on the occasion of the dedication of a new railroad. But because the academic examples are so widely known, we are not surprised to find such a reference in a novel, *Steppenwolf*, by a master German novelist, Hermann Hesse. His main character pauses to hear some jazz and then thinks, "it was repugnant to me, and yet ten times preferable to all the academic music of the day." Hesse then continues,

> One half of this music, the melody, was all pomade and sugar and sentimentality. The other half was savage, temperamental and vigorous. Yet the two went artlessly well together and made a whole. It was the music of decline. There must have been such music in Rome under the later emperors.

[107] Lodowick Bryskett, *A Discourse of Civill Life*, ed. Thomas Wright (Northridge: San Fernando Valley State College, 1970), 113.

[108] *The Colloquies of Erasmus*, trans. Craig Thompson (Chicago: University of Chicago Press, 1965), 256.

[109] *The Works of Voltaire* (New York: St. Hubert Guild, 1901), XXIII, 304.

Compared with Bach and Mozart and real music it was, naturally, a miserable affair.

One runs into this term, "real music," frequently over more than 2,000 years. It is a measure of the universality of aesthetic principles.

The Italian music theorist, Gioseffo Zarlino made the definition of the purpose of music being "edifying entertainment."

> To Mei, a sixteenth century Italian nobleman, such a mean goal was unworthy of an art extolled by the ancient philosophers. Music should not be content with delighting the ear; it should stir men's emotions.[110]

[110] Quoted in Claude Palisca, *Letters on Ancient and Modern Music* (American Institute of Musicology, 1960), 11.

Finally, since the performance of music is a live, experiential event, we must not fail to mention the importance of the role of the musicians who bring the work to life. The early critic, E. T. A. Hoffmann, illustrates this well in his description of Spontini, who for a time was the chief conductor in Berlin.

> In his hand the baton becomes a veritable magic wand, with which he wakens into life dormant forces which then rise up in majestic awareness of their power.[111]

[111] *E. T. A. Hoffmann's Musical Writings* (Cambridge: Cambridge University Press, 1989), 422.

And what if the performers fail to do this, fail to communicate the full emotional expression of the music they perform? Bruce Haynes gives an answer by Keith Hill.

> Even when players play music without an affect in mind, normal ordinary listeners like myself hear and feel the effects that result from not having a clear affect ... such as wandering, jerky, stilted, perfunctory, inane, bored, tired, get it over and done with as fast as possible, reluctant, and so on. I do not consider these affects worth my time, since I experience them too often on a daily basis.[112]

[112] Quoted in Bruce Haynes, *The End of Early Music* (New York: Oxford University Press, 2007), 168.

Catharsis—The Educational Purpose of Music

REFLECTING THE VERY WIDE interests of the man, Aristotle set out to write two books on the theater presentations of his day, one on Tragedy and one on Epic theater. His goal was, following his style of step by step rational investigation, to explain the constituent parts which made up these forms. Unfortunately his book on Epic theater is lost, but in the extant book on Tragedy, known as his *Poetics,* he lists the components: the story must be serious, the story must be complete in itself and of a sufficient magnitude, the characters must be noble and with appropriate language and the structure must be in action and not in narration. After he had discussed all these elements one by one and had seemingly completed his purpose, it apparently occurred to him that something remained to be discussed. Unlike the audience of Epic productions, which were of great interests visually, he was aware that in the audience member of Tragedy something remained after the end of the play. It was as if in the Epic the enjoyment was left in the theater at the work's conclusion, but in Tragedy the audience member was reached deeply inside and carried this with him when he left. This extra human dimension he called catharsis [*katharein*] and with his subsequent explanations he created the philosophic field of Aesthetics and at the same time distinguished the difference between aesthetic productions and those of mere entertainment. Following is his first mention of this subject in *Poetics*, a very famous literary passage. The reader will notice the inclusion of music, but as this book has also survived in an incomplete form we do not have his first-hand details of how music was used in Greek plays.

> Tragedy, then, is an imitation of an action that is serious, complete, and of a certain magnitude; in language embellished with each kind of artistic ornament, the several kinds being found in separate parts of the play; in the form of action, not of narrative; through pity and fear effecting the proper catharsis of these emotions. By "language embellished," I mean language into which rhythm, harmony[113] and song enter. By

[113] The ancient Greeks often used the word translated as "harmony" to mean music.

"the several kinds in separate parts," I mean, that some parts are rendered through the medium of verse alone, others again with the aid of song.[114]

[114] *Poetics*, 1449b.24t. Later speculation on what the role of music *really* was in Greek Tragedy led to the creation of opera.

First, it is clear that when Aristotle uses the word, "pity," he means "empathy." He makes this clear in a passage from his treatise on rhetoric.

> Pity may be defined as a feeling of pain caused by the sight of some evil, destructive or painful, which befalls one who does not deserve it, and which we might expect to befall ourselves or some friend of ours, and moreover to befall us soon.

With this in mind, when Aristotle speaks of "pity and fear" in the spectator, we believe he means the spectator empathizes and internalizes the moral problem seen on stage, causing him to meditate and perhaps even change his behavior. In the Epic form, which Aristotle otherwise praised as stage works, this does not happen. The spectator can be vastly entertained, but the experience "bounces off" and he leaves the theater unaffected. Thus, in drama criticism, most later writers, including Corneille, Racine and Lessing, understood Aristotle to mean by catharsis, in the case of the tragedy, that the play had an ethical or moral end. The word Aristotle used, *katharein*, was a Greek word meaning "to cleanse." For this reason English dictionaries tend to define it as meaning "to cleanse or purge," with older dictionaries focusing on the medical use of the term. For modern readers a better translation might be to "settle the mind," or after feeling upset by the action on the stage "to get if off one's chest."

We think a more familiar contemporary illustration of what Aristotle meant by this word can be found in our common experience in the cinema. One can think of going to the cinema with friends and during the film we are totally involved, we laugh, we cry. But as soon as the film ends, on the way out of the theater we immediately begin talking with our friends about other things, school, boy/girl friends and jobs, etc. On another occasion we go with friends to the cinema and when the film ends no one says a word, sometimes for a long time. We wish we could just sit there and that they would not turn on the lights. In the first example we were entertained. We were totally involved, but unaffected. In the second example the film reached us on a deeper level. It did not just "bounce off."[115] This is catharsis.

Aristotle uses this word, catharsis, two more times near the end of his treatise, *Politics*. It is especially interesting that the first reference here seems to refer specifically to music and education.

> We say, however, that music is to be studied for the sake of many benefits and not of one only. It is to be studied with a view to education, with a view to catharsis.

In this book he also describes the use of music in education in the same terms he used to define catharsis in drama.

> In education the most ethical modes are to be preferred, but in listening to the performances of others we may admit the modes of action and passions also. For feelings such as pity and fear, or, again, enthusiasm, exist very strongly in some souls, and have more or less influence over all. Some persons fall into a religious frenzy, whom we see as a result of the sacred melodies—when they have used the melodies that excite the soul to mystic frenzy—restored as though they had found healing and purgation. Those who are influenced by pity and fear, and every emotional nature, must have a like experience, and others in so far as each is susceptible to such emotions, and all are in a manner purged and their souls lightened and delighted. The purgative melodies likewise give an innocent pleasure to mankind.[116]

Following the early Greeks' strong interest in music therapy, in this passage Aristotle's main concern is using music to create a cathartic release from anxiety caused by hearing prior music.

> For educational purposes we must use those that best express character, but we may use melodies of action and enthusiastic melodies for concerts where other people perform. For every feeling that affects some souls violently affects all souls more or less; the difference is only one of degree. Take pity and fear, for example, or again enthusiasm. Some people are liable

[115] The reader will easily recall similar examples of both experiences following concerts.

[116] Ibid, 1342a. Some of these modes were apparently so associated with particular forms, that Aristotle cites [1342b.] an instance of a performer who attempted to perform a dithyramb, "acknowledged to be Phrygian," in the Dorian and could not do it.

to become possessed by the latter emotion, but we see that, when they have made use of the melodies which fill the soul with orgiastic feeling, they are brought back by these sacred melodies to a normal condition as if they had been medically treated and undergone a catharsis.

Those who are subject to the emotions of pity and fear and the feelings generally will necessarily be affected in the same way; and so will other men in exact proportion to their susceptibility to such emotions. All experience a certain purge [*katharein*] and pleasant relief. In the same manner cathartic melodies give innocent joy to men.[117]

[117] *Politics,* VIII: 7; 1341b35–1342a8. This translation is by J. Burnet.

Although the new Christian Church attempted to destroy all the works of Plato, Aristotle and the rest of the "pagan" philosophers, it is evident that the theater traditions which Aristotle described continued. We see this in a passage of St. Augustine where he gives a curious account of a personal experience with catharsis in the theater.[118]

[118] Owing to the Church, we know almost nothing of theater during the time Augustine lived.

Stage plays also carried me away, full of images of my miseries, and of fuel to my fire. Why is it, that man desires to be made sad, beholding doleful and tragical things, which yet himself would by no means suffer? Yet he desires as a spectator to feel sorrow at them, and this very sorrow is his pleasure. What is this but a miserable madness? For a man is the more affected with these actions, the less free he is from such affections. Howsoever, when he suffers in his own person, it is styled misery; when he compassionates others, then it is mercy. But what sort of compassion is this for feigned and scenical passions? For the audience member is not called on to relieve, but only to grieve: and he applauds the actor of these fictions the more, the more he grieves. And if the calamities of those persons (whether of old times, or mere fiction) be acted in such a way, that the spectator is not moved to tears, he goes away disgusted and criticizing; but if he be moved to passions, he stays intent, and weeps for joy.[119]

[119] *The Confessions,* Book III.

The most important Renaissance philosopher to write of catharsis was the great theorist, Johannes Tinctoris (1435–1511). In writing of the composers he most respected (Dufay, Dunstable and Okeghem, etc.) he describes himself after hearing their music as being "more refreshed and wiser."[120] This new phrase, "to be refreshed," is one that will be used

[120] *The Art of Counterpoint,* trans. Albert Seay (American Institute of Musicology, 1961), 14ff.

frequently to describe catharsis during the German Baroque. As for being "wiser," such as knowing one's emotional nature better through introspection, this too is certainly a facet of catharsis.

During the Renaissance several Italian writers speak of catharsis and they all focus on the "purge" character of its definition. Torquato Tasso, for example, uses the expression, "drawing the mind out of itself," as a synonym of "purge." He is writing of the old Greek modes and, like Aristotle, he finds the very ones which accomplish this end in the theater and in the church are the very ones considered too "powerful" for use in the education of children.

> The Phrygian and Lydian modes, and the one formed by combining them [Mixolydian] are much more desirable in tragedy and the canzone as in these they can move the mind and, so to speak, draw it out of itself. But they are not suitable for instruction ...
>
> Since music was invented not merely to entertain idleness or as a medicine and catharsis for the mind but for instruction as well ... A solemn and steady music like the Doric [Dorian] will serve the heroic poem better than any other.[121]

An important Italian writer on the Renaissance theater was Antonio Sebastiano, known as Minturno, Bishop of Ugento, who had represented that town in the Council of Trent. In his *The Art of Poetry* (1563) he first paraphrases the part of Aristotle's definition of tragedy which deals with catharsis.[122] In Minturno's words, Tragedy arouses,

> feelings of pity and terror, tending to purge the mind of the beholder of similar passions, to his delight and profit.[123]

Later he emphasizes the educational purpose of drama, saying that "the ennobling or purification of manners is the end toward which all effort is directed."

Minturno returns to catharsis, giving one of the most extended definitions to be found in early Italian literature and offers an analogy with art of the physician. The terror and pity which the observer experiences in tragedy, he contends,

[121] Tasso, *Discourses on the Heroic Poem*, trans. Mariella Cavalchini (Oxford: Clarendon Press, 1973), 199.

[122] He said dramatic works should be no less than three hours in length and no more than four.

[123] Ibid., 58.

frees us most pleasantly from similar passions, for nothing else so curbs the indomitable frenzy of our minds. No one is so completely the victim of unbridled appetites, that, being moved by fear and pity at the unhappiness of others, he is not impelled to throw off the habits that have been the cause of such unhappiness. And the memory of the grave misfortunes of others not only renders us more ready and willing to support our own; it makes us more wary in avoiding like ills. The physician who with a powerful drug extinguishes the poisonous spark of the malady that afflicts the body, is no more powerful than the tragic poet who purges the mind of its troubles through the emotions aroused by his charming verses.[124]

[124] Ibid., 58ff.

The prolific Italian writer Girolamo Cardano (1501–1576) gives the phrase, "cleansing of the spirit," as a synonym of "purge" in his definition of the parts of music.

[Music's] usefulness is divided into three parts, for it pertains to instruction and study, or to the cleansing of the spirit, or to spending time pleasurably in leisure, tranquility, and freedom from the pressure of more serious matters. It is often said that emotions in music reflect weakened and enervated morals, but I believe such emotions consist of gentle virtues, and correspond to those more appropriate to action and also to those most divine virtues suitable for intellectual endeavor. Accordingly music celebrates those moral virtues which are especially appropriate to that useful quality which pertains to learning. Teachers and disciplinarians have agreed on the expiative and purgative force of strong emotions. When these emotions subside they may become excessively reversed and softened by giving way especially to emotions of misery and pity, causing dejection and depression. Music also proposes to fill such moods with a certain innocuous pleasure.[125]

[125] Quoted in Clement Miller, *Hieronymus Cardanus, Writings on Music* (American Institute of Musicology, 1973), 105.

Finally among the Italians, there was the very conservative counter-Reformation Church philosopher, Giordano Bruno (b. 1548).[126] He left an allegorical reference to catharsis and extended its range to include arithmetic and geography.

[126] While he reads very conservative today, the Church at the time considered him too liberal and burned him at the stake.

Jove ordered his first-born, Minerva, to hand him the box he kept under the pillow on his bed, after which he drew forth nine boxes containing nine collyria, prescribed to purge the human mind in respect both to its knowledge and to its disposition. And to begin with he gave three of them to the first three Muses, [Arithmetic, Geometry and Music], saying to them: "Here for you is the best unguent with which you will be able to purge and make clear your perceptive virtue as regards the number, the size and the harmonious proportion of sensible things."[127]

From England we like the comment in 1516 by Sir Thomas More that "melodies wonderfullye move, stir, pearce, and enflame the hearers myndes."[128]

The greatest playwright of the sixteenth century, Shakespeare, wrote of music refreshing the mind of the student. In *The Taming of the Shrew*, when Lucentio, in criticizing a pretended music teacher, observes,

> Preposterous ass, that never read so far
> To know the cause why music was ordained!
> Was it not to refresh the mind of man
> After his studies or his usual pain?[129]

There is one Renaissance reference to catharsis which we really like. It is found in the music treatise, *Musica* (1537), by the German theorist Nicholaus Listenius, who was a student at Wittenberg when Luther was there. In this work he first defines music in the two familiar academic categories, the theoretical and practical (performance). In his definition of the performing musician, he finds for the listener an end beyond just listening to the music. The listener, he says, should be left with "something more," than the performance itself.

> Practical, whose goal is doing, is that which delights not only in the intricacies of skill, but extends into performance itself, leaving out no part of the act of performance. Hence the practical musician, who teaches others something more than the recognition of art, trains himself in it for the goal of any performance.

He employs this phrase again in a passage where he makes a real contribution to aesthetics by adding a third part to the traditional definition of music. In addition to the theoretical and the practical, he now adds what he calls the

---

[127] Giordano Bruno, *The Expulsion of the Triumphant Beast*, trans. Arthur Imerti (New Brunswick: Rutgers University Press, 1964), 181ff [II, iii].

[128] Quoted in Bruce Haynes, *The End of Early Music* (Oxford: Oxford University Press, 2007), 171.

[129] *The Taming of the Shrew*, III, i, 9ff.

"poetic." By this he is thinking of the meaning left with the listener when the performance is concluded. This he calls "*total* performance." It is most important and enlightening that he also observed in passing that the practical and the poetic always include the theoretical, "but the reverse is not true." When he says here that the total performance "leaves something more" after the conclusion of the performance, he is speaking of catharsis exactly in the sense of our cinema analogy above.

> Poetic is that which is not content with just the understanding of the thing nor with only its practice, but which leaves something more after the labor of performance, as when music or a song of musicians is composed by someone whose goal is total performance and accomplishment. It consists of making or putting together more in this work which afterwards leaves the work perfect and absolute, which otherwise is artificially like the dead.

The marriage of the first great composer of the German Baroque, Heinrich Schütz, was celebrated in a poem by Conrad Bayer, which makes a passing reference to music "renewing the heart."

> Music, sweet harmony,
> Over all the elements
> Rightly art thou exalted;
> Nothing can be compared to thee.
> To God's own praise and honor
> Dost thou most rightly turn,
> His fame to magnify.
>
> The human voice and song
> And sound of instrument
> Are pleasing thus to God;
> And in the whole wide world,
> Nothing doth please man more,
> Renew the heart and mind
> And drive away all sadness.[130]

Composers now began to add forewords and dedications to their scores which clearly gave catharsis as the goal of their music. Thus we find in the score of Bach's *Clavier Ubung*,

[130] Quoted in Hans Moser, *Heinrich Schütz* (St. Louis: Concordia, 1936), 104.

Part III, and also in the "Goldberg Variations," a statement to the effect that his purpose was to "refresh the spirits" of the listener. Similarly, when Bach was looking into a position in Halle, he was sent a contract which specified that the church music should have the result that "the members of the Congregation shall be the more inspired and refreshed in worship."[131]

We can document this transformation in the foreword of Georg Muffat's *Auserlesene Instrumental-Music* (1701). First, he explains that in his previous collections he has sought to draw "liveliness and grace" from the "Lullian well." In other words, previously he wrote in the French style, whose goal contemporaries often referred to as "tickling the ears." Now, in the present collection Muffat says his goal is to present "certain profound and unusual affects of the Italian manner." The purpose of this music, as he makes very clear, is what we would call "concert music" in the modern sense. That is, serious music intended for the contemplative listener. Muffat expresses it this way:

> These concerti, suited neither to the church ... nor for dancing ... [are] composed only for the express refreshment of the ear.

No representative of the power of music on the mind can surpass this description by Franz Liszt.

> Music embodies *feeling* without forcing it—as it is forced in its other manifestations, in most arts and especially in the art of words—to contend and combine with *thought*. If music has one advantage over the other means through which man can reproduce the impressions of his soul, it owes this to its supreme capacity to make each inner impulse audible without the assistance of reason, so restricted in the diversity of its forms, capable, after all, only of confirming or describing our affections, not of communicating them directly in their full intensity, in that to accomplish this even approximately it is obliged to search for images and comparisons. Music, on the other hand, presents at one and the same time the intensity and the expression of *feeling*; it is the embodied and intelligible essence of feeling; capable of being apprehended by our senses, it permeates them like a dart, like a ray, like

[131] Quoted in Hans T. David and Arthur Mendel, *The Bach Reader* (New York: Norton, 1966), 65.

a dew, like a spirit, and fills our soul ... Only in music does feeling, actually and radiantly present, lift the ban which oppresses our spirit with the sufferings of an evil earthly power and liberate us with the white-capped floods of its free and warmth-giving might from "the demon Thought," brushing away for brief moments his yoke from our furrowed brows. Only in music does feeling, in manifesting itself, dispense with the help of reason and its means of expression, so inadequate in comparison with its intuition, so incomplete in comparison with its strength, its delicacy, its brilliance. On the towering, sounding waves of music, feeling lifts up to heights that lie beyond the atmosphere of our earth and shows us cloud landscapes and world archipelagos that move about in ethereal space like singing swans. On the winds of the infinite art it draws us with it to regions into which it alone can penetrate, where, in the ringing ether, the heart expands and, in anticipation shares in an immaterial, incorporeal, spiritual life. What is it that, beyond this miserable, paltry, earthly shell, beyond these numbered planets, opens to us the meadows of infinity, refreshes us at the murmuring springs of delight, steeps us in the pearly dew of longing; what is it that causes ideals to shimmer before us like the gilded spires of that submerged city, that recalls to us the indescribable recollections that surrounded our cradles, that conducts us through the reverberating workshops of the elements, that inspires us with all that ardor of thirsting after inexhaustible rapture which the blissful experience; what is it that takes hold of us and sweeps us into the turbulent maelstrom of the passions which carries us out of the world into the harbor of a more beautiful life; is it not music, animated by elemental feeling like that which vibrates in us before, it manifests itself, before it solidifies and turns cold in the mold of the idea? What other art discloses to its adepts similar raptures, the more precious and ennobling in that they are veiled by a chaste and impenetrable mystery? What other art reveals to its votaries the heavens where angels lovingly hold sway and flies with them in Elijah's chariot through spheres of ecstasy?[132]

[132] Franz Liszt, "Berlioz and his Harold Symphony," *Neue Zeitschrift für Musik* (1855) XLIII.

Finally, the critic, Walter Jackson Bate, in his discussion of catharsis gives a bottom line we agree with as being very important with respect to music education, that catharsis unites left and right hemispheres of the brain.

For beneath the theory of *katharsis* lies the general Greek premise that art, in presenting a heightened and harmonious "imitation" of reality, is formative; that, in enlarging, exercising, and refining one's feelings, and in leading them outward, art possesses a unique power to form the "total man," in whom emotion may become reconciled to intelligence and harmoniously integrated with it.[133]

[133] Walter Jackson Bate, *Prefaces to Criticism* (New York: Doubleday Anchor Books, 1959), 31.

Catharsis is the End Goal for Public School Music Education

THIS QUESTION, and the following discussion, refers to the music performed in the classroom. We exempt from this discussion marching bands and similar activities which exist only for the purpose of being an activity and have nothing to do with indoor music education.

Any discussion of indoor music education with regard to wind bands must be synonymous with the repertoire they play because you cannot have a meaningful discussion about the educational concept of an ensemble of students sitting in chairs, holding instruments and playing nothing. The repertoire cannot be separated from the education. Consider, therefore, the following thoughts by two men with very bright minds.

> *Music allows us to gaze into the inmost Essence of ourselves.*[134]
> RICHARD WAGNER

> *Music whispers to us dim secrets that startle our wonder as to who we are.* EMERSON

[134] "Beethoven" (Leipzig: Fritzsch, 1870)

These two quotations refer to the educational purpose of catharsis, the employment of music to help the student come to know himself. Can we say this is presently the purpose of American public school education?

An objective observer would have to answer this question, No. It would appear to an objective observer that the emphasis of playing in a school band today is fun and that the purpose is to provide entertainment. Something is clearly wrong here; the Aristotelian concept of an aesthetic activity affecting the mind has been lost. How have we come to the point that the noble purpose of centuries of composers and performers, exemplified by the above quotations, has now become a simple provider of cause and effect entertainment?

I will skip over the question, "Should the purpose of the public schools be to provide entertainment to a public already saturated with entertainment alternatives," for the answer is obvious. So let me focus on the other question, centering on the concept of "fun" in the school music program.

I trust the reader will forgive my use of the following personal reflections, because I cannot address this question standing apart from them. I recall as a student player in a Middle School band performing a composition called *The One-Arm Paper Hanger*. I recall as a student player in the University of Michigan Symphony Band, under Dr. Revelli, performing a work called *Popcorn*. And not many titles between these two examples have remained in my mind. Even in Middle School I was confused by the purpose of such repertoire and as a young adult, in the 1960s, I began publishing numerous articles urging the improvement in the band's repertoire. One day, at a conference somewhere, I was sitting in a lobby talking with Bill Revelli when a young band director came by, looked at our name tags, and asked with some enthusiasm, "Are you *the* David Whitwell?" He ignored Revelli, a circumstance which did not go unnoticed by the latter. As a result of this surprise, Revelli later told me he went back to Ann Arbor and dug out his programs from the time I was a student there for the purpose of examining his own repertoire. And he said to me, "I looked at my repertoire and it made me want to vomit!" Imagine feeling that at the end of a long, successful career.

Today I regularly hear university band concerts which include one or more examples of really bad music. I simply cannot understand why a conductor would elect to play bad music. The answer, of course, was provided in a comment by a conductor to the audience, "The next work is not a good piece of music, but we had a lot of fun playing it!" I can think of university conductors whose driving principle is making sure the students (and public) have fun. I have seen a university conductor come out to the podium wearing a clown suit and walking on his hands. I have seen a university band play with students wearing monkey masks.

And here is where ethics enters our profession. If a public school band conductor provides his students a diet of superficial music, he cannot exempt himself from helping to produce superficial adults. We need to put a stop to this. We need a revolution which returns public school music education to the education of the student through music. We need to replace the goal of "fun" with the goal of catharsis. How do we do this?

First of all, some qualifications. There are no materials on the market suitable for this new purpose; an entirely new K-12 library needs to be created. I realize many educators expect to have teaching outlines and materials given them together with new ideas, but the duration of my life will not be long enough to do this. Second, most of the teaching must be in the form of rhetorical questions, for the idea is to get the student to think of his own feelings and not to provide an answer. In this regard it is important for the teacher to remember that in the right hemisphere there are individual answers but no "right" answers. The teacher must constantly remind the class that if a student provides an answer or comment it does not mean theirs is *ipso facto* wrong. Third, the repertoire used in class must be of high quality aesthetic music. No popular tunes or jazz will work. In selecting high quality aesthetic repertoire it is most expedient to choose something from a composer who is universally honored, like perhaps a Schubert song.

The development of teaching strategies for catharsis must be in both listening and playing formats. For the listening exercises one might begin with a very simple question, does this example sound happy or sad? Let's assume the music you selected was sad. I would not recommend asking the class why it sounds sad, for that gets into left hemisphere prejudices. Better to ask "Does anyone have any comments." Even if they don't they will all be thinking "inside of themselves" in response to the question. If one child raises his hand and says he doesn't think it sounds sad, this is a valuable teaching point. Asking why he thinks that makes him and the class concentrate more deeply inside. Again, try to formulate questions that do not require declarative answers.

For playing exercises I would recommend taking something like a simple Schubert song and having one student play it. Ask the student what feeling he was trying to express in his performance. If he says, "sad," then ask him to play it again but instead communicate "contemplative." All other students in the class will be concentrating fully and thus learning lessons about their own emotional templates.

The overall goal is to help the student come to know himself in the right hemisphere—emotionally. The rest of the educational world does not even try to do this and leaves it to the students to learn about emotions on their own; their failure is trumpeted in headlines in every daily newspaper. We are the most qualified faculty to help the student learn to know himself in this way.

In addition to the change we could make in American society over time (consider how Rock changed society), there will be important cultural profits. In the process of the kind of introspection involved in the examples given above, the student will come to notice the difference between aesthetic music and pop music which just bounces off him and does not become part of him through catharsis. In so doing we will finally be helping to create a generation of new audience members for aesthetic concerts such as orchestral or chamber music. After all, the decline of classical music must clearly, one way or the other, be placed at the door-step of education.

There is currently a great deal of discussion internationally about the disappearance of classical music. Certainly the wide movement of orchestras playing pop music is the worst possible answer. Rather, the orchestra needs to concentrate on what it does which no one else can do.

SOMEWHERE the spirits of Bach, Mozart, Beethoven and five hundred years of others must be watching over us and wondering who will save their noble profession.

Ethics 101: A Concert is not a "show"

If it is art, it is not for all; and if it is for all, it is not art.[135]
   SCHÖNBERG

I assert that it is impossible for anything to be truly good if it is reckoned in advance for presentation to the public.[136] WAGNER

[135] Quoted in Nat Shapiro, *An Encyclopedia of Quotations About Music* (New York: Da Capo, 1977), 237.

[136] *Wagner's Prose Works,* trans. William Ashton Ellis (New York: Broude), III, 96.

IF YOU ADVERTIZE A *concert*, the public will arrive expecting a concert and not an entertainment event. This understanding of what a *concert* is has been formed by the public, even those of the lowest levels of education and personal experience, through years of exposure to such an event in movies, paintings and in literature. They will arrive in expectation of a special experience in music and this is true no matter how young the performers are. The conductor who steps across the line into entertainment, even if it be a single composition of brief duration, therefore not only disappoints the audience but he *ipso facto* appears to presume he thinks he can compete with an extraordinary broad, trillion dollar professional entertainment industry with a medium badly suited for competition in entertainment. Most of the time what the conductor thinks will be perceived as funny will, in fact, be viewed by the public as silly.

I use the heading "Ethics 101" because the concert will always be a public statement of the conductor's personal professional ethics. No other member of the education establishment, at any level, ever has to stand before the public and reveal his true self in so fundamental a way. The American Literature professor may feel forced to violate his personal perception of what his profession demands and organize his teaching to meet some social pressure, but he does this in the closed door of his classroom. He never has to stand up in public and present his class as a representation of his professional ethics.

This is an ethical question every American band conductor must give more thought to. He must put behind him the fact that the very history of his medium in America is one of entertainment. This history took place in a time where small towns had no other forms of live entertainment. But in the third decade of the twentieth century the environment changed very rapidly. Fred Fennell once told me that the tradition of the Sousa Band came to an end with the arrival of the five cent movies.[137]

But aside from this history, it takes a man of considerable strength of character to publicly demonstrate that he understands that his duty is to his art and not to the public. The temptation to take the easy road and slip over into entertainment will always be there and is ancient as the Greek myth of the Sirens, the three sea nymphs who lured sailors to their death with a bewitching song. Robert Schumann wrote of this with respect to composers in Vienna in the early nineteenth century.

> The same thing has been said, with the same result, of a hundred other Viennese composers. They want one thing, yet cannot give up the other. They want to be artists, and yet please the crowd. Boundless failures in this endeavor have not yet opened their eyes to the fact that nothing can be attained on such a path. Only one path leads to an artistic end and to reach that we must fulfill our duty to ourselves and to art.[138]

Franz Liszt summarized this duty very well.

> The word "Evening entertainment" must, as is self-evident, be entirely dispensed with. Our business is to raise, to educate the audience, not to amuse them; and if indeed, as Goethe very pertinently says, "deep and earnest thinkers are in a bad position as regards the public," we will therefore not so much the less, but so much the more earnestly maintain this position.[139]
>
> .....
>
> With notes alone nothing can be accomplished; one thirsts for soul, spirit, and actual life![140]

Beginning with the nineteenth century, one begins to find much interest in using music to raise the general culture. Henry Cleveland wrote in 1840,

> Music must be made popular, not by debasing the art; but by elevating the people.[141]

---

[137] See Paul Yoder's personal description of the sad end of Sousa's career in David Whitwell, *The Sousa Oral History Project,* ed. Craig Dabelstein (Austin: Whitwell Books, 2010).

[138] "Trios for Pianoforte, Violin and Violoncello," in *Neue Zeitschrift für Musik,* 1842.

[139] Liszt, letter to an unknown person, Spring, 1859.

[140] Liszt letter to Franz Brendel, August 29, 1862.

[141] National Music (1840), quoted in Nat Shapiro, *An Encyclopedia of Quotations About Music* (New York: Da Capo, 1977), 233.

Wagner wrote to Hans von Bülow contending that their purpose was to,

> persuade our audiences, by means of the correct illusion, to acquire, without noticing it, a greater refinement of taste.[142]

[142] Letter of December 27, 1868.

Weingartner wondered,

> will the courts, states and towns never understand that the [opera] theater must be a place not of luxury and thoughtless amusement, but of *popular education* like the school, only in a more spiritualized sense, and at any rate of a higher ethical significance than the church?[143]

[143] Felix Weingartner, *On Conducting* (New York: Kalmus), 49.

We are especially fond of a passage by Bruno Walter:

> There are people for whom life begins anew every morning. It is they who are ever more deeply touched by every renewed encounter with Schubert's *Unfinished*, it is they whom the perusal of a familiar Goethe poem moves with the force of a first impression; people over whom habit has no power; people who, in spite of their increasing years and experience, have remained fresh, interested, and open to life. And there are others who, when they watch a most glorious sunset or listen to the *Benedictus* in Beethoven's Missa Solemnis, feel scarcely more than "I know this already"; and who are upset by everything new and unusual—in other words, people whose element is habit and comfort. It is for the former that our poets have written, our artists created, and our musicians composed; and it is for them, above all, that we perform our dramas, our operas, oratorios, and symphonies. As regards the latter, we artists must try, time and time again, to burst open the elderly crust they have acquired, or with which many of them may have been born; our youthful vigor must call upon theirs or revive whatever is left of it.[144]

[144] Bruno Walter, quoted in Carl Bamberger, *The Conductor's Art* (New York: McGraw-Hill, 1965), 176ff.

And once again, Liszt summarizes, in a letter to Chopin in 1852.

> Instead of laboring so to attract and please listeners at any price, let us rather strive to leave a celestial echo of what we have felt, loved, and endured! Let us learn to demand of ourselves whatever ennobles in the mystical city of art rather than to seek from the present, without regard to the future, those easy crowns which, scarce assumed, are at once dulled and forgotten![145]

[145] Liszt letter to Chopin, 1852.

All this brings us to the point, the modern conductor must also take some responsibility over the environment in which the concert takes place. A concert is not an entertainment event but something much more spiritual in character and everything surrounding the concert affects this quality: the setting of the stage, the hall, the lighting, what the players wear, etc. Of particular importance is how the conductor begins each composition, how he frames and establishes the character of the music even before the first tone is sounded.

Solti speaks of the discomfort of the audience which has to listen to someone talking before a performance. "People go to hear music, not to listen to speeches,"[146] he reminds his readers. This is actually a very important psychological, and even physiological, issue. We have seen many concerts where the conductor, erroneously believing he was making music more palatable to the audience, introduced each work with lengthy comments. Physiologically this only makes it difficult for the listener to shift gears to listen to music and we guarantee that any musical fragments pointed out beforehand, such as "later the composer presents this upside down," will never be heard by the listener—nor should they. We want the listener to be caught up in the emotional meaning of the music, not in the grammar which has nothing to do with the purpose of listening to music, as we have repeatedly stressed in this book.

Even worse is the conductor who comes out at the beginning of a concert and wanders around the stage, whispering little things to players who giggle. This kind of "inside humor" is very offensive to the audience.

The importance of the environmental aspects of a concert has long been discussed. Francis Bacon observes that sounds are better if one's mind is concentrated on only one sense, hearing. Therefore he suggests that music sounds better at night than during the day.[147] It is for this reason why we wear black clothes for classical concerts; colors would distract the listener by introducing a stimulus for another sense, the eye. Charles Gounod raised the question of tempo, relative to the hall. He believed that tempi should go slower in a

[146] Georg Solti, *Memoirs* (New York: Knopf, 1997), 101.

[147] "Natural History," Section 230ff, in *The Works of Francis Bacon*, ed. James Spedding (Cambridge: Cambridge University Press, 1869). In Bacon's utopian study, *The New Atlantis*, he presents an extraordinary proposal for an acoustic studio, a "sound-house."

large hall than a smaller one.[148] William Finn, the choral conductor, also emphasizes this point, as well as the question of whether various concert halls are themselves sensitive to specific keys.[149] We once conducted in a sixteenth century hall in Austria which resonated vibrantly to each Eb major chord as it sounded.

The above issues are all relative to the perspective of the listener, which is also an interesting problem with respect to recordings. Eugene Ormandy once told me that for recordings one should always perform slow movements at a faster tempo than one would use in a live performance, the argument being that the listener at home would be distracted and would not have the attention span necessary for contemplative listening to a slow movement. Von Karajan once mentioned that the recording engineers tried to get him to use faster tempi in general for recordings. He called the idea nonsense and refused.[150] Haggin, during his conversations with Toscanini, found that the maestro, while pleased with his perception of tempo in concert, was often displeased with his tempi when hearing his own recordings.[151]

Of course, few composers give thought to acoustics or the environment of the performance. Conductors are left to struggle with a number of additional problems which affect the performance, such as the nature and size of group, hall, acoustics and the size of audience. An early exception was Anton Reicha, who included an extraordinary handwritten note in the score of his *Symphony for Band* (1815),[152] in which he discusses the nature of the performance site he had in mind, the space between players, exact adherence to the instrumentation—together with his plea for a good conductor who will study the score!

Peter Paul Fuchs has written at some length about the psychological frame of mind of the conductor immediately before a concert.[153] He acknowledges that the conductor will always have some apprehension, since he knows that no performance is ever fully rehearsed. On the other hand, we, and we would suppose most conductors as well, have found that there is great compensation in the fact that for once one

[148] *Mémoires.*

[149] William J. Finn, *The Conductor Raises his Baton* (London: Dobson, 1946), 75, 62, 69, 71. He also discusses the influence on acoustics by such things as floral displays.

[150] Richard Osborne, *Conversations with Von Karajan* (New York: Harper & Row, 1989), 128.

[151] B. H. Haggin, *Conversations with Toscanini* (Garden City: Doubleday, 1959), 18.

[152] "*Musique pour célébrer la memoire das grands hommes et des grands événements.,*" available today from Maxime's Music (http://maximesmusic.com).

[153] Peter Paul Fuchs, *The Psychology of Conducting* (New York: MCA, 1969), 71ff.

truly has one hundred per cent attention and concentration from the ensemble, a state which can sometimes produce miracles. For the period before the concert Fuchs cautions the conductor against such things as drinking, or having arguments which might detract from his concentration. This is a time to gather his thoughts together, to prepare himself for the "holy office." We might add that the same is necessary before ordinary rehearsals. A school conductor should make every effort to keep the hour before rehearsal free.

In the final seconds before the first down-beat, Fuchs stresses that the conductor must have no thought of the audience, or how he might look. He must appear as if saying to the orchestra, "this is our great moment: now we shall make beautiful music together." The highest priority is to "concentrate completely on the intended sound of the first measures of music he is about to conduct."

Leonard Bernstein, writing of these final moments before the concert, found a magical moment, a moment when the audience is ready, the players are focused and the conductor has brought his mental and spiritual forces to a point of concentration.

> How can I describe to you the magic of the moment of beginning a piece of music? There is only one possible fraction of a second that feels exactly right for starting. There is a wait while the orchestra readies itself and collects its powers; while the conductor concentrates his whole will and force toward the work in hand; while the audience quiets down, and the last cough has died away. There is no slight rustle of a program book; the instruments are poised and—bang! That's it. One second later, it is too late, and the magic has vanished.[154]

[154] Quoted in Carl Bamberger, *The Conductor's Art* (New York: McGraw-Hill, 1965), 271.

The use of the term "holy office," by Fuchs, above, seems appropriate to me, for I have always considered a concert to be a very serious spiritual occasion. For me the closest analogy would be something like high Mass at St. Peter's in Rome—and I feel that way even if it is a Middle School concert.

But, however serious our attitude toward aesthetic music is, human nature always makes it a constant test. The greatest French writer of the sixteenth century, Michel Montaigne (1533–1592), acknowledged this struggle.

> Whether it is art or nature which stamps on us that characteristic of living by what others say, it does us much more harm than good. We cheat ourselves of what is rightly useful to us in order to conform our appearances to the common opinion. We are not so much concerned with what the actual nature of our being is within us, as with how it is perceived by the public.[155]

And it is often by a very human path that the artist fails to make the distinction between the concept of the audience finding *pleasure* in the universality of music with the concept of the artist setting out *to please* the audience. The aesthetic danger is in progressing from the one to the other, as might be illustrated in the following chronology:

1. The artist performs and the audience finds pleasure in his performance.

2. The artist observes he has pleased the audience.

3. The artist now tries to please the audience.

4. His art has become entertainment.

For Robert Schumann the personal struggle one has to make to prevent falling into this trap was like the effort of swimming against the stream.

> So it has often happened that those who did not understand this, but struggled against the stream, have been obliged to do so alone and unapplauded, while those who abandoned their higher aim and yielded, swam with a hundred others in the current and disappeared without leaving a trace behind them.[156]

Richard Wagner, who spent his life swimming against the stream, wrote of the same metaphor.

[155] Michel de Montaigne, *Essays*, trans. M. A. Screech (London: Penguin, 1993), III, ix, 1081.

[156] Schumann, "Trios," in *Neue Zeitschrift für Musik,* March, 1840.

To take a last look back upon the picture afforded us by the public astir in Time and Space, we might compare it with a river, as to which we must decide whether we will swim against or with its stream. Who swims with it, may imagine he belongs to constant progress; it is so easy to be borne along, and he never notes that he is being swallowed in the ocean of vulgarity. To swim against the stream must seem ridiculous to those not driven by an irresistible force to the immense exertions that it costs.[157]

And Wagner's judgment of those who failed in this effort was severe.

The man who strays into the realm of triviality must pay for his transgression at the cost of his own more noble nature. But he who seeks it deliberately, that man is fortunate, for he has *nothing* worth losing.[158]

Finally, we include three comments on repertoire by famous musicians, beginning with Georg Solti.

What you really remember is not the performance itself, but whether a performance touched you.[159]

Bruno Walter was also agitated over the fact that we only have one word, "music," to cover everything.

And how can it happen that music may descend from its lofty place, stooping to banality and vulgarity; how can one call by the same name of music what spills out from dance-halls and bars, or assaults us, with yowls and screeches, in the grotesquely distorted melodies, harmonies, and rhythms of jazz and allied forms of dance-music?
The character of music, as that of every other art, can be superlatively ennobled by chosen individuals, or debased beyond recognition by the inept, inferior or perverse.[160]

And finally, a very important reminder from Franz Liszt that there will be some members of the audience who applaud the performance, and not the music.

A successful performance cannot as a rule be considered as a criterion of artistic worth.[161]

---

[157] *Wagner's Prose Works,* trans. William Ashton Ellis (New York: Broude), VI, 94.

[158] Letter to Eduard Hanslick, January 1, 1847.

[159] Georg Solti, *Memoirs* (New York: Knopf, 1997), 211.

[160] Bruno Walter, *Of Music and Music-Making* (New York: Norton, 1957), 18.

[161] Franz Liszt, letter to Fedor von Milde, June 3, 1857. Wagner, in *Wagner's Prose Works,* IV, 291, gives a different perspective,

> The audience is incapable of distinguishing between a poor performance and a poor composition.

Contesting Bands: The Great Pretense

I HAVE NEVER MET a band or orchestra conductor who enjoyed the idea of his ensemble being judged by strangers at a music contest, or to use the misnomer, a music festival. Therefore I do not anticipate any conductor will disagree with my list of objections to the whole idea of contesting in music.

[1] Contrary to the implication of the title, a music contest never judges music, nor grades music performance. The question, Which band was the most musical?, can never be answered because the answer is found only in the right hemisphere of the listener, where every listener has a different answer and where they are all right, none is wrong. The only thing which can be judged, and hence compared against some standard, is the grammar found in the left hemisphere. But the components of grammar, which usually is all that is found on adjudication sheets, is, in part and sum, not music at all. The definition of these elements of grammar is what the eye sees on the page, courtesy of the publisher. Every great musician feels free to vary all these elements for musical purposes and, in any case, we should be judging the students and not the publisher.

Let me offer a personal illustration of how wrong-headed this whole process is. I was once invited to be the President of the Jury for an international piano contest held in Italy. The contestants were from all over the world and each, in addition to the personal cost of flying from Japan or someplace, had no doubt devoted months of practice in advance of this contest. Ten of the judges were famous piano teachers, whereas I, as number eleven, was supposed to represent "the listener." Like Roman emperors of old, we voted with our thumbs—up or down after each performance in five rounds of performances, the final one accompanied by a full orchestra. In cases where the majority of thumbs were down, even in the first round, the student was abruptly eliminated from the contest, sent home never to be seen again. To my embarrassment, when the arms were extended and the thumbs employed it rather frequently resulted in ten thumbs down and one up, or one down and ten up. After a very musical performance of a Beethoven Sonata by a young lady from Finland, whose beautiful playing earned only my single thumb pointing up, I asked another judge, a friend from Argentina, "I don't understand what is going on here. She was extremely musical and now she has been sent home." His answer, a completely honest answer characteristic of the great touring artist he himself is, was, "Oh, a piano contest doesn't have anything to do with music!" The other ten judges were judging the results of specific piano teaching techniques, in other words they were really just judging each other. Which leads to Objection Number 2.

[2] In the case of a band contest, the adjudication form addresses only the degree of perfection in the musical grammar which the band exhibits. There is no question on the form which reflects either the general musicality or the conductor. Yet, in truth we are judging the conductor, not the band. Everyone knows this, it is a big lie no one will dispute.

[3] If the real object were to judge musicality, in my mind it would rest in the teaching the conductor had offered his students in performance practice. But we do not teach performance practice. We only teach playing what is on the page, which is not music to begin with, "music" not being a noun.

I very frequently hear, for example, performances of the first movement of the Mozart *Gran Partita*, K. 361/270a, where the final note is made into a fermata, whereas Mozart intended it to be played one-half the written value, for reasons of a Vienna performance practice, and would have never imagined it would be held longer than half its written value. It makes a very big difference, for if the final note is elongated the listener will feel that yet another downbeat is needed to end the movement. How many university band conductors understand that in Mozart the dot over a single note-head has nothing to do with staccato? And in Baroque music which simply cannot be played as written on paper, what does the conductor tell the student about improvisation—oh, oh! a forbidden word!

[4] Adjudication fees reflect disrespect. In most cases we pay the adjudicator an hourly fee far less than we would pay, without a moment's complaint, a beginning plumber. The last time I judged for the Southern California Band and Orchestra Association, while granted many years ago, I figured out I was paid about $11.00 per band. Would you trust the judgment of a plumber who charged $11.00 to give an estimate of a major plumbing problem? Would you trust a doctor who gave you a bill for $11.00 for a physical exam?

As a result the adjudicator sits there all day doing his best just to remember one band from another and whatever comments he offers for the improvement of the performance are given no attention at all. I would venture to wonder if in many cases they are even read.

[5] In any contest there is one winner and everyone else is a loser. In terms of education how is this justified when the object is in the right hemisphere where everyone is right and no one wrong?

[6] There is usually no audience. Music makes no sense if there is no listener, since the whole point of music is the communication of feeling.[162] Perhaps the most accurate form of discovery of the success of a band's performance might be found if we videotaped the faces of the members of the audience, and not the band. Because the face is the only part of the body which both left and right hemisphere can operate, and the right hemisphere is by nature incapable of a lie.[163]

Competition is a fact of life which no doubt dates from the earliest period of man. There are philosophers who credit much of the advance of man to competition, but in music I am not so sure. In any case, for those who might be

[162] Is the recorded music played in an elevator to be called music if there is no one in the elevator to hear it? The answer is "No." In the famous riddle, does a tree falling in a forest make a sound if there is no one there to hear it? The answer is "No."

[163] The reader is strongly advised to read David Whitwell, *Essays on the Modern Wind Band*, ed. Craig Dabelstein (Austin: Whitwell Books, 2013), where one will find an essay on "A Proposal for a New Festival Format," which helps overcome most of the objections given above.

interested, the following provides a brief background on how our earlier profession viewed competition.

In one of the earliest references to competition among musicians, Hesiod, a Greek poet (c. seventh century BC), we get the impression that such competition was old enough to become controversial. Hesiod says that when a man sees his wealthy neighbor planting and plowing with zeal, it makes him also "long for work" and that this form of competition is good. However, artists should not compete, nor create for the market place.

> Then potters eye one another's success and craftsmen, too;
> the beggar's envy is a beggar, the singer's a singer.
> Perses, treasure this thought deep down in your heart,
> do not let malicious [competition] curb your zeal for work [only]
> so you can see and hear the brawls of the market place.[164]

There are references to trumpet contests which began with the 96th Olympiad of 396 BC. These seem to have been more physical contests, rather than musical, and perhaps the modern Olympic motto, *citius, altius, fortius* (faster, higher, stronger) describes them well. We know the names of a few of the famous winners and the information about them reads like a description of sumo wrestlers. We are told, for example, that Heradorus of Megara consumed, in a typical meal, six pints of wheat bread, twenty pounds of meat and six quarts of wine! We also know of a woman trumpeter who participated in these contests, Aglais, the daughter of Megacles. She wore a wig with a plume on her head and had an appetite similar to the male trumpeter, eating in a typical meal twelve pounds of meat, four pints of wheat bread and a pitcher of wine![165]

In the public athletic festivals the performance of music was included and centered in competition, called *krisis*, judged by adjudicators called, *kritai*. No doubt we may assume that *kritai* will be critics, for a fragment by Archilochus responds to some criticism he received.

> Upbraid me for my songs:

[164] *Works and Days*, 25–29. Aethenaeus, in *Deipnosophistae*, VII, 310, mentions a singing contest at this time in which the prize was "a lad with the fair bloom of youth," for the enjoyment of the winner!

[165] Athenaeus, Ibid., X, 414.

> Catch a cricket instead,
> And shout at him for chirping.[166]

According to comments by Pindar, the best known of the seventh century BC lyric poets, the choral competition at these festivals was one among professionals.[167] This seems to be the meaning of a fragment of Bacchylides as well.

> The keenly-contested gifts of the Muses are not prizes open to all, which the first comer may win.[168]

Pindar also tells us in one Ode that the music lovers of Aegina loved these competitions.

> For his city is one of music lovers,
> The sons of Aeacus, bred to the clash of spears;
> And glad are they to embrace a spirit, that shares
> Their love of contest.[169]

Indeed, one of the extant Odes of Pindar was written for "Midas of Acragas, Winner of the Aulos Playing Contest," composed for the Pythian Festival of 490 BC.

In this lyric poetry performed by the solo singer, he was accompanied by either the lyre or the aulos. In the tradition of the Greek myths, the Greeks seemed compelled to assign the beginning of everything to a specific god. In the case of the lyre, the inventor was said to be Hermes, however some Greek writers said it was invented by Hermes, the son of Zeus and Maia, daughter of Atlas, while others assigned its origin to the Egyptian Hermes, or Thoth, the god of learning.[170] Plutarch, on the other hand, says that the lyre used by these lyric poets was invented by a student of Terpander.

> As to the form of the lyre, it was such as Cepion, one of Terpander's students first caused to be made, and it was called the Asian lyre, because the Lesbian lyre players bordering on Asia always made use of it. And it is said that Periclitus, a Lesbian by birth, was the last lyre player who won a prize by his skill, which he did at one of the Spartan festivals called Carneius; but he being dead, that succession of skillful musicians which had so long continued among the Lesbians, expired.[171]

---

[166] Guy Davenport, *Archilochos, Sapo, Alkman: Three Lyric Poets of the Late Greek Bronze Age* (Berkeley: University of California Press, 1980), 76.

[167] Gregory Nagy, *Pindar's Homer: The Lyric Possession of an Epic Past* (Baltimore: Johns Hopkins University Press, 1982), 342.

[168] Bacchylides, R., *The Poems and Fragments*, trans. Richard Jebb (Hildesheim: Georg Olms, 1967), 423.

[169] *Ode for Sogenes of Aegina*, Winner of the Boys' Pentathlon, in Geoffrey S. Conway, *The Odes of Pindar* (London: Dent, 1972), 204.

[170] W. Chappell, *The History of Music* (London: Chappell), I, 27.

[171] Quoted by Plutarch in *Concerning Music*.

This musician called Terpander of Lesbos, who flourished c. 710–670 BC, is said to have won the first music contest at the Feast of Carneius, in Sparta, in 676 BC, and to have invented the practice of lyre singing.[172]

Xenophon provides us with some enlightening details of the choral competitions held as part of the festivals which have been mentioned by the epic and lyric poets in the pages above. First of all, he attributes competition itself as the essential catalyst which brings about the highest levels of performance. He credits Lycurgus as having instituted this philosophy.

> He saw that where the spirit of rivalry is the strongest among the people, there the choruses are most worth hearing and the athletic contests afford the finest spectacle.[173]

Xenophon also tells us that long periods of training and large sums of money were necessary to prepare a chorus for competition and he seems almost perplexed that they do this when the goal is only a "paltry" prize. He apparently failed to realize that it is the honor of winning which propels the competition, not the value of the trophy the winner receives. In a conversation with a political leader, Hiero, Xenophon speaks through the character of Simonides, one of the lyric poets.

> In case you fear, Hiero, that the cost of offering prizes for many subjects may prove heavy, you should reflect that no commodities are cheaper than those that are bought for a prize. Think of the large sums that men are induced to spend on horse races, gymnastic and choral competitions, and the long course of training and practice they undergo for the sake of a paltry prize.[174]

The chief end of this "long course of training," which he sees in terms of artistic value, is discipline.

> There is nothing so convenient nor so good for human beings as order. Thus, a chorus is a combination of human beings; but when the members of it do as they choose, it becomes mere confusion, and there is no pleasure in watching it; but when they act and sing in an orderly fashion, then those same men at once seem worth seeing and worth hearing.[175]

[172] Chappell, *The History of Music*, 32. We can assume this practice was actually much older, in view of the icons we seen in the Egyptian tombs. Jebb, *The Poems and Fragments*, 28, says Terpander founded a school of cithara performance in Lesbos which continued for several centuries.

[173] *The Lacedaemonians*, IV., trans. E. C. Marchant, *Scripta Minora* (Cambridge: Harvard University Press, 1956).

[174] *Hiero*, IX, in Ibid.

[175] *Oeconomicus*, VIII, trans. E. C. Marchant, *Memorabilia and Oeconomicus* (Cambridge: Harvard University Press, 1953).

Xenophon, now in the voice of Socrates, also tells us that the most successful choruses are those which have as their leaders, "the best experts."[176] Although speaking of a battle in another place, he also gives an interesting clue as to how these choruses may have stood when they performed.

> They took position in lines of about a hundred each, like the choral dancers ranged opposite one another.[177]

As we have seen above, these choral performances often were accompanied by an aulos player. Socrates, speaking on the subject of imposture, gives us a picture of this aulos player which suggests that some of them must have played the role of the prima donna.

> Suppose a bad aulos player wants to be thought a good one, let us note what he must do. Must he not imitate good players in the accessories of the art? First, as they wear fine clothes and travel with many attendants, he must do the same. Further, seeing that they win the applause of crowds, he must provide himself with a large claque. But, of course, he must never accept an engagement, or he will promptly expose himself to ridicule as an incompetent player and an impostor to boot.[178]

Finally, in another discussion relative to war, Xenophon mentions in passing the fact that musicians of his experience were both performing older compositions and creating new ones.

> However, my son, since you are desirous of learning all these matters, you must not only utilize what you may learn from others, but you must yourself also be an inventor of stratagems against the enemy, just as musicians render not only those compositions which they have learned but try to compose others also that are new. Now if in music that which is new and fresh wins applause, new stratagems in warfare also win far greater applause, for such can deceive the enemy even more successfully.[179]

Thucydides also mentions these choral competitions, in a brief reference to the Festival of Delia, held by the Ionians of Delos every fifth year. He quotes a *Hymn to Apollo* which

[176] *Memorabilia*, III, in Ibid.

[177] *The Anabasis of Cyrus*, V, trans. Carleton L. Brownson, *Anabasis* (Cambridge: Harvard University Press, 1947).

[178] *Memorabilia*, I.

[179] *Cyropaedia*, I, trans. Walter Miller, *Cyropaedia* (Cambridge: Harvard University Press, 1960).

speaks of "music's magic" in reference to the listener, suggesting to us that the audiences were still listening to these performances as music, and not as entertainment.

> In Delos, Phoebus, lies thy chief delight,
> Thy isle's warm landscapes cheer thy gladden'd sight,
> When long-rob'd Ions throng around thy fane,
> Whose blushing spouses swell the festal train,
> Whose ruddy children's lisping accents sound thy name.
> Thy feast to celebrate the leapers vig'rous bound,
> The champions box, the dancers' footsteps beat the ground,
> While music's magic echoes wide resound.[180]

Plutarch also mentions the sponsorship of music competitions by Pericles and his construction of a special hall for the performance of music.

> The Odeum, or concert hall, which in its interior was full of seats and ranges of pillars, and outside had its roof made to slope and descend from one single point at the top, was constructed, we are told, in imitation of the king of Persia's Pavilion ...
>
> Pericles, also, eager for distinction, then first obtained the decree for a contest in musical skill to be held yearly at the Panathanaea, and he himself, being chosen judge, arranged the order and method in which the competitors should sing and play on the aulos and harp. And both at that time, and at other times also, they sat in this music room to see and hear all such trials of skill.

The extant speeches of Antiphon, a famous fifth century speaker, and early interpreter of dreams, include some interesting references to the famous choral contests. In a fragment of a speech[181] discussing the fact that pleasure often follows pain, he mentions contests in general and observes,

> For honors, prizes, the baits which God has given to mankind, bring them to the necessity of great toil and sweat.

Of particular interest is a speech, known as "On the Chorus Boy," which Antiphon wrote for an unknown defendant who was in charge of the chorus[182] at Thargelia in 412 BC. This speech provides valuable details regarding the establishment and provisions of a boy's chorus.

---

[180] S. T. Bloomfield, *The History of Thucydides* (London: Longman, Rees, Orme, Brown, and Green, 1829), III, civ.

[181] Quoted in Rosamond Kent Sprague, *The Older Sophists: A complete translation by several hands of the fragments in Die Fragmente der Vorsokratiker* (Columbia: University of South Carolina Press, 1972), 228.

[182] Athenaeus, *Deipnosophistae*, XIV, 633, says *choregus* originally was used to mean the conductor of the chorus, not, as later, the administrator, or "provider."

> When I was appointed in charge of the chorus [*choregus*] at Thargelia..., I performed the office as well and conscientiously as I could. In the first place, I provided a room for training in the most convenient part of my house, where I used to train when I was *choregus* at the Dionysia. Secondly, I enrolled a chorus in the best way I could, not penalizing anyone nor forcibly exacting security nor making an enemy of anyone; but, as was most agreeable and convenient to both parties, I made my requests and demands, while the parents sent their sons with good grace and willingly...
>
> I appointed Phanostratus to look after the chorus in case they needed anything. Phanostratus is a fellow demesman of the prosecutors and a kinsman of mine, in fact, my son-in-law, and I expected him to look after them well. I appointed two other men too, Ameinias of the tribe Erechtheis, whom the tribesmen themselves regularly elected to enroll and look after the tribe, a man with a good reputation; and the second man from the Cecropid tribe, who regularly convened that tribe. Then I appointed a fourth, Philippus, who was commissioned to buy and spend any money necessary on the authority of the poet or of any other of the officials, so that the boys should enjoy the best possible *choregia* and should go in want of nothing because of my inability to give them my attention.

There were apparently also contests held in the realm of music education, in both instrumental and choral music. Plato provides an interesting discussion on the goals and organization of such contests.

> It will be proper to appoint directors of music and gymnastic, two kinds of each—of the one kind the business will be education, of the other, the superintendence of contests.... In speaking of contests, the law refers to the judges of gymnastics and of music; these again are divided into two classes, the one having to do with music, the other with gymnastics; and the same who judge of the gymnastic contests of men, shall judge of horses; but in music there shall be one set of judges of solo singing, and of imitation—I mean of rhapsodists, players on the harp, the flute and the like, and another who shall judge of choral songs. First of all, we must choose directors for the choruses of boys, and men, and maidens, whom they shall follow in the amusement of the dance, and for our other musical arrangements;—one director will be enough for the choruses, and he should be not less than forty years of age.

One director will also be enough to introduce the solo singers, and to give judgment on the competitors, and he ought to be not less than thirty years of age. The director and manager of the choruses shall be elected after the following manner:—Let any persons who commonly take an interest in such matters go to the meeting, and be fined if they do not go, but those who have no interest shall not be compelled. Any elector may propose as director someone who understands music, and he in the scrutiny may be challenged on the one part by those who say he has no skill, and defended on the other hand by those who say that he has. Ten are to be elected by vote, and he of the ten who is chosen by lot shall undergo a scrutiny, and lead the choruses for a year according to law. And in like manner the competitor who wins the lot shall be leader of the solo and concert music for that year; and he who is thus elected shall deliver the award to the judges.[183]

[183] *Laws*, 764d.

Aristotle seemed to believe that music education should continue only to the extent that it accomplishes the goals he has thus far mentioned: preparing one for adult intellectual leisure, formation of character, and the ability to judge musical performances. To go beyond this, to create professional musicians for example, should not be an aim of public education.

> The right measure will be attained if students of music stop short of the arts which are practiced in professional contests, and do not seek to acquire those fantastic marvels of execution which are now the fashion in such contests, and from these have passed into education.[184]

[184] *Politica*, 1341a.10.

From ancient Rome there is one description of an actual repertoire work played at the contests of this period, and we even know the name of the composer, one Timosthenes (fl. c. 270 BC). This work, performed by rhapsodists with either aulos or lyre accompanying, told the story of a contest between Apollo and a dragon. It consisted of a prelude, the battle, the triumph following the victory, and the expiration of the dragon—with the aulos player imitating the last hissings of the dragon.[185]

From the famous Roman historian, Polybius, we find a reference to contests.

[185] *The Geography of Strabo*, trans. Horace L. Jones (Cambridge: Harvard University Press, 1960), IX.3.10.

For it is a well-known fact, familiar to all, that it is hardly known except in Arcadia, that in the first place the boys from their earliest childhood are trained to sing in measure the hymns and paeans in which by traditional usage they celebrate the heroes and gods of each particular place; later they learn the measures of Philoxenus and Timotheus, and every year in the theater they compete keenly in choral singing to the accompaniment of professional aulos players, the boys in the contest proper to them and the young men in what is called the men's contest. And not only this, but through their whole life they entertain themselves at banquets not by listening to hired musicians but by their own efforts, calling for a song from each in turn. Whereas they are not ashamed of denying acquaintance with other studies, in the case of singing it is neither possible for them to deny a knowledge of it because they all are compelled to learn it, nor, if they confess to such knowledge can they excuse themselves, so great a disgrace is this considered in that country. Besides this the young men practice military parades to the music of the aulos and perfect themselves in dances and give annual performances in the theaters, all under state supervision and at public expense.[186]

[186] Polybius, *The Histories*, IV.20.5ff, trans. W. R. Paton (Cambridge: Harvard University Press, 1954).

There are some surviving memorial stones from ancient Rome and one carries the name of a choral conductor, suggesting that the choral contests were, at least on some occasions, still *musical* contests.

Damomenes the choirmaster put us this tripod,
Dionysus, and your image, blest and blythest god.
Measured in all things, he won the victory
With his male choir, observing beauty and degree.[187]

[187] Theocritus, *Epigram XII*.

In the Roman poetic literature there are many references to musical contests among the rural people. One of the most interesting describes the shepherd, Menalcas, challenging the cattle boy, Daphnis, to a musical duel.[188] Daphnis won and, we are told, celebrated by "clapping his hands and jumping for joy, as a fawn might have jumped all around its own mother." But, since one of the problems of all musical contests is that there must of necessity be a "loser," Menalcas, "smoldered and worried his heart with his sorrow."

[188] Theocritus, *Idyll* Nr. VIII.

One of the most frequently discussed singers of ancient Rome was the famous emperor, Nero. We are fortunate to have a few insights into the nature of artistic contests of this period in Suetonius' account of Nero's participation in them.

> Nero was greatly taken too with the rhythmic applause of some Alexandrians, who had flocked to Naples from a fleet that had lately arrived, and summoned more men from Alexandria. Not content with that, he selected some young men of the order of knights and more than five thousand sturdy young commoners, to be divided into groups and learn the Alexandrian styles of applause (they called them "the bees," "the roof-tiles," and "the bricks"), and to ply them vigorously whenever he sang ...
>
> Considering it of great importance to appear in Rome as well, he repeated the contest of the Neronia before the appointed time, and when there was a general call for his "divine voice," he replied that if any wished to hear him, he would favor them in the gardens; but when the guard of soldiers which was then on duty seconded the entreaties of the people, he gladly agreed to appear at once. So without delay he had his name added to the list of the lyre players who entered the contest, and casting his own lot into the urn with the rest, he came forward in his turn, attended by the prefects of the Guard carrying his lyre, and followed by the tribunes of the soldiers and his intimate friends. Having taken his place and finished his preliminary speech, he announced through the ex-consul Cluvius Rufus that "he would sing Niobe"; and he kept at it until late in the afternoon, putting off the award of the prize for that event and postponing the rest of the contest to the next year, to have an excuse for singing oftener ...
>
> Not content with showing his proficiency in these arts at Rome, he went to Achaia, as I have said, influenced by the following consideration. The cities in which it was the custom to hold contests in music had adopted the rule of sending all the lyric prizes to him.[189] These he received with the greatest delight, not only giving audience before all others to the envoys who brought them, but even inviting them to his private table. When some of them begged him to sing during dinner and greeted his performance with extravagant applause, he declared that "the Greeks were the only ones who had an ear for music and that they alone were worthy of his efforts." So he took ship without delay and immediately

[189] Suetonius, *Lives of the Caesars*, VI, xii, relates, unfortunately without explaining the significance, that on one such occasion Nero, when the prize for lyre playing was offered him, knelt before it and ordered that it be laid at the feet of Augustus's statue.

on arriving at Cassiope made a preliminary appearance as a singer at the altar of Jupiter Cassius, and then went the round of all the contests.

To make this possible, he gave orders that even those which were widely separated in time should be brought together in a single year, so that some had even to be given twice, and he introduced a musical competition at Olympia also, contrary to custom. To avoid being distracted or hindered in any way while busy with these contests, he replied to his freedman Helius, who reminded him that the affairs of the city required his presence, in these words: "However much it may be your advice and your wish that I should return speedily, yet you ought rather to counsel me and to hope that I may return worthy of Nero."

While he was singing no one was allowed to leave the theatre even for the most urgent reasons. And so it is said that some women gave birth to children there, while many who were worn out with listening and applauding, secretly leaped from the wall, since the gates at the entrance were closed, or feigned death and were carried out as if for burial. The trepidation and anxiety with which he took part in the contests, his keen rivalry of his opponents and his awe of the judges, can hardly be credited. As if his rivals were of quite the same station as himself, he used to show respect to them and try to gain their favor, while he slandered them behind their backs, sometimes assailed them with abuse when he met them, and even bribed those who were especially proficient.

Before beginning, he would address the judges in the most deferential terms, saying that he had done all that could be done, but the issue was in the hands of Fortune; they however, being men of wisdom and experience, ought to exclude what was fortuitous. When they bade him take heart, he withdrew with greater confidence, but not even then without anxiety, interpreting the silence and modesty of some as sullenness and ill-nature, and declaring that he had his suspicions of them.

In competition he observed the rules most scrupulously, never daring to clear his throat and even wiping the sweat from his brow with his arm. Once indeed, during the performance of a tragedy, when he had dropped his scepter but quickly recovered it, he was terribly afraid that he might be excluded from the competition because of his slip, and his confidence was restored only when his accompanist swore that it had passed unnoticed amid the delight and applause of the people. When the victory was won, he made the announcement himself; and for that reason he always took part in the contests of the heralds. To obliterate the memory of all other victors in the games and leave no trace of them, their statues and busts were all thrown down by his order, dragged off with hooks, and cast into privies.[190]

[190] Ibid., VI, xx.

By the time the Renaissance arrives we begin to find some writers making rather negative assessments of the idea of contests in music. Vives, for example, in his famous book on Education discourages the spirit of competition, which he says leads to "quarrels, wrangling and dissensions."[191]

[191] *Vives: On Education,* trans. Foster Watson (Cambridge: University Press, 1913), II, i.

Cervantes makes an interesting observation about poetry contests.

> If it's for a poetry competition, you ought to aim at the second prize, your grace, because the first prize is always awarded as an act of patronage or in recognition of social standing, but second prize strictly on merit, so that third prize really amounts to second, and what's called first prize, if you calculate matters this way, has to be truly the third—much in the fashion that universities award advanced degrees.[192]

[192] Miguel de Cervantes, *Don Quijote,* trans. Burton Raffel (New York: Norton, 1995), II, xviii.

Finally, Roger North, an important English critic found that competition in music has largely negative results.

> Instead of encouraging the endeavors of all, the happy victor only was pleased, and all the rest were discontented and some who thought they deserved better, were almost ready to [give up music] ... So much a mistake it is to force artists upon a competition, for all but one are sure to be malcontents.[193]

[193] Roger North, *Memoirs of Music*, ed. Edward Rimbault (London: Bell, 1846), 118ff.

Unique Benefits of Performance-based Music Education, which are not possible under the current Conceptual Music Education Doctrine

THE PREVIOUS PAGES presented and discussed the stipulations which must be met if a genuine revolution in music education in America is to be achieved. These stipulations are not variable. They must all be achieved and there is no middle ground, if the following benefits to the students are to be realized. If we were to create a new philosophy of music education based on those stipulations then the whole series of very important educational achievements listed below would ensue. None of these educational accomplishments are possible under the present philosophy of "talking about" music instead of making music.

An entire new library of materials and the development of new teaching strategies must be developed upon which the principle of all children experiencing the performance of music, from kindergarten through high school. The overriding goal must be experiential learning by the child and not entertainment for the child. It is for this reason that the achievements listed below are obtainable only if aesthetic musical materials and no popular music of any kind are used.

Students receive the only Direct Right Hemisphere Education in the School

NEARLY ALL EDUCATION MATERIALS are in print or vocal language in format, hence *ipso facto* left hemisphere and past tense. In addition nearly all educational materials and techniques objectives are geared to the class, not the individual. The experiential nature of Music is found in the right hemisphere; the elements of music which are in the left hemisphere, namely music grammar, notation, etc., are not music.

Therefore the personal emotional development in the right hemisphere which is possible through music performance is unique to the individual.

Students receive the only Present Tense Education in the School

> Education can neither consist entirely of mere unfolding—for everything that keeps living unfolds—nor of developing all the powers, because we can never act upon all of them at once.
>
> The child is not to be educated for the present—this will happen without our help unceasingly—but for the remote future and in opposition to the immediate one.
>
> JEAN-PAUL RICHTER, *Levana* (1806)

WHAT THE GREAT ROMANTIC CRITIC, Jean-Paul Richter is drawing our attention to here is the fact that most general education is presented in a kind of time-warp. Everything presented is in the past tense, while telling the student he will need this in the future, and yet the object, the student, sits there in the present tense. It is a formula inviting disorientation and lack of interest because the information leaps over the student, from past to future. Because of the focus on the past, the student in a graduate Music of the Renaissance course sits there struggling with endless dates of people whose music he has never heard and fails to understand that this course could possibly have anything to do with his life—and then after class he leaves for a rehearsal which includes Renaissance music.

Jean-Paul Richter is correct that we should not educate as if the present is the only object, but on the other hand we must educate in the present, as that is where the student is. And in the case of music, since the educational subject is his emotions, his present will also be his immediate future at least.

The first person in the field of music to concern himself with this topic was the great early theorist, Johannes Tinctoris (1435–1511), author of the first music dictionary. Here, for the smallest element of time, the single note, Tinctoris quite correctly reminds the reader that notation is only a symbol of the real music.

> A note is the symbol of a sound, and is of either definite or indefinite time value.[194]

The next level of time he associates with present tense performance.

> Measure is the correct division of the notes, as far as their delivery is concerned.[195]

Nothing is more clearly in the present tense than performing music. Each of us has a folder in a drawer or closet somewhere where we keep old programs of concerts we participated in. We faithfully keep them but we never look at them and have no desire to. We have no desire to listen to recordings of our past performances, which seem so cold and lifeless. Any type of educational material which falls in the left hemisphere category [anything written] has the same effect on us.

The music performance class is, therefore, perhaps the only classroom instruction in which the material is in the present tense, the student is in the present tense and the instruction is in the present tense. Maybe that is one reason why students love to perform music.

[194] Tinctoris, *Dictionary of Musical Terms*, trans. Carl Parrish (New York: Free Press of Glencoe, 1963), 47.

[195] Ibid., 41.

Students experience a Direct Association with Great Minds

Great thoughts often circulate in similar words and tone through different minds. ROBERT SCHUMANN, unpublished diary, c. 1833

THE VERY EARLY WRITERS, in noticing how a man's mind was influenced by another, thought of this as being a kind of music therapy. Cassiodorus (485–585 AD), statesman and philosopher, offers this explanation:

> The artist changes men's hearts as they listen; and, when this artful pleasure issues from the secret place of nature as the queen of the senses, in all the glory of its tones, our remaining thoughts take to flight, and it expels all else, that it may delight itself simply in being heard. Harmful melancholy he turns to pleasure; he weakens swelling rage; he makes bloodthirsty cruelty kindly, arouses sleepy sloth from its torpor, restores to the sleepless their wholesome rest, recalls lust-corrupted chastity to its moral resolve, and heals boredom of spirit which is always the enemy of good thoughts. Dangerous hatreds he turns to helpful goodwill, and, in a blessed kind of healing, drives out the passions of the heart by means of sweetest pleasures.

He thought there must be an analogy of this process in the example of a string made to vibrate by the movement of an adjacent string.

> For, although many instruments of this delight have been discovered, nothing has been found more effective to move the soul than the sweet resonance of the hollow cithara. Hence, we suppose that the strings of the instrument were called chords because they easily move the heart [*corda*]. So great is the concord of the diverse notes assembled there that a string, once struck, makes it neighbor vibrate spontaneously, although itself untouched. For such is the power of harmony that it makes a lifeless object move spontaneously because it so happens that its fellow is in motion.[196]

The important early fifteenth century Florentine philosopher, Leon Battista Alberti (b. 1404), one of those who believed strongly that Reason, and not the senses or the emotions, must rule man, comments that one must read only the finest of the ancient writers.

[196] Letter to Boethius, in *Variae*, trans. Thomas Hodgkin (London: Frowde, 1886), II, xl.

> The intellect, they say, is like a drinking vessel; if you first fill it with bad stuff it always retains something of the taste. This is why one should avoid crude and rough writers. One should follow the finest and most polished, keep them ever at hand, never tire of rereading them, recite them aloud frequently, and commit them to memory. I do not say anything against the knowledge found in any erudite and abundant source, but I decidedly prefer the good writers to the poor ones, and as there are enough whose work is perfect, I am sorry when people select the others.[197]

This standard is seconded by Pietro Bembo (1470 in Venice–1547), a colorful supporter of the arts, who reflects the standard for painters at the time, that they should surpass Nature. It was in reference to this that Bembo wrote the lines inscribed on Raphel's tomb,

> Here lies Raphael.
> Nature feared to be conquered when he lived,
> And to die when he died.[198]

The greatest French writer of the sixteenth century was unquestionably Michel Montaigne (1533–1592). After an education in law at Toulouse, he became in turn a soldier, courtier, traveler and mayor of Bordeaux. In his essay in defense of Seneca and Plutarch, he makes an eloquent statement regarding how one can be lifted by the great minds of others. His discussion here, it seems to us, applies as well to Art in general and Music in particular.

> It seems to each man that the master Form of Nature is in himself, as a touchstone by which he may compare all the other forms. Activities which do not take his form as their model are feigned and artificial. What brute-like stupidity! I consider some men, particularly among the Ancients, to be way above me and even though I clearly realize that I am powerless to follow them on my feet I do not give up following them with my eyes and judging the principles which raise them thus aloft, principles the seeds of which I can just perceive in myself, as I also can that ultimate baseness of minds which no longer amazes me and which I do not refuse to believe in either. I can clearly see the spiral by which those great souls wind themselves higher. I admire

---

[197] Leon Battista Alberti, *I Libri dela Famiglia*, trans. Renèe Watkins (Columbia: University of South Carolina Press, 1969), I, 83.

[198] Quoted in Frank Chambers, *The History of Taste* (New York: Columbia University Press, 1932), 59. The modern font, Bembo, is named in honor of this man.

the greatness of those souls; those ecstasies which I find most beautiful I clasp unto me; though my powers do not reach as far, at least my judgment is most willingly applied to them.[199]

In another place he writes of the other side of this coin, an observation which again seems to us particularly valid with respect to the exposure to inferior music.

> Just as our mind is strengthened by contact with vigorous and well-ordered minds, so too it is impossible to overstate how much it loses and deteriorates by the continuous commerce and contact we have with mean and ailing ones. No infection is as contagious as that is.[200]

Giraldi Cinthio, in his *Discorso intorno al comporre dei romanzi* (1549), makes a comment very similar to the Schumann quotation at the beginning of this discussion.

> Often the same spirit that inspired the poet whom he reads will work also in him and will kindle in him flames which will little by little set his spirit afire and fill it with the same frenzy the Greeks called enthusiasm, by which he, as though touched by a stinging inspiration, will be as though he were driven to set forth on paper those things born in his mind through the reading of his author.[201]

His more precise explanation of how this occurs is a remarkable early recognition of the genetic universality of emotions.

> This I believe comes about through what our minds naturally have in common to receive that inspiration of which we spoke.[202]

It is interesting that Giraldi also stipulates that this exchange with a great mind depends on the attitude of the student as well.

> It should be pointed out that it is not enough that he who speaks explain and teach faithfully but it is necessary also that he who listens be able to adapt himself to learning, to set aside an arrogant manner and the belief (which is the mortal poison of him who thinks he knows a great deal) that he needs no teacher. Such individuals frequently remain in an

[199] Michel de Montaigne, *Essays*, trans. M. A. Screech (London: Penguin, 1993), II, xxxii, 822.

[200] Ibid., III, viii, 1045.

[201] Giraldi Cinthio, *Discorso intorno al comporre dei romanzi*, trans. in Henry Snuggs, *Giraldi Cinthio On Romances* (Lexington: University of Kentucky Press, 1968), 27.

[202] Ibid.

elementary state or are enveloped in a thousand errors which fill them with distorted and perplexed conceits, afterward expressed so tortuously that they seem as drunkards talking in the madness of wine that takes away their sense.[203]

[203] Ibid., 26.

A frequently quoted line, with respect to the subject of learning from great minds, relates to the very powerful personality in England, Samuel Johnson (1709–1784). One who studied with him was Sir Joshua Reynolds who observed that Johnson "brushed from his mind a great deal of rubbish."

This line reminds us of a passage by the early nineteenth century critic, E. T. A. Hoffmann. In encouraging a young composer to study the music of Gluck, he reflects,

> Even if his wings are not strong enough to match the eagle's flight of that great genius, he will certainly rise above the mire in which the common herd so contentedly graze.[204]

[204] *E. T. A. Hoffmann's Musical Writings* (Cambridge: Cambridge University Press, 1989), 261.

For the student of music education we are fortunate, for it is the nature of our Art of Music that the composer communicates directly with the student, without any person or object standing in between, something which happens in no other art. Thus, through our selection of material, the student has an opportunity to communicate with some of the greatest minds of all time, men such as Bach, Mozart, Beethoven and Wagner. But at the same time, we also have our version of Hoffmann's "common herd." So in selecting any popular entertainment music the teacher must ask himself, just what kind of person does he wish to expose his students to?

For more than fifty years I have asked, "Is it appropriate for the public school to be expected to provide entertainment for the public?" Now I wish to make it more personal. Clinical research has proven that the brain is physically changed by the music we hear. As "We are what we eat," so "We are what we hear." The conductor/educator is the only adult in the school building who is in intimate contact with the right hemisphere of the student. Perhaps the time has come when the conductor/educator must ask just how expensive "fun" really is? The great masters before you, in speaking of the goal of their art, did not use the word "fun." They used the word, "Joy."

Students profit from the Discovery and Development of their Unique Emotional Template

> I Hate Music, but I Love to Sing!
> Song by Leonard Bernstein

THE MUSIC EDUCATORS NATIONAL CONFERENCE, in a 1991 publication, presented the following arguments in support of music in the public schools.

> Common sense lends support to the belief that music and music education foster a number of nonmusical factors important for success in school and life. Three areas are important here:
>
> 1. development goals such as self-esteem, self-discipline, and individual creativity;
>
> 2. the development of important academic and personal skills; and
>
> 3. the contributions of music to other areas of study, particularly to their integration.[205]

On the contrary, the "common sense" of parents and administrators, all of whom carry genetic musical knowledge, tells them these things are not unique values of music at all and might as well be a list of goals for employees working in a bank. Every school board will quickly conclude that music is simply too expensive a program to maintain for the purpose of helping to instill "self-discipline."

These kinds of arguments for why we have music in the curriculum have a kind of desperate quality about them, like a preacher arguing for the benefits of love without being allowed to use the actual word "love." That is a pretty good analogy for why these kinds of arguments do not work. They are an attempt to conceptualize music, to force the left hemisphere of the brain to make up arguments even though it has no idea what goes on in the right hemisphere of the brain where the experiential nature of music lies.

Why did not these educators instead talk about the values of music itself—something self-evident to every professional

[205] *The Report of the National Commission on Music Education* (Reston: MENC, 1991), 23.

musician? The reason is that the profession of music education collectively made a gamble in the mid-twentieth century to place all their bets on talking about music instead of making music. That is a philosophy never before tried in the previous 12,500 documented years of music education and it is one that, as an educational experiment, has failed. Here we ask the reader to begin to think in terms of the direct educational values in the right hemisphere of the brain which can be accessed through the performance of music.[206]

First, taking the ancient Greek goal of all education, "Know Thyself!," in light of the historic results of clinical brain research during the past fifty years everyone today should now understand that "self" means all of us, both a left and a right hemisphere of the brain. The failure of the educational institutions to acknowledge this is documented in a moving testimonial by the famous recording artist, Rosanne Cash.

> We rely heavily on logic and cognitive processes and, indeed, that is half of our condition as human beings. But the other, subtler half—the intuitive, creative part—we treat like a shameful alien cousin to our personalities... In my own life, I spent my formative years feeling like a freak of nature, because that alien cousin was the part I completely identified with, but was not valued or validated by my teachers.[207]

Because the right hemisphere of the brain is mute, and cannot write or speak, teachers, as Ms Cash points out, do not value this part of the person. It is exactly the circumstance which brought the famous French philosopher, François de la Rochefoucauld (1613–1680), to write,

> Nature would seem to have hidden deep within us talents and abilities we know nothing about; only strong emotion is able to bring them to light, and to give us at times insights beyond the reach of ordered thought.[208]

La Rochefoucauld in another place mentions yet another benefit in developing the child's understanding of his right hemisphere in his confidence gained in self-expression, for as we know it is the emotional content which the right

---

[206] The reader can find additional information in Chapter 7 of David Whitwell, *Music Education of the Future*, ed. Craig Dabelstein (Austin: Whitwell Books, 2011).

[207] Quoted in *The Report of the National Commission on Music Education*, 9.

[208] *The Maxims of La Rochefoucauld*, trans. Louis Kronenberger (New York: Random House, 1959), Nr. 249. François de la Rochefoucauld joined the army at an early age and spent most of his life in public service. The *Maxims*, his most famous work, was published anonymously in 1665.

hemisphere adds to the language of the left hemisphere which gives meaning to the sentences.

> Tone of voice, look and manner can prove no less eloquent than choice of words.[209]

[209] Ibid., Nr. 404.

The ability of music to aid such confidence in the right hemisphere, was a subject noted by Plato, who said that "Music could thus be used to correct any discord which may have arisen in the courses of the soul."[210]

The seventeenth century poet known as Angelus Silesius refers to these two parts of ourselves not by left and right hemisphere, of which he knew nothing, but as "the intellect" and the "heart." And now that he understands these two poles of his mind he mentions precisely the problem lying at the foundation of contemporary music education in America, "words cannot describe it."

[210] Quoted in Stuart Isacoff, *Temperament* (New York: Vintage Books, 2003), 48. It is interesting that Plato's use of the word "discord" (out of tune) is still used today with regard to the mind. Isacoff here also adds,

> Quintilian, Roman orator, gives opposite: an aulos player was accused of manslaughter because he played music in the wrong mode to accompany a sacrifice "with the result that the person officiating went mad and flung himself over a precipice."

> Now that my eye
> Has seen the essence of the mind,
> No words that could describe it
> Can I find.
>
> The longest way to God,
> The indirect,
> Lies through the intellect.
> The shortest way lies through the heart.
> Here is my journey's end
> And here its start.
>
> Unknowable, unnamable,
> You seem the other pole.
> And yet
> My human heart
> Contains You whole.[211]

Yet another benefit to the student through the use of music is to help the student learn to recognize his emotional template in the right hemisphere, from which it follows that understanding himself better helps him understand others. This was noticed by the very early poet, Juan Ruiz (1283–1350).

[211] *The Book of Angelus Silesius* [Johann Scheffler, 1624–1677], trans. Frederick Franck (New York: Knopf, 1976), 103ff. Scheffler (1624–1677) studied at the Elizabeth Gymnasium and as a medical student at the University of Strasbourg and at the University of Padua. In 1653 he became a Catholic and took the name Angelus Silesius ("God's Silesian Messenger").

> Examine, then, your inner self, inspect your feelings well,

And by your heart you'll judge how others' passions surely go.[212]

The need to achieve greater balance in our educational institutions is clearly urgent. Our present educational system is so completely one-sided that we need not ever fear of going too far in the other direction, as pointed out by C. S. Lewis.

> For every one pupil who needs to be guarded from a weak excess of sensibility there are three who need to be awakened from the slumber of cold vulgarity. The task of the modern educator is not to cut down jungles but to irrigate deserts.[213]

For the listener of music, can there be such a thing as "too much sensibility?" Mendelssohn debated this with a pastor in Berlin in an exchange of letters in 1833. Mendelssohn's view was,

> There is no such thing as an excess of sensibility, and what is called "too-much" is always rather "too-little." The soaring, elevated emotions inspired by music—so welcome to the listeners—are no excess; let him, who is capable of emotions, feel them to the utmost of his capacity—and more so, if possible.[214]

At least one contemporary educator has agreed with this value. The proper artistic education of the young, he says, is,

> a training in perception and expression, which in its full results would develop to the fullest measure of which the child is capable, his ability to be an artist; that is to say, to apprehend the world finely through his own sensibility, and to express it in spontaneous activity purely for the joy in doing so.[215]

I would like to add the suggestion that when we begin to create new teaching strategies for the education in the right hemisphere, we first allow the students to experience their own emotions in their experiencing of the music before we begin to conceptualize, talk about it, or analyze it. I am reminded of the old European rule of etiquette regarding one's coming into contact with an aristocrat: "Don't speak

[212] Juan Ruiz, *The Book of True Love*, trans. Saralyn Daly (University Park: Pennsylvania State University Press, 1978), 565.

[213] C. S. Lewis, *The Abolition of Man* (New York: Macmillian, 1967), 24.

[214] Letter to Pastor Bauer, March 4, 1833.

[215] John Macmurray, *Reason and Emotion* (London: Faber and Faber, 1972), 74ff.

until spoken to." In other words, we must give the music itself a chance to speak to the students before we begin talking and analyzing it to death.

The goal here is to "Know Thy Self," the whole self, the total man. The very distinguished philosopher, Walter Jackson Bate, wrote that he believed this was the real goal of education at the time of the ancient Greeks.

> Fine arts complete nature through imitation in order to enlarge, nourish and develop human awareness and insight. The classical view emphasizes, then, that art is formative in the most valuable sense by assisting man to fulfill *his* own end. For man's end is to *complete himself:* to carry out, in the fullest extent, what is best in him.
>
> .....
>
> Hence the confidence of the Greeks in the immense power of art—which they called *psychagogia* (a *leading* or *persuading* of the soul) as a molding or formative agent in developing human feelings and motivations ... The Greeks raised the whole concept of education far above the routine acquirement of simple memory, mechanical skills and vocational apprenticeship.[216]

[216] Walter Jackson Bate, *Prefaces to Criticism* (New York: Doubleday Anchor, 1959), 8ff. 10, and 31.

Bates calls this goal of education, catharsis.

If we can learn to do this right, to reach the real child in the right hemisphere and to teach music there as a special language through which the individual student learns about himself, his feelings and his emotions, we may be sure that society will then come to appreciate music education. Society will come to understand,

- That it is music teachers, not philosophy teachers, who can help the student discover his real self.

- That it is music teachers, not English teachers, who can help the student communicate his feelings.

- That it is music teachers, not science teachers, who help the student connect his *own* experiences and feeling with his environment.

- That it is music teachers, not history teachers, who can help the student associate earlier periods of time *with himself*.

- That English grammar teachers teach students to speak alike, while music teachers teach students to express themselves as individuals.

- That Foreign language teachers teach students the language of another country, while music teachers share a language spoken by all peoples.

These are not examples of how music *helps* other courses. These are examples of things music can teach, which other courses cannot.

Music education which is performance based, and not concept based, which is a language of the feelings, and not a skill, can produce an adult who understands and can communicate his own feelings, who is a balanced and more holistic person, who will be capable of participating in the world as an *individual* acting on the basis of his experience rather than acting on the basis of learned responses, and who will continue to use what he learned the rest of his life. What other "core subject" could claim as much?

Students experience Beauty as a form of Truth

> The Beautiful is the splendor of the True.
> FRANZ LISZT, in *The Gipsy in Music*

THE READER WILL RECALL that at the end of Chapter One we presented a long discussion on the concept of Truth in the right hemisphere of the brain. Here we should like to add only a few additional comments as it relates to what might be absorbed in the student's performance.

It is not unusual to find writers associating ideal Beauty with the concept of perfection, which is also a natural goal of music performance. The French philosopher, La Rochefoucauld, wrote,

> Truth is the body and breath of perfection and beauty. Nothing, whatever its nature, can be beautiful or perfect that is not all it ought to be or has not all it ought to have.[217]

And the twentieth century philosopher, George Santayana, concluded,

> Beauty is truth, that it is the expression of the ideal, the symbol of divine perfection, and the sensible manifestation of the good.[218]

The student performer will learn that his new understanding of Beauty in the right hemisphere finds its natural expression in performance. For the critic, Walter Jackson Bate, this may be a gradual assimilation.

> "The heart," as Coleridge later said, "should have fed upon the truth, as insects on a leaf, until it is tinged with its food and shows the color … in every minutest fibre." By gradually enlarging and unconsciously shaping man as a desiring, reacting, and living organism, and by calling forth his ability to convert insight or awareness into feeling, art is capable of developing his capacity to react vitally and sympathetically to the truth. It thus assumes dignity and genuine value as a nourisher, enlarger, and shaper of the mind and heart, offering insight through a true representation and at the same time stimulating and arousing a dynamic and feeling response.[219]

[217] *The Maxims of La Rochefoucauld*, trans. Louis Kronenberger (New York: Random House, 1959), Nr. 626.

[218] George Santayana, *The Sense of Beauty* (New York: Collier Books, 1961), 23.

[219] Walter Jackson Bate, *Prefaces to Criticism* (New York: Doubleday Anchor Books, 1959), 11.

Franz Liszt found the musical expression of these feelings to be not only natural but important for aesthetic reasons.

> Music by itself does not develop the reason; but from it proceed those emotions of the heart from which the will is developed. It would avail nothing merely to *see* the True, to *know* the Good, or to *judge* the Beautiful if, in the meantime, the will to act were lacking.
>
> .....
>
> The Greeks, who were naturally gifted with an incomparable appreciation of the Beautiful, well understood the subtle connecting link provided by music between the perceptible and the impalpable between that which is understood and that which is felt.[220]

[220] Franz Liszt, *The Gipsy in Music*.

But what if the student only just plays the notes on paper and is not inspired, or does not understand his duty to communicate emotions to the listener. The result of such a performance was mentioned already in the twelfth century. Gottfried Strassburg (d. 1210) interrupts his famous story of Tristan to make one of the most important statements on aesthetics in music of the Middle Ages. His definition of Truth in performance assumes the honest intent of the performer to communicate genuine feelings.

> But the pleasure they had from him was short-lived, since the sounds that he made for them with hands or lips did not come from the depths—his heart was not in his music. For it is of the nature of music that one cannot play for any length of time unless one is in the mood. Although it is a very common thing, what one plays superficially in a heartless and soulless way cannot really claim to be music.[221]

[221] Gottfried von Strassburg, *The Maxims of La Rochefoucauld*, trans. Louis Kronenberger (New York: Random House, 1959), *Tristan*, trans. Arthus Hatto (Harmondsworth: Penguin Books, 1960), 141.

Students experience the World of Higher Spirituality

> Art has been defined as Man's highest spiritual expression, and in one respect superior to religion in that it is the only activity that does not lead to killing.[222] JACQUES BARZUN

[222] Jacques Barzun, *From Dawn to Decadence* (New York: Harper Collins, 2000), 713.

FOR MANY YEARS our understanding of early music has been influenced by the fact that the Church, which produced nearly all early music treatises, promoted mostly the kind of music which supported Reason, in particular the mathematics based polyphonic style. With what we know of our bicameral brain today, with its recognition of the physical existence of the experiential side of our nature, it seems reasonable to conclude that outside the Church, music had always represented its primary purpose of communicating the emotions. It follows that while the Church missed its opportunity to take advantage of the spiritual qualities in music, for many early regular listeners this characteristic of music must have been evident.

In our time, when discussion of religion in any form is prohibited in the schools, there may be some educators who nevertheless want to provide some spiritual opportunities for contemplation by their students and aesthetic music is an opportunity to do so. For those educators the discussion below may perhaps stimulate their own thinking along these lines.

Beginning with the sixteenth century composers began to make great advances in composing music which was overtly emotional in character. At the same time commentators began to adopt the Church's word, "soul," as a surrogate for the experiential side of man's nature. This general topic was one discussed by the Baïf Academy in Paris, which, in turn, influenced the composer Claude Le Jeune to explain in the preface of his *Printemps* that he deplored the fact that the ancient art of the music of the Greeks had been lost and that it was his purpose to restore music to its rightful place that it might stir "the soul of man to such passions as [the Greeks] intended."[223] One of his contemporaries, Odet de la Noue,

[223] Quoted in François Lesure, *Musicians and Poets of the French Renaissance*, trans. Elio Gianturco (New York: Merlin Press, 1955), 111.

believed he had been successful, for he writes in an eulogy,

> By the efforts of his melody he flings out soul wherever he pleases;
> He casts it down to grievous death, or stirs it up to joy;
> He instills courage into the most dejected heart;
> And to raving men he restores meekness.[224]

By the early nineteenth century this new emphasis on the spiritual qualities of music found a logical home in the focus of Romanticism in Nature. For the influential early critic, E. T. A. Hoffman, the romantic mystery of Nature offered an opportunity to explain the mysterious spiritual qualities of Music.

> Music is a universal language of Nature; it speaks to us in magical and mysterious resonances; we strive in vain to conjure these into symbols, and any artificial arrangement of the symbols provides us with only a vague approximation of what we have distantly heard.[225]

This association of Nature and Music had definite roots in the seventeenth and eighteenth centuries, as we can see in a comment by François de La Rochefouauld (1613–1680).

> Nature would seem to have hidden deep within us talents and abilities we know nothing about; only strong emotion is able to bring them to light, and to give us at times insights beyond the reach of ordered thought.[226]

We particularly like a comment by Jean Paul Richter, which points out the association between Nature and the spiritual world.

> The beautiful does not dwell in the things of nature themselves, but only in the spirit, which can divine the idea within them, because it brings this from God; they are only the echo of our inner music.[227]

Hoffmann in his writings on music placed great emphasis on this special realm of the mind, unknown to Reason, where music introduces us to spiritual longings. We need to remind the reader of the qualification, which must have

---

[224] Quoted in Ibid., 112.

[225] *E. T. A. Hoffmann's Musical Writings*, ed. David Charlton (Cambridge: Cambridge University Press, 1989), 165. The editor, on page 11, says that the above was based on a work by Caspar Rütz (1708–1755), *Sendschreiben eines Freundes*, quoted in Friedrich Marpurg, *Historisch-Kritische Beyträge zur Aufnahme der Musik* (Berlin, 1754), 273–311, cited by Hellamy Hosler, *Changing Aesthetic Views in Instrumental Music in Eighteenth-Century Germany* (Ann Arbor, 1981), 126.

> Music actually causes feelings in us; and music has as its own peculiar property thousands of other feelings to which a musical heart is susceptible, but which no orator or poet can awaken through words or moving delivery. In this latter case music is not a copy of nature, but the original itself. Music is a universal language of nature which is only intelligible to harmonious souls. And its peculiar expressions, which it does not borrow from anywhere else, have a secret understanding with these souls.

[226] *The Maxims of La Rochefoucauld*, trans. Louis Kronenberger (New York: Random House, 1959), Nr. 404.

[227] Eduard Berend, *Jean Pauls Sämtliche Werke* (Weimar, 1927), I: 16:411

been assumed by Hoffmann, that these deep thoughts are only possible with respect to the contemplative listener of important aesthetic music. Popular music, which essentially bounces off the listener does not produce this level of experience.

> Music reveals in man an unknown realm, a world quite separate from the outer sensual worlds surrounding him, a world in which he leaves behind all precise feelings in order to embrace an inexpressible longing.[228]
>
> .....
>
> Our kingdom is not of this world, say musicians, for where in nature do we find the prototypes for our art, as painters and sculptors do? Sound resides in all things; but notes, that is to say melodies, which speak the higher language of the spirit-realm, repose only in the breast of men. But like the spirit of sound, does not the spirit of music also permeate the whole of nature? A sounding body, when it is mechanically animated and thus brought to life, gives expression to its existence, or rather its inner organism consciously emerges. Cannot the spirit of music, when it is awakened by its votaries, similarly express itself melodically and harmonically in secret resonances intelligible only to them?[229]
>
> .....
>
> What an utterly miraculous thing is music, and how little can men penetrate its deeper mysteries! But does it not reside in the breast of man himself and fill his heart with its enchanting images, so that all his senses respond to them, and a radiant new life transports him from his enslavement here below, from the oppressive torment of his earthly existence? Indeed , he is suffused by a divine power, and by abandoning himself with a childlike and pious mind to whatever influence the spirit arouses within him, he is able to speak the language of that unknown, romantic spirit-realm.[230]

This idea that music causes one to contemplate areas of thought previously unknown to the listener is one which continued for some time. The English philosopher, Herbert Spencer (1820–1903), wrote,

> And thus we may in some measure understand how it happens that music not only strongly excites our more familiar feelings, but also produces feelings we never had before— arouses dormant sentiments of which we had not conceived

[228] *E. T. A. Hoffmann's Musical Writings*, 96.

[229] Ibid., 163. Hoffmann supports this view in a footnote mentioning Johann Wilhelm Ritter (1776–1810), *Fragmente*, I, 162, Section 250, "Every sounding body, or rather its note, is as it were the colored shadow of its inner quality."

[230] Ibid., 88.

the possibility and do not know the meaning; or as Richter says—tells us of things we have not seen and shall not see.[231]

And similarly, the great Arthur Schopenhauer (1788–1860), observed,

> This deep relation which music has to the true nature of all things also explains the fact that suitable music played to any scene, action, event or surrounding seems to disclose to us the most secret meaning, and appears as the most accurate and distinct commentary on it. This is so truly the case, that whoever gives himself up entirely to the impression of a symphony, seems to see all the possible events of life and the world take place in himself, yet if he reflects, he can find no likeness between the music and the things that passed before his mind.[232]

One of the important benefits of this kind of spiritual contemplation for the student is a tendency to raise his standard of taste. Hoffmann comments on this as a goal not understood by the common consumers of music.

> While the Philistines use music as a social commodity, the 'true' musician or music-lover understands the relevance of 'real' music as an expression of transcendental reality, and as a transcendental expression of surrounding nature. It reveals those same 'higher natures' as does genuine Romantic opera.[233]

We can see this concept developing in an interesting early discussion of Taste by Johann Heinichen (1683–1729).

> If experience is necessary in any art or science, it is certainly necessary in music. In this *Scientia practica*, first of all, we must gain experience either at home, provided opportunities are sufficient, or through traveling. But what is it that one believes one must seek in the experience? I will give a single word ... *Taste*. Through diligence, talent, and experience, a composer must achieve above all else an exquisite sense of good taste in music ... The definition of *Taste* is unnecessary for the experienced musician; and it is as difficult to describe in its essentials as the true essence of the soul. One could say that good taste was in itself the soul of music, which so to speak it doubly enlivens and brings pleasure to the

[231] Herbert Spencer, *Essays on Education and Kindred Subjects* (London: J. M. Dent, 1966), 323.

[232] Arthur Schopenhauer, *The World as Will and Idea* (London: Broadway House, 8th edition), I, 330.

[233] *E. T. A. Hoffmann's Musical Writings*, 172.

senses. The *Proprium 4ti modi* of a composer with good taste is contained solely in the skill with which he makes his music pleasing to and beloved by the general, educated public, or which in the same way pleases our ear by experienced artifices and moves the senses ... In general, this can be brought about through a good well-cultivated, and natural invention or through the beautiful expression of words. In particular, through an ever dominating *cantabile*, through suitable and affecting accompaniments, through a change of harmonies recommended for the sake of the ears, and through other methods gained from experience and frequently looking poor on paper, which in our times we only label with the obscure name of "rules of experience ..." An exceptional sense of good taste is so to say the musical *Lapis philisophorum* and the principal key to musical mysteries through which human souls are unlocked and moved and by which the senses are won over ... For even the natural gift or talent endowed with most invention resembles only crude gold and silver dross that must be purified first by the fire of experience before it can be shaped into a solid mass—I mean into a finely cultivated and steadfast sense of good taste.[234]

[234] Johann David Heinichen, *General-Bass Treatise* [1711], quoted in George Buelow, *Thorough-Bass Accompaniment according to Johann David Heinichen* (Ann Arbor: UMI Research Press, 1986), 285ff.

Students experience Principles of Morality through Music Performance

The laws of morality are also those of art.[235] ROBERT SCHUMANN

[235] Robert Schumann, *Album for Youth*, 1848.

AT FIRST GLANCE, this topic may seem strange to many readers, especially in these times when "political correctness" governs so much of what happens in a classroom. But in performance based music education we have a natural platform for subtle instruction in morals, for a wrong note is indisputably wrong and cannot be excused under any circumstances. In addition, when the performance has an audible relationship with the overtone series, then "right or wrong" is juxtaposed with a natural law of physics. In these cases the student is prepared for life in a pluralistic world where often there is no middle ground between right or wrong.

While music teachers today still must of necessity be concerned with right and wrong notes, etc., it is unusual when a teacher imparts such information from a moral perspective. But we find that perspective in one of the first treatises devoted to performance, the *Practica musicae* by Franchino Gaffurio (1451–1518). In his dedication, he begins by stressing how important music is for its role in moral education.

> It is readily apparent, illustrious Prince, how much influence the profession of the art of music had and with what veneration it was held among the ancients. We know this both from the example of the greatest philosophers, who, when they were very old, devoted themselves to this discipline as if in it they put the finishing touch to their studies, and from the practice of the strictest governments, which with the utmost diligence saw to it that whatever was harmful to public morals should be eliminated. Not only did these states not banish the art of music; they cultivated it with the utmost zeal as the mother and nurse of morals.[236]

[236] *The Practica musicae of Franchinus Gafurius,* trans. Irwin Young (Madison: University of Wisconsin Press, 1969), 3.

He adds that music plays an active role in affecting morals and makes the interesting observation that it was thought that Music was the first of the Liberal Arts.

Now music is not, like the other learned disciplines, merely a speculative pursuit: it reaches out into practice, and as was said previously, is connected with morality ...

Thus this field of music theory is valuable not only because of the knowledge it gives music itself, but also because its roots extend very far; it aids other disciplines. This has been verified by the testimony of very influential men who have acknowledged that they learned literature from music above all else. Fabius Quintilian declares, on the authority of Timagenes, that this art "is the most ancient of all studies in liberal education."[237]

[237] Ibid., 5ff.

In perhaps the most famous book of the Renaissance, *The Courtier*, by Baldassare Castiglione (1478–1529),[238] we find,

[238] Castiglione was a diplomat for the Duke of Urbino and for popes Leo x and Clement VII and from his experience he attempts to describe the attributes of the perfect gentleman.

> The central purpose of the teacher must be to instill moral values. It is necessary to have a master who by his teaching and precepts stirs and awakens the moral virtues whose seed is enclosed and buried in our souls and who, like a good farmer, cultivates and clears the way for them by removing the thorns and tares of our appetites which often so darken and choke our minds as not to let them flower or produce those splendid fruits which alone we should wish to see born in the human heart.[239]

[239] *The Courtier*, trans. George Bull (New York: Penguin Books, 1967), III, 291.

He follows this with a quotation from Socrates which states that this kind of teaching fosters ideal learning attitudes in the student.

> Socrates was perfectly right in affirming that in his opinion his teaching bore good fruit when it encouraged someone to strive to know and understand virtue; for those who have reached the stage where they desire nothing more eagerly than to be good have no trouble in learning all that is necessary.[240]

[240] Ibid., I, 88.

Tosi, author of a famous singing treatise of the Baroque, makes it clear that the quality of one's morals must be considered as a prerequisite to lessons in singing.

> After a strict care of his morals, he should give the rest of his attention to the study of singing in perfection, that by this means he may be so happy as to join the most noble qualities of the soul to the excellencies of his art.[241]

[241] P. F. Tosi, *Observations on the Florid Song* (London: Wilcox, 1743), VI, ii.

Tosi's thought here reminds one of Bacon's reflection, "Virtue is nothing but inward beauty; beauty nothing but outward virtue."[242]

The relationship between moral ethics and performance itself can be seen throughout the early philosophic literature of ancient Greece. Plutarch says the reason the Greeks "were so careful to teach their children music," was,

> For they deemed it requisite by the assistance of music to form and compose the minds of youth to what was decent, sober, and virtuous; believing the use of music beneficially efficacious to incite to all serious actions.[243]

Strabo gives a slightly different explanation for the use of music to form morals. The ancient Greeks, he said,

> Assumed that every form of music is the work of the gods ... And by the same course of reasoning they also attribute to music the upbuilding of morals, believing that everything which tends to correct the mind is close to the gods.[244]

If music was considered this important to education, it stands to reason that someone must oversee the quality of the music itself. Much as Plato would recommend later for his utopian city, Plutarch suggests that the music used in education was subject to civic censors.

> They adjudged it necessary for the preservation of that gravity and seriousness of manners which was required of their youth for the attainments of wisdom and virtue, never to admit of any light and wanton, any ludicrous or effeminate poetry; which made them allow of no poets among them but such only who for their grave and virtuous compositions were approved by the public magistrate; that being hereby under some restraint, they might neither act nor write anything to the prejudice of good manners, or to the dishonor of their laws and government.[245]

The last in the tradition of important early Greek philosophers was the third century AD writer, Aristides Quintilianus. We have quoted above his recognition in the ancient Greeks of the importance of using music to instill moral standards, but he gives some hints on how this was made part of education.

[242] *The Advancement of Learning*, in *The Works of Francis Bacon*, ed. James Spedding (Cambridge: Cambridge University Press, 1869), IX, 156.

[243] "Concerning Music."

[244] *The Geography of Strabo*, trans. Horace L. Jones (Cambridge: Harvard University Press, 1960), X.3.10.

[245] *Customs of the Lacedaemonians.*

> Why then are we surprised to find that it was mostly through music that people in ancient times produced moral correction?—for they saw how powerful a thing it is, and how effective its nature makes it. Just as they applied their intelligence to such other human attributes as health and bodily well-being, seeking to preserve one thing, working to increase another, limiting to what is beneficial anything that tended towards excess, so also with the songs and dances to which all children are naturally attracted. It was impossible to prohibit them without destroying the children's own nature: instead, by cultivating them, little by little and imperceptibly, they devised an [educational] activity both decorous and delightful, and out of something useless made something useful.

For Aristides, the most important role in the effectiveness of music to develop moral objectives in education was the quality of the repertoire used. We must, he wrote, "separate out the best from the worst." If we fail at this, then our students "are left undisciplined, lapsing into base or brutal passions."

> Of those among whom music has been perverted against its nature into depravity and cultural corruption, the peoples that cultivate the appetites have souls that are too slack, and improper bodily affectations, like those who live in Phoenicia and their descendants in Africa; while those that are ruled by the spirited part lack all mental discipline—they are drunkards, addicted to weapon-dances no matter whether the occasion is right, excessive in anger and manic in war, like the Thracian peoples and the entire Celtic race. But the races that have embraced the learning of music and dexterity in its use, by which I mean the Greeks and any there may be who have emulated them, are blessed with virtue and knowledge of every kind, and their humanity is outstanding. If music can delight and mold whole cities and races, can it be incapable of educating individuals? I think not.

Beginning with the late seventeenth century composers began to place less emphasis on observing the "rules" and more emphasis on expressing their own feelings. During the nineteenth century, with the arrival of Romanticism, the decision on what is good became a matter of individual feeling, as Goethe's Faust said, "Feeling is all." This led to the twentieth century where rules and aesthetics become a matter of the individual artist, filling our lives with abstract painting, sculpture made of junk and aleatoric music. One may decide for one's self what the value is of such art work, but for the important critic, Jacques Barzun, these endeavors tell the world that "art as an institution with a moral or social purpose is dead."[246]

[246] Jacques Barzun, *From Dawn to Decadence* (New York: Harper Collins, 2000), 722.

Performance based Music Education aids in developing Character

Music is a semi-discipline and taskmistress, which makes people milder and more gentle, more civil and more sensible.[247]
  MARTIN LUTHER

[247] Quoted in Walter Buszin, "Luther on Music," *The Musical Quarterly* (January, 1946), 92.

THE ALMOST EXCLUSIVE use of music for the purpose of forming the character of the student was an educational principle believed in and acted on for thousands of years. And yet, what music teacher in our time will dare speak of this subject in class? How many music teachers today make this priority number one in the selection of repertoire for their students to study and perform?

Of the ancient Egyptian people who pre-date the ancient Greeks, our primary record is the tomb paintings. Very little literature exists, but references by the later Greeks give us a few clues regarding the use of music in that earlier society. It is an important question for it appears that much of the character of the ancient Greek society, including music, came from Egypt. Strabo, for example, writing during the first years of the Christian Era, says that the Egyptians instructed their children with music established by the government and that musicians were in charge of the development of character in the young.[248]

> The musicians in giving instruction in singing and playing the lyre or aulos considered this virtue as essential, since they maintain that such studies are destined to create discipline and develop the character.[249]

[248] This remains true today, however, today neither the teachers nor the parents have any idea who the musicians are who are forming the character of their children.

[249] Quoted in Lise Manniche, *Music and Musicians in Ancient Egypt* (London: British Museum Press, 1991), 41. More on this subject can be found in David Whitwell, *Early Views on Music and Ethics,* ed. Craig Dabelstein (Austin: Whitwell Books, 2013).

It is also very clear, as the reader has seen above in the discussion of aesthetic repertoire, that for the early Greeks the success in developing character in the student was tied to the quality of the music used. Indeed, in the play, *The Thesmophoriazusae*, by Aristophanes, it would seem that the character of the music and the musician were one and the same.

> Answer me. But you keep silent. Oh! just as you choose; your songs display your character quite sufficiently.

Plato (427–347 BC) studied for nineteen years in Egypt and he writes of the long era before the rise of Greece when the Egyptians carefully controlled the use of music and art in the education of young students. One can get a sense of this discipline when Plato discusses the control even of the audiences.

> All these forms and others were duly distinguished, nor were the performers allowed to confuse one style of music with another. And the authority which determined and gave judgment, and punished the disobedient, was not expressed in a hiss, nor in the most unmusical shouts of the multitude, as in our days, nor in applause and clapping of hands. But the directors of public instruction insisted that the spectators should listen in silence to the end; and boys and their tutors, and the multitude in general, were kept quiet by a hint from a stick. Such was the good order which the multitude were willing to observe; they would never have dared to give judgment by noisy cries.[250]

[250] *Laws*, trans. B. Jowett (Oxford: Clarendon Press, 1953), 656d.

From this it is already apparent that Plato believed that the greatest period of Greek music, culturally speaking, was already past. He blames the musicians, composers and performers themselves, for this decay and squarely places the blame on them for seeking to please the audience without any perceptions of the subsequent danger to their art.[251]

[251] Ibid., 700ff.

Plato also tells us that the ancient Greeks also placed great emphasis on the use of music to form the character of the young. In a widely quoted definition, he wrote,

> Education has two branches,—one of gymnastic, which is concerned with the body, and the other of music, which is designed for the improvement of the soul.[252]

[252] Ibid, 795d.

For Plato it was in this area of the improvement of the soul where he found the great value of music education. The importance of the educational value of this mysterious art of music, which could not even be seen, was first based on an idea shared by other early philosophers, that while the other senses, smell, touch, taste and sight all seemed to be a form of information outside the body and therefore accessible to discussion, music seemed to enter through the ears to affect us inside the body reaching the heart, meaning our feelings. Second, since the feelings heard in the music were by nature so similar to those felt in the heart, it followed that an educational pedagogy based on imitation, or modeling, held the promise of improving the character of the listener. This was why Plato sensed the great power of music.

> Therefore musical training is a more potent instrument than any other, because rhythm and harmony find their way into the inward places of the soul, on which they mightily fasten, imparting grace, and making the soul of him who is rightly educated graceful, or of him who is ill-educated ungraceful; and also because he who has received this true education of the inner being will most shrewdly perceive omissions or faults in art and nature, and with a true taste, while he praises and rejoices over and receives into his soul the good, and becomes noble and good, he will justly blame and hate the bad, now in the days of his youth, even before he is able to know the reason why; and when reason comes he will recognize and salute the friend with whom his education has made him long familiar. Yes, he said, I quite agree with you in thinking that it is for such reasons that they should be trained in music.[253]

On the other hand, Plato was very clear about the kinds of music which were not appropriate for use in music education.[254] Popularity is not a criterion[255] and not just whatever kind of music the students want.[256] Indeed he speaks at length on the bad educational influence which comes from popular music.[257] Four hundred years later one of the last of the ancient Greek philosophers, Philodemus (first century AD), still reflected this basic contention. Music, he wrote, which is devoid of significance naturally "equates with disorderliness and lack of restraint."[258]

Aristotle (384–322 BC), the great philosopher who followed Plato, recognized that the use of music to form character was important for its own sake, even though it was not part of the usual educational training to provide skills for work.

> It is evident that there is a sort of education in which parents should train their sons, not as being useful or necessary, but because it is liberal or noble.[259]

---

[253] *Republic*, 401d. Because of the power of this modeling, Plato also added that probably too much music, as well as too much gymnastics, was probably undesirable. Aristotle agrees with this basic pedagogy in *Problemata*, 920b.28.

[254] *Politica*, 1342a.17.

[255] *Republic*, III, 397c.

[256] *Laws*, 656f and 659d.

[257] Ibid.

[258] Warren D. Anderson, *Ethos and Education in Greek Music* (Cambridge: Harvard University Press, 1966), 153.

[259] *Politica*, 1338a.30.

Aristotle not only believed in the use of music to form the character of the young, but he believed that of the five senses hearing (music) is the *only* one which can affect character.

> Why is it that of all things which are perceived by the senses that which is heard alone possesses moral character? For music, even if it is unaccompanied by words, yet has character; whereas a color and an odor and taste have not.[260]

[260] *Problemata*, 919b.26.

For Aristotle the means by which music education affects character lies, as in the case of the experience of Tragedy, in catharsis. When we hear emotions in music our feelings move in sympathy.

> Rhythm and melody supply imitations of anger and gentleness, and also of courage and temperance, and of all the qualities contrary to these, and of the other qualities of character, which hardly fall short of the actual emotions, as we know from our own experience, for in listening to such strains our souls undergo a change. The habit of feeling pleasure or pain at mere representations is not far removed from [the real feelings].[261]

[261] *Politica*, 1340a.19.

The key in making this work, according to Aristotle, was in the selection of the highest music. Only certain kinds of music produce the catharsis with the empathy and introspection (pity and fear) necessary to character formation.[262]

[262] *Politica*, 1342a; 1342a. 27; 1342b.14; 1340a.40.

In summary, Aristotle concludes,

> Enough has been said to show that music has a power of forming the character, and should therefore be introduced into the education of the young.[263]

[263] *Politica*, 1340b.10.

During the final years of the ancient Greek period there was an apparent decline in the quality of music performances which the writers complained of. Some, such as the philosopher, Eratosthenes (276–194 BC), took the position that the role of music is to entertain, not instruct. The philosopher, Strabo (63 BC–24 AD), attacked him for this viewpoint, which suggests that Eratosthenes was an exception.

> Why, even the musicians, when they give instruction in singing, in lyre playing, or in aulos playing ... maintain that these studies tend to discipline and correct the character.[264]

[264] *The Geography of Strabo*, trans. Horace L. Jones (Cambridge: Harvard University Press, 1960), I.2.3.

We have quoted above, in the final pages of the discussion of Aristotle and music education, the extraordinary account by the historian, Polybius (203–120 BC), of the impact of music on the character on whole societies of persons.

With the beginning of the Christian Era, the Church assumed the role of character formation and officially cast out all the old Greek philosophical ideas about music as being merely "pagan." The Church transferred music into a branch of mathematics, as far removed from its natural role in communication of feeling as possible.

It is only when we come to Boethius (475–524 AD) that we find a Church mathematician who understood the importance of music and after him music gradually begins a long trip back to its proper place in education. Because of the importance of this philosopher still today, we wish to call the reader's attention to four very significant arguments by Boethius.[265]

First, he elevates music above the other liberal arts with respect to its sole role in affecting character ("morality").

Second, he makes the intuitive conclusion that we ourselves are somehow made in the likeness of music. Indeed a group of physicists working with Dr. Hans Jenny in Switzerland have been studying the fact that all our organs produce specific pitches. One of the physicists has concluded that we look as we do as a species due to the combined influence of this internal "harmony" and gravity.

Three, on the basis of the second idea, it follows that his explanation of how music affects character is solidly based on ancient Greek philosophy, pagan or not.[266]

Four, his conclusion that "there is no greater ruin of morals in a republic than the gradual perversion of music" requires no better witness than our own time.

At the dawn of the Renaissance, one who was bothered by the music he was hearing was Jacques de Liege in Paris. One of the most famous representatives of the *ars antiqua*, he was the author, in about 1313, of *Speculum Musicae*. All art, he contended, must be judged on moral grounds.

[265] Boethius, *Fundamentals of Music*, trans. Calvin Bower (New Haven: Yale University Press)

[266] His tendency to ignore the positions of the Church had the result, on another occasion, of the pope arranging for his murder.

> For though art is said to be concerned with what is difficult, it is nevertheless concerned with what is good and useful, since it is a virtue perfecting the soul through the medium of the intellect.[267]

And it was from this perspective that he found "modern music" (*ars nova*) to be a harmful influence on the character of man.

> For, if I may say so, the old art seems more perfect, more rational, more seemly, freer, simpler, and plainer. Music was originally discreet, seemly, simple, masculine, and of good morals; have not the moderns rendered it lascivious beyond measure?[268]

With the arrival of the High Renaissance we find renewed interest among leading philosophers in the role of music in character formation. The important critic of music, Vincenzo Galilei (1533–1591), began his *Fronimo*[269] by reflecting on his admiration for the views of the ancient civilizations on the virtues of music with respect to character development.

In Germany, Martin Luther also comments on the ability of music to affect the character. He seems to have noticed this first in the quality of people he knew who were also musicians. We may presume that it was his recognition of this purpose of music which fostered his frequent recommendation that music be part of the school curriculum.

> I have always loved music. Those who have mastered this art are made of good stuff, they are fit for any task. It is necessary indeed that music be taught in the schools. A teacher must be able to sing; otherwise I will not as much as look at him. Also, we should not ordain young men into the ministry unless they have become well acquainted with music in the schools ... We should always make it a point to habituate youth to enjoy the art of music, for it produces fine and skillful people.[270]

Luther mentioned this purpose in another dinner conversation, where he also comments on the difference between good and bad music.

> Music is a semi-discipline and taskmistress, which makes people milder and more gentle, more civil and more sensible.

---

[267] Quoted in Oliver Strunk, *Source Readings in Music History* (New York: Norton, 1950), 184.

[268] Ibid., 189.

[269] Vincenzo Galilei, *Fronimo* (1584), trans. Carol MacClintock (Neuhasen-Stuttgart: Hanssler-Verlag, 1985), Preface to the Readers, 27. He was the father to the famous Galileo Galilei.

[270] Quoted in Walter Buszin, "Luther on Music," *The Musical Quarterly* (January, 1946), 85.

The wicked gut-scrapers and fiddlers serve the purpose of enabling us to see and hear what a fine and wholesome art music really is; for white is more clearly recognized when it is contrasted with black.[271]

[271] Ibid., 92.

Shakespeare held a view very similar to Luther's, as we can read in the *Merchant of Venice*.

> The man that hath no music in himself,
> Nor is not moved with concord of sweet sounds,
> Is fit for treasons, stratagems, and spoils;
> The motions of his spirit are dull as night,
> And his affections dark as Erebus:
> Let no such man be trusted.[272]

[272] *The Merchant of Venice*, V, i, 91ff.

In the dramatic literature of the Renaissance there are a number of references to the question, "Can a man play in tune if he himself is out of tune?" In Fernando de Rojas' *Celestina* we find,

> CALISTO. Sempronio!
> SEMPRONIO. Sir!
> CALISTO. Reach me that lute.
> SEMPRONIO. Sir, here it is.
> CALISTO [singing]. Tell me what grief so great can be as to equal my misery?
> SEMPRONIO. This lute, sir, is out of tune.
> CALISTO. How can he tune it, who himself is out of tune? Take this lute and sing me the most doleful song thou canst devise.[273]

[273] Fernando de Rojas, *Celestina*, trans. James Mabbe (New York: Applause Publishers, 1986), 4ff.

In Lope de Vega's *Dorotea* we find, in a similar dialog, an interesting additional observation.

> DOROTEA. You're quite right, Celia, for the genius of music, as my master Enrique used to tell me, lies not in skilled fingers nor in a voice well trained, but in the soul itself—so the theory of music teaches.[274]

[274] Lope de Vega, *La Dorotea*, trans. Alan Trueblood and Edwin Honig (Cambridge: Harvard University Press, 1985), V, ix.

References to the importance of music for aiding the development of character in the schools continue into the Baroque. In Johann Mattheson (1681–1764), who was not only a very prolific writer on a wide variety of musical subjects, but an experienced singer, performer on organ and harpsichord and respected composer, we find,

The eyesight, the sense of smell, the sense of taste and the sense of touch serve the body; but only the sense of hearing is reserved for the soul and our morals.[275]

[275] Johann Mattheson, *Der vollkommene Capellmeister* (1739), trans. Ernest Harriss (Ann Arbor: UMI Research Press, 1981), I, v, 33ff.

The foregoing is a sample of a remarkable 3,000 years of testimony by some of civilization's greatest minds regarding the role of music in forming character. Why, after 3,000 years, is this subject no longer discussed? Who is otherwise responsible for the formation of character today?

In American society we have a constitution framed specifically for separating church and state. Thus the church is without influence in the schools. Their influence is limited to the church itself and upon the students who choose to attend. But, as we have seen too often in the news, the church has its own problems with character formation. The influence of the government is not wanted by the schools, only its money is welcome.

Parents, whose interest in character development should begin with the prenatal period, too often tend to leave the rearing of their children to the schools. And so, as a last resort, character development falls to the school. If music education can do this its focus must lie in the development of the experiential side (right hemisphere of the brain) of the child. This is the side of the personality where character formation must lie, not on the rational side (left hemisphere) of the personality. The ancients were right about that. Music education should approach this through a focus on the emotions, in helping the child to come to know himself in that half of his personality. Nothing can do this like music and music teachers, provided only the highest quality classical art music is used.

But professional music educators, shortly after the mid twentieth century, elected to abandon the emphasis on performance experience in the field of music education. Why? First, under the fear of "accountability" music educators have created a system of music education based on "concepts." But whatever is "conceptual" or "rational" about music, is not music at all. Of course it is easy to grade concepts, but what about the students? Students want the actual experience with music, they want to perform music and learn how to perform music. Students, every last one of them, *love* music even before beginning school. But music educators are not offering what the students are interested in, so the students go home and teach themselves to sing, to play a keyboard instrument and to compose.

Second, instead of following the ancient advice that only the highest quality music should be used in education, music educators have lowered the quality of the music they use to the lowest common denominator. We regard it as largely a last desperate attempt to increase the number of students in music education classes by making them more "popular" with the students. The past fifty years have also seen a subsequent broadening of the repertoire to include sometimes culturally primitive "world music." These exponents say, "all music is equal." The great masterpieces of European art music thus become just one more choice on the buffet table. Let the student pick whatever he is interested in. But this is like an astronomy teacher placing before the student the completely wrong theories of Ptolemy, Kepler and others in addition to the known scientific facts of today and saying, "students, pick the theory you like best." It makes a mockery of the ancient notion that society should pass on to the next generation the best of what it has learned.

What, then, has been the result of this new concept American music education over the past fifty years? Have we created a more sophisticated music culture in America? Or is it becoming lower? Is music education in the public schools now viewed by the parents and public as being representative of Art or entertainment? Are school music budgets growing larger? Is public support stronger?

There are other countries which have maintained the emphasis on the performance of music as the primary vehicle of music education. I have heard in Hungary, for example, elementary school and middle school performers with technical and sophisticated musical abilities our public schools cannot match. And then there is the amazing accomplishment by the Japanese, among whom Shinichi Suzuki has observed,

Teaching music is not my main purpose. I want to make good citizens.[276]

[276] *Reader's Digest*, November, 1973.

Performance based Music Education aids in developing Manners

The right molding or ruin of ingenuous manners and civil conduct lies in a well-grounded musical education.[277]
   ARISTOXENUS (FL. 335 BC)

It is true that, as Saint Paul says, every evil word corrupts good manners, but when it has the melody with it, it pierces the heart much more strongly and enters within; as wine is poured into the cask with a funnel, so venom and corruption are distilled to the very depths of the heart by melody.[278]
   JOHN CALVIN (1509–1564)

[277] Quoted by Plutarch in *Concerning Music*, from a now lost book by Aristoxenus, a student of Aristotle.

[278] Jean Calvin, *Geneva Psalter*, quoted in Oliver Strunk, *Source Readings in Music History* (New York: Norton, 1950), 346ff.

IN ANCIENT TIMES the most frequent advice about controlling the manners of the young involved music. Since music was considered fundamental in establishing character, the ancients considered a problem in manners to be more on the order of the young person being temporarily "out of tune" and in need of a musical "tune up." Indeed, Vasari, in his *Lives* (of artists) of 1550, uses this very analogy:

> If we bring in music, with its most sweet connections and its very suave intervals, we shall be able to tune, almost like strings, the contrary and diverse motions of our souls.[279]

Italians of his period used the term "distemper" (literally, to be out of tune) for a person who "is out of tune." Today we use this term only for mad dogs.

An early biography of Pythagoras (sixth century BC) gave to that famous philosopher the credit for discovering the power in music to affect manners. Pythagoras, we are told, discovered ancient knowledge,

> which subsists through music's melodies and rhythms, and from these he obtained remedies of human manners and passions, and restored the pristine harmony of the faculties of the soul.[280]

But Athenaeus (c. 200 AD) maintained that the practice of using music to "keep in tune" manners was much more ancient, dating back to the rhapsodists who sung epic poems

[279] Quoted in Claude V. Palisca, *Humanism in Italian Renaissance Musical Thought* (New Haven: Yale University Press, 1985).

[280] Porphyry (c. 233–305 AD), "Life of Pythagoras," trans. Kenneth Guthrie, *The Pythagorean Sourcebook* (Grand Rapids: Phanes Press, 1987).

before the age of written Greek. Singing of the great men of the past at their banquets, according to Athenaeus, enabled the noble guests to restore balance in their character.

> It is plain that Homer observes the ancient Greek system when he says, "We have satisfied our souls with the equal feast and with the lyre, which the gods have made the companion of the feast," evidently because the art is beneficial also to those who feast. And this was the accepted custom, it is plain, first in order that everyone who felt impelled to get drunk and stuff himself might have music to cure his violence and intemperance, and secondly, because music appeases surliness; for, by stripping off a man's gloominess, it produces good-temper and gladness becoming to a gentleman ... It is plain, therefore, that while most persons devote this art to social gatherings for the sake of correcting conduct and of general usefulness, the ancients went further and included in their customs and laws the singing of praises to the gods by all who attended feasts, in order that our dignity and sobriety might be retained through their help. For, since the songs are sung in concert, if discourse on the gods has been added it dignifies the mood of every one ... It is plain, therefore, in the light of what we have said, that music did not, at the beginning, make its way into feasts merely for the sake of shallow and ordinary pleasure, as some persons think.[281]

In another place Aethenaeus offers his personal observation that "indeed music trains character, and tames the hot-tempered and those whose opinions clash."[282]

From the perspective of all early Greek philosophy the key word is the "soul." The ancient Greeks often used the analogy of the string instrument, the lyre, to illustrate the relationship of body and soul. One can see the lyre, as a material object like the body, but the sounds it makes are unseen, like the soul. They added to this analogy the word "harmony," meaning "music," using it to express not only the unity of the various elements of music, but also to express the soul in its ideal state. Plato believed music was given to man by the Gods for this purpose, and not for the more common use of it as entertainment.[283]

If music was considered this important to shaping the soul, it stands to reason that someone must oversee the quality of

[281] Aethenaeus, *Deipnosophistae*, XIV, 627ff.

[282] Ibid., XIV, 623.

[283] *Timaeus*, 47d.

the music itself. Much as Plato would recommend for his utopian city, Plutarch (46–122 AD) suggests that the music and sung poetry used in education was subject to civic censors.

> They adjudged it necessary for the preservation of that gravity and seriousness of manners which was required of their youth for the attainments of wisdom and virtue, never to admit of any light and wanton, any ludicrous or effeminate poetry; which made them allow of no poets among them but such only who for their grave and virtuous compositions were approved by the public magistrate; that being hereby under some restraint, they might neither act nor write anything to the prejudice of good manners, or to the dishonor of their laws and government.[284]

[284] "Customs of the Lacedaemonians."

With the arrival of the Christian Era we find a comment by one of the church fathers, Clement of Alexandria (c. 150–215 AD), which also mentions the ancient banquet tradition. Here he specifically speaks of the use of music to improve manners and emphasizes the importance of using only good music for this purpose.

> Music is then to be handled for the sake of the embellishment and composure of manners. For instance, at a banquet we pledge each other while the music is playing; soothing by song the eagerness of our desires, and glorifying God for the copious gift of human enjoyments, for His perpetual supply of the food necessary for the growth of the body and of the soul. But we must reject superfluous music, which enervates men's souls, and leads to variety,—now mournful, and then licentious and voluptuous, and then frenzied and frantic.[285]

[285] Clement of Alexandria, in "The Miscellanies," trans. William Wilson (Edinburgh: T. & T. Clark, 1884), Book VI, xi.

We have an extraordinary survey of the aesthetics of music by Cassiodorus (480–573 AD), in a letter to the famous Boethius. His purpose in writing was to ask Boethius to find a harp player to fulfill a request by Clovis, King of the Franks, whom Cassiodorus suggests has "heard of the fame of my banquets." He requests Boethius to find someone "who is skilled in musical knowledge," who with his "sweet sound can tame the savage hearts of the barbarians." In this letter he mentions the power of music to affect manners.

> The artist changes men's hearts as they listen; and, when this artful pleasure issues from the secret place of nature as the

queen of the senses, in all the glory of its tones, our remaining thoughts take to flight, and it expels all else, that it may delight itself simply in being heard. Harmful melancholy he turns to pleasure; he weakens swelling rage; he makes bloodthirsty cruelty kindly, arouses sleepy sloth from its torpor, restores to the sleepless their wholesome rest, recalls lust-corrupted chastity to its moral resolve, and heals boredom of spirit which is always the enemy of good thoughts. Dangerous hatreds he turns to helpful goodwill, and, in a blessed kind of healing, drives out the passions of the heart by means of sweetest pleasures.

Guido of Arezzo, in his important music treatise, *Micrologus* of c. 1026–1028 AD, provides an illustration of the ability of music to affect behavior in an anecdote not found elsewhere. As to the explanation how music does this, he cannot say, offering only the observation that this is known only to Divine Wisdom.

> Another man was roused by the sound of the cithara to such lust that, in his madness, he sought to break into the bedchamber of a girl, but, when the cithara player quickly changed the mode, was brought to feel remorse for his libidinousness and to retreat abashed.[286]

Marsilio Ficino, the fifteenth century founder of the Florentine Academy, was a philosopher who believed music served man's "spirit" in the same way medicine serves the body and theology the soul.

Through these many centuries there was frequently expressed concern for the difference between "good" music and "bad" music. The important English Church philosopher, Richard Hooker (1553–1600), a rational voice which attempted to counter the radical Puritans, shared the concern of Erasmus for the influence of vulgar music. For Hooker it was not a question of philosophical description but common sense.

> For which cause there is nothing more contagious and pestilent than some kinds of [music]; then some nothing more strong and potent unto good. And that there is such a difference of one kind from another we need no proof but our own experience.[287]

---

[286] Hucbald, "Melodic Instruction" in *Hucbald, Guido, and John on Music*, trans. Warren Babb (New Haven: Yale University Press, 1978), 160.

[287] Richard Hooker, *On the Laws of Ecclesiastical Polity*, V, xxxviii, in *The Works of Mr. Richard Hooker* (Oxford: Clarendon Press, 1888), II, 159.

In France, Charles IX, in a patent document relative to the establishment of Baïf's Academy, noted that,

> It is of great importance for the morals of the citizens of a town that the music current and used in the country should be retained under certain laws, for the minds of most men are formed and their behavior influenced by its character, so that where music is disordered, there morals are also depraved, and where it is well ordered, there men are well disciplined morally.[288]

We find additional valuable information regarding the aesthetic purpose of Baïf's Academy in the form of a document discovered by Yates, written early in the seventeenth century by the famous Marin Mersenne. It is apparently based on personal information given Mersenne by an older man who had been a member of the Academy. This document is the principal source for our understanding that the Academy studies ranged far beyond music and poetry.

> [The Academicians] did not wish to bring in a new kind of music, unless you call that new when something is restored to wholeness, but wished to recover those effects which, as we read, were once produced by the Greeks, by joining Gallic verses to our carefully cultivated music. For they hoped to exhilarate the depressed spirit, to reduce the over-elated spirit to modesty, and to stir themselves to other feelings by their own music.
>
> .....
>
> When Jean Antoine de Baïf and Joachim Thibault de Courville labored together to drive barbarism from Gaul, they considered that nothing would be of more potency for forming the manners of youth to everything honorable than if they were to recover the effects of ancient music and compose all their songs on the models of the fixed rules of the Greeks.[289]

Juan Vives, author of a famous sixteenth century book, *On Education*, contends that music should be part of education for the purpose of stabilizing the students' manners and he specifies the importance of using only good music.

> Only let the pupil practice pure and good music which, after the Pythagorean mode, soothes, recreates, and restores to

[288] Quoted in Frances Yates, *The French Academies of the Sixteenth Century* (London: University of London, 1947; Nendeln: Kraus Reprint, 1968), 23.

[289] Ibid.

itself the wearied mind of the student; then let it lead back to tranquility and tractability all the wild and fierce parts of the student's nature.[290]

[290] Ibid.

Lodowick Bryskett (1546–1612), in his *A Discourse of Civill Life*, advises young men to be very selective of what they listen to.

> Let it suffice that young men are to take great account of that part of music which bears with it grave melodies, fit to compose the mind to good order by virtue of the rhythms and sound … But those which by variety in tunes, and warbling variations, confounds the words and melodies, and yields only a delight to the exterior sense, and no fruit for the mind, I wish them to neglect and not to esteem.[291]

[291] Quoted in Henry Morley, *Ideal Commonwealths* (Port Washington: Kennikat Press, 1968), 110.

Marin Mersenne (1588–1648), author of the great French *Harmonie universelle* of 1636, wonders why man was made with the ability to make only one sound at a time.[292] He doubts that man would be able to accomplish anything he cannot do with one voice and concludes that God made it necessary for man to need another man to make harmony, "so that the harmony of voices might invite men to the harmony of manners."[293]

The first great philosopher of the English Baroque was Francis Bacon (1561–1626). In his *Natural History* he devotes a lengthy discussion of the role of music in affecting manners and attempts to explain how it works.

[292] Marin Me Richard Hooker, *On the Laws of Ecclesiastical Polity*, V, xxxviii, in *The Works of Mr. Mersenne, Harmonie universelle* (1636), III, i, 21. In III, i, 22, Mersenne mentions that the "son of Pierre d'Avignon" astonished everyone by singing one part and whistling another simultaneously.

[293] Ibid., III, i, 6.

> The cause is, for that the sense of hearing strikes the spirits more immediately than the other senses, and more incorporeally than the smelling. For the sight, taste, and feeling, have their organs not of so present and immediate access to the spirits, as the hearing has.[294]

[294] *Natural History*, Section 114, in *The Works of Francis Bacon*, ed. James Spedding (Cambridge: Cambridge University Press, 1869).

While the humanists, who concentrated on sung poetry, always emphasized that it was the words, and not the music, which produced the greater impact on feelings, Jean Calvin, in the passage from which the quotation at the top was taken, found a greater danger in the music than the words for reasons similar to Bacon.

For this reason the early doctors of the Church often complain that the people of their times are addicted to dishonest and shameless songs, which not without reason they call mortal and Satanic poison for the corruption of the world. Now in speaking of music I understand two parts, namely, the letter, or subject and matter, and the song, or melody. It is true that, as Saint Paul says, every evil word corrupts good manners, but when it has the melody with it, it pierces the heart much more strongly and enters within; as wine is poured into the cask with a funnel, so venom and corruption are distilled to the very depths of the heart by melody.[295]

Sixteenth century nobles, especially in Italy, had felt that after a dinner party, during which there was much debating and arguing, it was important to conclude the evening by singing in order to bring everyone into "harmony." We find it somewhat charming, therefore, that Johann Kuhnau makes a similar argument when discussing the virtues of the collegium musicum.

> The musicians in cities commonly hold a collegium musicum every week or two. That is indeed a laudable undertaking, in part because it provides them with the opportunity to refine further their excellent art, and in part, too, because they learn from the pleasing harmonies how to speak together concordantly, even though these same people mostly disagree with one another at other times.[296]

We find this topic discussed by one of the nineteenth century's great composers *and* philosophers, Richard Wagner. His discussion is not limited to the individual, but entire societies.

> No less than Drama, Music is able to work on taste, yes, also on *manners*: the first point will be disputed by no one, even in our day …
>
> .....
>
> Let us think back to our own immediate past; with tolerable certainty we may contend that those inspired by Beethoven's music must have been more active and energetic citizens of the State than those bewitched by Rossini, Bellini and Donizetti, a class consisting for the most part of rich and lordly do-nothings. A speaking proof is further afforded by Paris: anyone might have observed during the last

[295] Jean Calvin, *Geneva Psalter*, quoted in Olive Strunk, Source Readings in Music History (New York: Norton, 1950), 346ff.

[296] Johann Kuhnau, *Der musicalische Quack-Salber* (Dresden, 1700), Chapter I. Kuhnau (1660–1722), like Bach, was the music director of St. Thomas in Leipzig. Although known today as a composer, he was educated in law and mathematics and was capable in Hebrew, Greek and Latin.

decades that in exact degree as the morals of Parisian society have rushed into that unexampled corruption, its music has floundered in a sphere of frivolous taste; one has only to hear the latest compositions of an Auber, Adam and so on, and to compare them with the odious dances performed in Paris at the time of Carnival, to perceive a terrible connection. If this rather proves that Morals operate on Music, yet the mutual relation of the two is manifest; it consequently is the State's affair to apply to this art, as well, that demand addressed by Kaiser Joseph to the theater: "that it shall work for the ennobling of taste *and* manners."[297]

[297] Quoted in *Wagner's Prose Works*, trans. William Ashton Ellis (New York: Broude), VII, 355ff.

Now *there* is a nice line by Franz Joseph! Wouldn't it be nice if today that line appeared in some school's mission statement?

Music education shall work for the ennobling of taste *and* manners.

Certainly it must be recognized today that the popular music has become so degenerate as to have been unimaginable in earlier times. Who is there to speak out on the subject of the vulgar popular music of today?

Most music educators shrug their shoulders at this and simply assign it to the world of entertainment. But history will not do that for history has seen this problem appear over and over for three thousand years. History will record that this was a failure of music education for not understanding that aesthetics, a fundamental branch of philosophy, must be the foundation of their teaching. At the graduation ceremonies of 2016 universities will send out a new crop of music educators with no background in aesthetics. And they consequently will expose their students to the dark side of the impact of emotions on the right hemisphere of the student's brain which follows from the teaching that "all music is equal." And for the trophies they will add to their trophy case, they will have paid a price measured not in dollars but in human lives.

The music teacher will say, "But it is not my job to teach aesthetics, ethics, character and manners to my music students." OK. Who, then?

About the Author

Dr. David Whitwell is a graduate ("with distinction") of the University of Michigan and the Catholic University of America, Washington DC (PhD, Musicology, Distinguished Alumni Award, 2000) and has studied conducting with Eugene Ormandy and at the Akademie für Musik, Vienna. Prior to coming to Northridge, Dr. Whitwell participated in concerts throughout the United States and Asia as Associate First Horn in the USAF Band and Orchestra in Washington DC, and in recitals throughout South America in cooperation with the United States State Department.

At the California State University, Northridge, which is in Los Angeles, Dr. Whitwell developed the CSUN Wind Ensemble into an ensemble of international reputation, with international tours to Europe in 1981 and 1989 and to Japan in 1984. The CSUN Wind Ensemble has made professional studio recordings for BBC (London), the Köln Westdeutscher Rundfunk (Germany), NOS National Radio (The Netherlands), Zürich Radio (Switzerland), the Television Broadcasting System (Japan) as well as for the United States State Department for broadcast on its "Voice of America" program. The CSUN Wind Ensemble's recording with the Mirecourt Trio in 1982 was named the "Record of the Year" by *The Village Voice*. Composers who have guest conducted Whitwell's ensembles include Aaron Copland, Ernest Krenek, Alan Hovhaness, Morton Gould, Karel Husa, Frank Erickson and Vaclav Nelhybel.

Dr. Whitwell has been a guest professor in 100 different universities and conservatories throughout the United States and in 23 foreign countries (most recently in China, in an elite school housed in the Forbidden City). Guest conducting experiences have included the Philadelphia Orchestra, Seattle Symphony Orchestra, the Czech Radio Orchestras of Brno and Bratislava, The National Youth Orchestra of Israel, as well as resident wind ensembles in Russia, Israel, Austria, Switzerland, Germany, England, Wales, The Netherlands, Portugal, Peru, Korea, Japan, Taiwan, Canada and the United States.

He is a past president of the College Band Directors National Association, a member of the Prasidium of the International Society for the Promotion of Band Music, and was a member of the founding board of directors of the World Association for Symphonic Bands and Ensembles (WASBE). In 1964 he was made an honorary life member of Kappa Kappa Psi, a national professional music fraternity. In September, 2001, he was a delegate to the UNESCO Conference on Global Music in Tokyo. He has been knighted by sovereign organizations in France, Portugal and Scotland and has been awarded the gold medal of Kerkrade, The Netherlands, and the silver medal of Wangen, Germany, the highest honor given wind conductors in the United States, the medal of the Academy of Wind and Percussion Arts (National Band Association) and the highest honor given wind conductors in Austria, the gold medal of the Austrian Band Association. He is a member of the Hall of Fame of the California Music Educators Association.

Dr. Whitwell's publications include more than 127 articles on wind literature including publications in *Music and Letters* (London), the *London Musical Times,* the *Mozart-Jahrbuch* (Salzburg), and sixty books, among which is his 13-volume *History and Literature of the Wind Band and Wind Ensemble* and an 8-volume series on *Aesthetics in Music.* In addition to numerous modern editions of early wind band music his original compositions include six symphonies.

David Whitwell was named as one of six men who have determined the course of American bands during the second half of the twentieth century, in the definitive history, *The Twentieth Century American Wind Band* (Meredith Music). A doctoral dissertation by German Gonzales (2007, Arizona State University) is dedicated to the life and conducting career of David Whitwell through the year 1977. David Whitwell is one of nine men described by Paula A. Crider in *The Conductor's Legacy* (Chicago: GIA, 2010) as "the legendary conductors" of the twentieth century.

> "I can't imagine the 2nd half of the 20th century—without David Whitwell and what he has given to all of the rest of us."
> Frederick Fennell (1993)

About the Editor

CRAIG DABELSTEIN began studying the piano at age seven and took up the saxophone at age twelve. Mr Dabelstein has Bachelor of Arts (Music) and Bachelor of Music degrees from the Queensland Conservatorium of Music and a Graduate Diploma of Learning and Teaching and a Graduate Certificate in Editing and Publishing from the University of Southern Queensland. He has held the principal saxophone chairs in the Australian Wind Orchestra and has been an augmenting member of the Queensland Philharmonic and Symphony Orchestras. He was a member of the Queensland Saxophone Quartet and has previously been a saxophone teacher at the Queensland Conservatorium of Music. He is a regular conductor of the Queensland Wind Orchestra and has been a research associate for the *Teaching Music Through Performance in Band* series of books. He is the editor of more than forty books by Dr. David Whitwell including *A Concise History of the Wind Band, Foundations of Music Education, Music Education of the Future, The Sousa Oral History Project, Wagner on Bands, Berlioz on Bands, The Art of Musical Conducting, Aesthetics of Music* (8 volumes) and *The History and Literature of the Wind Band and Wind Ensemble* (13 volumes). He currently teaches saxophone and clarinet, and conducts bands at St Joseph's College, Gregory Terrace.

Books by David Whitwell

- The Sousa Oral History Project
- The Art of Musical Conducting
- The Longy Club: 1900–1917
- La Téléphonie and the Universal Musical Language
- Extraordinary Women
- A Concise History of the Wind Band
- Essays on the Modern Wind Band
- Essays on Performance Practice
- A New History of Wind Music
- The College and University Band
- The Early Symphonies of Mozart
- Band Music of the French Revolution
- Stories from the Podium

On Composers

- Wagner on Bands
- Berlioz on Bands
- Chopin: A Self-Portrait
- Liszt: A Self-Portrait
- Schumann: A Self-Portrait in His Own Words
- Mendelssohn: A Self-Portrait in His Own Words

Aesthetics of Music

- Aesthetics of Music in Ancient Civilizations
- Aesthetics of Music in the Middle Ages
- Aesthetics of Music in the Early Renaissance
- Aesthetics of Music in Sixteenth-Century Italy, France and Spain
- Aesthetics of Music in Sixteenth-Century Germany, the Low Countries and England
- Aesthetics of Baroque Music in Italy, Spain, the German-Speaking Countries and the Low Countries
- Aesthetics of Baroque Music in France
- Aesthetics of Baroque Music in England
- Aesthetics of Music, Annotated Index, Volumes 1–8

The History and Literature of the Wind Band and Wind Ensemble Series

- Volume 1 The Wind Band and Wind Ensemble Before 1500
- Volume 2 The Renaissance Wind Band and Wind Ensemble
- Volume 3 The Baroque Wind Band and Wind Ensemble
- Volume 4 The Wind Band and Wind Ensemble of the Classical Period (1750–1800)
- Volume 5 The Nineteenth-Century Wind Band and Wind Ensemble
- Volume 6 A Catalog of Multi-Part Repertoire for Wind Instruments or for Undesignated Instrumentation before 1600
- Volume 7 Baroque Wind Band and Wind Ensemble Repertoire
- Volume 8 Classical Period Wind Band and Wind Ensemble Repertoire
- Volume 9 Nineteenth-Century Wind Band and Wind Ensemble Repertoire
- Volume 10 A Supplementary Catalog of Wind Band and Wind Ensemble Repertoire
- Volume 11 A Catalog of Wind Repertoire before the Twentieth Century for One to Five Players
- Volume 12 A Second Supplementary Catalog of Early Wind Band and Wind Ensemble Repertoire
- Volume 13 Name Index, Volumes 1–12, The History and Literature of the Wind Band and Wind Ensemble

On Education

- Philosophic Foundations of Education
- Foundations of Music Education
- Music Education of the Future

Ancient Voices

- Ancient Views on Music and Religion
- Ancient Views on the Natural World
- Ancient Views on What Is Music
- Contemporary Descriptions of Early Musicians
- Early Views of Music and Ethics
- Early Thoughts on Performance Practice
- Music Performance in Ancient Societies

Renaissance Voices

- Essays on Renaissance Philosophies of Music
- Renaissance Men on Music

www.whitwellbooks.com

www.ingramcontent.com/pod-product-compliance
Lightning Source LLC
Chambersburg PA
CBHW080543230426
43663CB00015B/2688